THE CONSTITUTION OF SOUTH KOREA

The current South Korean Constitution of 1987 is the culmination of decades-long efforts by the South Korean people to achieve democratic selfgovernment. It is the fruition of untold sacrifices made by dedicated citizens who tirelessly fought to rein in the power of the government under some form of constitutional rule. In that sense, it should be understood against the backdrop of Korea's long experimentation with constitutionalism that goes back to the dynastic period. Yet, it also represents a radical break, the beginning of a new era which ended years of authoritarian rule that prioritised development over democracy. For the first time in the history of the Korean nation, the written constitution has become a living norm rather than an ornament, or a façade, for illegitimate or ineffectual governments. It has proven to be a binding law that matters not only for government leaders but also for private individuals. With the adoption, especially, of a system allowing the adjudication of constitutional issues at an independent court, citizens have begun to realise that the constitution can be invoked to protect their rights and advance their interests. As a result, the South Korean Constitutional Court is being stretched to its limits with a great number of cases filed at its docket. The constitutional system of South Korea is, therefore, very much a work in progress, whose shape and contours are still being hammered out. The primary goal of this volume will be to flesh out, and make intelligible to foreign readers, that process within the specific political and historical context of modern South Korea.

Pictorial Narrative

This fragmented multi-dimensional image is comprised of mainly geometric shapes and other forms emerging from blocks of colour which serve as visual metaphors for South Korea as a constitutional democracy in its historical and international context.

In the upper inverted triangle, seemingly chased by a charging dragon of traditional Korean values with its saw tooth jaws open, is a soaring KAI KF-21 Boramae fighter jet. This ultra-modern aircraft alludes to both the cutting-edge sophistication of South Korea's industrial technology and the need for constant vigilance to safeguard the nation against external threats. Centre stage within this navy-blue triangle hangs an orange copy of the current 1987 Constitution, a symbol of South Korea's transition to democracy.

The central part of the composition features a deconstructed national flag of South Korea with its emblematic design of *t'aegŭk* (red and blue paisley-like images) and the 'trigrams' (three lines). The smaller semi-circular design to the right refers to the royal standard of the Chosŏn dynasty, a reminder of the historical roots of modern Korea. The number '38' on the left refers to the division of the Korean nation at the 38th parallel and the continuing confrontation with North Korea. Behind the *t'aegŭk* appears the Stars and Stripes, a reference to South Korea's deep alliance with the USA.

On another diagonal from the left-hand corner is a yellow-white pentagon shape, continuing into two unequal triangles dotted with yellow chrysanthemums, a reminder of the long shadow of Japanese colonialism. This is interrupted by the pointed mauve quadrilateral cut through with vertical shafts and zigzags, which evoke South Korea's modern and postmodern geometric architecture, and more generally its rapid economic growth. The light blue and white chevrons next to it represent the South Korean Constitutional Court's role in activating and giving substance to the 1987 Constitution. To the left in the foreground is the studded rustication of the exterior walls of the Court building. A small black eagle is shown behind the chevrons to suggest the German influence on South Korean legal system.

Putachad
Artist

Constitutional Systems of the World
General Editors: Benjamin L Berger, Rosalind Dixon, Andrew Harding, Heinz Klug, and Peter Leyland

In the era of globalisation, issues of constitutional law and good governance are being seen increasingly as vital issues in all types of society. Since the end of the Cold War, there have been dramatic developments in democratic and legal reform, and post-conflict societies are also in the throes of reconstructing their governance systems. Even societies already firmly based on constitutional governance and the rule of law have undergone constitutional change and experimentation with new forms of governance; and their constitutional systems are increasingly subjected to comparative analysis and transplantation. Constitutional texts for practically every country in the world are now easily available on the internet. However, texts which enable one to understand the true context, purposes, interpretation and incidents of a constitutional system are much harder to locate, and are often extremely detailed and descriptive. This series seeks to provide scholars and students with accessible introductions to the constitutional systems of the world, supplying both a road map for the novice and, at the same time, a deeper understanding of the key historical, political and legal events which have shaped the constitutional landscape of each country. Each book in this series deals with a single country, or a group of countries with a common constitutional history, and each author is an expert in their field.

Published volumes

The Constitution of the United Kingdom; The Constitution of the United States; The Constitution of Vietnam; The Constitution of South Africa; The Constitution of Japan; The Constitution of Germany; The Constitution of Finland; The Constitution of Australia; The Constitution of the Republic of Austria; The Constitution of the Russian Federation; The Constitutional System of Thailand; The Constitution of Malaysia; The Constitution of China; The Constitution of Indonesia; The Constitution of France; The Constitution of Spain; The Constitution of Mexico; The Constitution of Israel; The Constitutional Systems of the Commonwealth Caribbean; The Constitution of Canada; The Constitution of Singapore; The Constitution of Belgium; The Constitution of Taiwan; The Constitution of Romania; The Constitutional Systems of the Independent Central Asian States; The Constitution of India; The Constitution of Pakistan; The Constitution of Ireland; The Constitution of Brazil; The Constitution of Myanmar; The Constitution of Czechia; The Constitution of New Zealand; The Constitution of Italy; The Constitutional System of the Hong Kong SAR; The Constitution of South Korea.

Link to series website

www.bloomsbury.com/uk/series/constitutional-systems-of-the-world/

The Constitution
of South Korea

A Contextual Analysis

Chaihark Hahm

·HART·
OXFORD · LONDON · NEW YORK · NEW DELHI · SYDNEY

HART PUBLISHING

Bloomsbury Publishing Plc

Kemp House, Chawley Park, Cumnor Hill, Oxford, OX2 9PH, UK

1385 Broadway, New York, NY 10018, USA

Bloomsbury Publishing Ireland Limited, 29 Earlsfort Terrace, Dublin 2, D02 AY28, Ireland

HART PUBLISHING, the Hart/Stag logo, BLOOMSBURY and the Diana logo are
trademarks of Bloomsbury Publishing Plc

First published in Great Britain 2024

First published in hardback, 2024

Paperback edition, 2025

A catalogue record for this book is available from the British Library.

A catalogue record for this book is available from the Library of Congress.

Library of Congress Control Number: 2023952405

ISBN: PB: 978-1-50997-634-8
        ePDF: 978-1-50991-920-8
        ePub: 978-1-50991-919-2

Typeset by Compuscript Ltd, Shannon

For product safety related questions contact productsafety@bloomsbury.com

To find out more about our authors and books visit www.hartpublishing.co.uk.
Here you will find extracts, author information, details of forthcoming events
and the option to sign up for our newsletters.

For Jumi

Acknowledgements

THIS BOOK HAS been too long in the making. During that period, I have benefitted greatly from conversations and feedback from many individuals. I wish to first express my gratitude to my colleagues at Yonsei University. Chulwoo Lee, Jong-cheol Kim, and Inyoung Cho at the Law School were all kind enough to read parts of the manuscript and provided helpful comments. At the Political Science Department, Sung Ho Kim, my partner on a previous book project, has continued to be a wonderful source of intellectual stimulation and inspiration. Joe Phillips of the Underwood International College went far beyond the call of duty to offer countless suggestions for better phrasing and economy of expression.

I am also indebted to numerous scholars located outside Korea. Jimmy Hsu, Marie Kim, Sung-moon Kim, Holning Lau, David Law, and Kevin Tan encouraged me to formulate and articulate my thoughts about various aspects of the South Korean constitution, all of which proved to be valuable preparation for this book. During my stay at the Center for Advanced Study in the Behavioral Sciences, where sections of the manuscript were written, Ruth Chang, Diane Desierto, Terry Maroney, and Jack Rakove (the 'law-types' among that year's fellows) helped me fine-tune the way I present and explain Korea's constitutional system to foreign audience.

And, of course, I must thank the editors of the Hart series *Constitutional Systems of the World* for sticking it out with me over the many years when the completion of this volume must have seemed doubtful. Andrew Harding, in particular, deserves a special word of appreciation – without his kind encouragement, astute observations and limitless patience, this book would not have seen the light of day.

Thanks are also due to my many research assistants, past and present. I wish to thank especially Juhyung Yoon for his excellent and speedy responses to my inquiries. Lastly, I should mention the generations of students who attended my courses, including numerous exchange students from abroad. This book is in great measure the result of years of engagement with them. It is hoped that they may find in it answers to questions that were left unanswered in class.

Contents

Table of Abbreviations

BAI   Board of Audit and Inspection

CCA   Constitutional Court Act

COA   Court Organisation Act

DMZ   Demilitarised Zone

JRTI   Judicial Research and Training Institute

KILA   Korean Interim Legislative Assembly

KPG   Provisional Government of the Republic of Korea

NAA   National Assembly Act

NCA   National Court Administration

UNTCOK   United Nations Temporary Commission on Korea

UPP   Unified Progressive Party

USAMGIK   US Army Military Government in Korea

Table of Cases

Table of Legislation

Republic of Korea

Other National Legislation

International Instruments

Introduction

OR FOREIGNERS, THE Republic of Korea[1] signifies many different things. For those interested in pop culture, it is the origin of K-pop such as the band BTS, or dramas like *Squid Game*. For the more economically inclined, Korea is home to such business conglomerates as Samsung, Hyundai, and LG. Those into international relations or military affairs might think of the Demilitarised Zone (DMZ), the heavily fortified 155-mile-long border that separates the prosperous and vibrant South Korea from its impoverished totalitarian northern neighbour. To those who visited the country during the 1970s and 1980s, South Korea may be remembered as a garrison state under ex-military leaders. For those with an even longer memory, Korea's most salient feature might be the Korean War (1950–1953) with all the destruction and destitution it left behind.

These various signifiers reveal that South Korea is a country rife with intriguing tensions, if not paradoxes. It is technically still at war because the Korean War ended only with a ceasefire agreement. Military service is compulsory for male citizens and the entire population must cope with the constant security threat from North Korea. At the same time, to survive and to rebuild, South Koreans have had to work and invest in the future as if there was no war. Self-induced 'amnesia' of the security threat was a daily requisite for their pursuit of economic prosperity.

South Korea is practically a new state that was rebuilt after the devastation of war. Formally, too, it is a new republic that became independent after the Second World War, when Japan's colonial occupation (1910–1945) came to an end. Yet, its constitution states in the preamble that the Korean people have 'a resplendent history and traditions dating from time immemorial'. According to common parlance, their history as one nation goes back 'five thousand years'.

Observers both foreign and domestic have described South Korea as the world's most Confucian society. Yet, it is also the only Asian country (besides the Philippines) where Christianity is thriving. Moreover,

---

[1] Throughout this book, Republic of Korea and South Korea will be used interchangeably. 'Korea' will also be used where there is no risk of confusion with North Korea.

despite the supposed Confucian heritage which emphasises seniority and prioritises the family over the individual, South Koreans are one of the most contentious and litigious people in Asia. They are not hesitant to take to the streets to challenge the government or to utilise the courts to defend the rights of the individual.

This co-presence of seemingly conflicting traits that characterises the Republic of Korea may be attributed to the 'compressed development' it went through during the last century. In 1953, it was one the world's poorest countries with an estimated income per person of US$67. In 2021, it was the world's tenth largest economy with a gross domestic product (GDP) per capita of US$34,983. It became a member of the Development Assistance Committee of the Organisation for Economic Co-operation and Development (OECD) in 2009, signifying its transformation from a former recipient of development aid to a donor state. This phenomenal growth was once led by an overbearing state, which must now find a new role in a much more complex and globalised economy led by private enterprises. Authoritarian governments that called for nationwide discipline and suspension of political freedom for the sake of economic development eventually became victims of their own success. The emergence of a well-educated, politically self-assured middle class meant that competitive electoral democracy and individual rights could no longer be postponed. In 1987, the political system was changed to allow for direct popular election of the president and liberalisation of the political process. As of 2022, Korea has seen four transfers of power to opposition parties and a marked improvement in its human rights records. Yet, that also means that Korean has been a democracy for a little over three decades. The citizens' ever-expanding appetite for liberal democracy is bound to clash with the demands of national security as well as inherited cultural norms and practices. According to the 2021 Democracy Index, published by the weekly *Economist*, South Korea was ranked at 16 in the world, above the United Kingdom, France, and the United States. Yet, in terms of gender inequality, it ranked 99th out of 146 countries in the World Economic Forum's 2022 report.

South Korea's constitutional system has gone through many changes during the years of compressed development. The constitution, first adopted in 1948, has been revised nine times. The last revision took place in 1987 to formalise the citizens' demand for democratisation. The current constitution, which is by far the longest lasting one Korea has seen, has overseen the process of democratic consolidation. By invoking it, Koreans have learned to defend their rights and freedom and to challenge and discipline their political leaders. This is partly due to the creation of a Constitutional Court, which has acted as a forum for adjudicating social tensions and citizens' discontents. Through the Court's interpretations, the constitution has become a living, flexible norm that can adjudicate conflicting demands from the people. Yet, even before the Court was established, Koreans knew that a state's legitimacy depends on adherence to its constitution. That is why the current system is more than the result of the 1987 transition to democracy. Even during the periods of authoritarian governments and colonial occupation, Koreans have aspired to practice constitutional politics. Indeed, even during dynastic times, constitutional norms were invoked to both legitimise and contest political power. South Korea's constitutional system is thus the culmination of the Korean people's long history of constitutional aspirations.

This book will begin in Chapter 1 with a sketch of Korea's constitutional past from the earliest recorded history to the founding of the modern Republic in 1948. By presenting the workings of dynastic constitutional norms based on Confucian teachings, it will describe how the ideal of restraining and disciplining the ruler has long been a part of Korean history. It will then look at the path toward the adoption of South Korea's Founding Constitution, after liberation from Japan's colonial occupation, under conditions of national division and the incipient Cold War. This will be followed in Chapter 2 by an account of the nine constitutional revisions that South Korea went through since its founding. By reviewing the process and substance of the changes, it will explain how the constitution reflected and affected the nation's often turbulent politics, as Korea sought to overcome abject poverty and practice liberal democracy.

Chapter 3 will be a thematic discussion of the major principles of the 1987 Constitution. It will discuss how such universal principles as republicanism, popular sovereignty, separation of powers, and the rule of law are interpreted and implemented in the Korean context. The chapter will also discuss how such principles are affected by the presence of the North Korean regime across the DMZ and the need to work toward national reunification, while safeguarding South Korean democracy.

Chapters 4 to 6 will examine the status and function of the three branches of the government. The powers of the president and the issue of 'imperial presidency' will be the focus of Chapter 4. Chapter 5 will then discuss the role and function of the National Assembly, South Korea's legislature, as well as the electoral system and political parties. Next, Chapter 6 will examine the judiciary's powers and its structure, as well as the challenges it faces in terms of the proper balance between judicial independence and democratic accountability. Chapter 7 will be devoted to the Constitutional Court. Although a part of the judiciary in a broad sense, the Court merits separate discussion given its central role in interpreting and implementing the current constitution. The various types of cases adjudicated by the Court, as well as its occasionally strained relationship with the Supreme Court, will be explained.

The last two chapters are topical essays designed to place the Korean constitution in its unique context. Chapter 8 will discuss the expansion of constitutional rights in Korea. After a brief sketch of the history of Korean rights discourse, it will describe how the scope of constitutionally protected rights has expanded through the Constitutional Court's jurisprudence on 'human dignity and worth'. Some recent debates on rights as Korea becomes a more diverse and internationalised society will also be noted. Chapter 9 will be a more abstract discussion on the Korean constitution's role as a medium for assessing the past and imagining the future. By reviewing cases that dealt with three topics (transitional justice, Confucian family norms, and overseas Koreans), we will see that the constitution is often called upon to both reject regrettable pasts and affirm meaningful pasts, while projecting a vision for the future.

The book will conclude with a short reflection on three themes that have characterised South Korea's constitutional experience since the founding: the hybrid form of government, the tension between democracy and the rule of law, and the polarising influence of nationalism.

It is suggested that this book be read with the following 'polarities' in mind. First is the coexistence of change and continuity. South Korea's constitutional system will be better understood when we know what changed and what stayed the same over the years. Second is the polarity between sameness and difference. It should be remembered that the Korean constitution is at once an expression of the people's common identity and aspirations and a medium for navigating and adjudicating their diverse viewpoints and conflicting interests. The third polarity is that between universality and particularity. A proper understanding of Korea's constitution requires recognising how abstract principles and values found in most constitutional democracies were made concrete and sometimes contested through their encounter with Korean political history and cultural traditions. The story of the Korean constitution will come alive when read through the lens of these polarities.

Finally, a note on citations: unless otherwise indicated, all references to articles in the main text without specific attribution are to provisions of the current 1987 Constitution. References to provisions of other laws (acts, treaties, regulations, etc) are given in the footnotes. All translations of Korean legal materials are by the author.

1

The Road to a Democratic Republic

The Dynastic Legal Heritage – Confucian Constitutionalism – Hope for Constitutional Monarchy – Japanese Colonial Occupation and the Notional 'Democratic Republic' – Constitutional Debates after Liberation – Drafting the Founding Constitution

THE FIRST MODERN constitution of Korea was promulgated on 17 July 1948. A month later, on 15 August 1948, an official ceremony was held in Seoul to commemorate the establishment of the Republic of Korea under the new constitution. That date also marked the third anniversary of the end of Japanese colonial rule, and so the event was heavy with multiple meanings. As a symbol of national independence regained, the 'Founding Constitution' was a powerful statement against imperialism and foreign subjugation. As a proclamation of popular sovereignty, it was also a resolute expression of the people's determination to embrace democracy rather than return to the pre-colonial dynastic order. And, as the legal basis for a government with *de facto* control over only the southern part of the Korean Peninsula, it was a painful reminder of the externally imposed division of the Korean nation. The 1948 Constitution was thus an embodiment and reflection of the complex geopolitical and ideological difficulties facing Korea at the time. From a broader historical perspective, however, its adoption was without doubt a milestone in the legal and political history of Korea. The year 1948 is therefore commonly viewed as the starting point of modern constitutionalism in Korea.

This should not, however, be taken to mean that prior to 1948 there was no constitutional tradition in Korea. Of course, if one defines constitutionalism in terms of individual rights, popular sovereignty, separation of powers, and judicial view, then it might be difficult to say that Korea had any familiarity with constitutionalism in the pre-modern era. If, by contrast, one views constitutionalism more as a project aimed at restraining arbitrary use of state power, while providing the terms of its legitimacy, then one might describe certain periods and actors of pre-modern Korean history as evidencing knowledge and practice of constitutional politics, albeit through a vocabulary and institutions very different from the ones we use today. This chapter will trace the development of constitutionalist ideas and institutions from Korea's earliest known history to the adoption of the Founding Constitution.

I. THE DYNASTIC LEGAL AND POLITICAL HERITAGE

According to Korea's founding myth, Tan'gun, an offspring of the heavenly ruler, founded the first Korean state called Chosŏn in 2333 BCE. Historical records show that by fourth century BCE a state by that name vied with neighbouring states for control of what is now the Liaodong Peninsula and southern part of Manchuria. Now called 'Old Chosŏn' to distinguish it from a later dynasty of the same name, this kingdom is important for our purposes because this was the period when Confucianism was first introduced to Korea. As discussed below, Confucian texts and ideas provided the foundation for what might be called dynastic constitutionalism.

Old Chosŏn lasted until the first century BCE, when the three kingdoms of Koguryŏ, Paekche, and Silla emerged on the Korean Peninsula and Manchuria. They began utilising, to different degrees, Confucianism as a tool in state administration. At first, these states' ruling classes were attracted to Confucian learning because it could be used to enforce hierarchical social distinctions and to elevate the ruler's status. Their law codes included provisions on treason and *lèse majesté*.[1] Yet, with its emphasis on rule by virtuous and benevolent sage-kings, Confucianism also provided resources for holding the ruler responsible for the commoners' wellbeing. For example, in the third century CE, a prime minister of Koguryŏ reportedly said to the king: 'If a prince does not relieve the sufferings of his people, he is not good. If a subject does not offer remonstrance, he is not loyal.'[2] As the three kingdoms established, at different times, national academies for promoting Confucian learning and training government officials, Confucianism began to take root as an important part of the political establishment. In the seventh century CE, Silla vanquished Koguryŏ and Paekche to unify most of Korean Peninsula under its rule. While Silla had a strict caste system and was strongly influenced by Buddhism, it also began recruiting officials based

---

[1] Park B-h, *Han'guk Pŏpchesa* [*Korean Legal History*] (Minsogwŏn 2012) 31–32.
[2] PH Lee and WT de Bary (eds), *Sources of Korean Tradition*, vol I (Columbia University Press 1997) 22.

on their proficiency in Confucian learning. A full-fledged merit-based civil service examination was implemented in 958 during the Koryŏ dynasty (918–1392 CE), which also established a national academy and local schools to propagate Confucian teachings. It also disseminated Confucian texts through a national library and printing office. By late Koryŏ period, a class of Confucian intellectuals emerged who advocated reforms to strengthen the state to resist the intrusion of the Mongols and criticised the influence of Buddhist monks on state affairs.

A. Chosŏn Dynasty: A Model Confucian Polity

Chosŏn dynasty (1392–1910) was founded by Yi Sŏng-gye, a former general under Koryŏ, but the support of Confucian intellectuals and statesmen was indispensable. They provided the new dynasty's governing ideology. They justified Chosŏn's founding by invoking the Confucian theory of 'Mandate of Heaven' to suggest that Heaven had withdrawn the mandate to govern from the last king of Koryŏ due to his iniquities and had anointed Yi to be the new ruler. Chosŏn promoted Confucianism as not just a tool for statecraft but also a universal norm for family life and even spirituality. By the seventeenth century, even illiterate commoners were expected to practice Confucian rituals and values.

In the original design for Chosŏn's government, proposed by the Confucian intellectual Chŏng To-jŏn, the king was to play a largely ceremonial role. A 'prime minister', who presided over the government and oversaw its daily operations, was expected to 'rectify the king' according to Confucian ideals. While this plan was never fully realised, it was an indication of the degree to which Confucianism would dominate Chosŏn politics. The king eventually exercised substantial power throughout the dynasty, but the Confucian scholar-officials made sure that the government structure included numerous agencies dedicated to preventing arbitrary rule and ensuring that the king adhered to Confucian norms. One such bureau was the Royal Lectures (*Kyŏngyŏn*) which conducted daily lectures for the king on Confucian classics. The goal was to ensure that that the king be continually inculcated with the ideals and values of Confucian government to become a virtuous ruler. By law, the lectures were held three times a day and were led by respected scholar-officials from within the bureaucracy.

Another bureau designed to 'rectify the king' was the Censorate, which comprised two separate agencies. One was the Office of Remonstrance (*Saganwŏn*) whose official responsibility was to 'remonstrate and contest, discuss and refute' the king in all government matters. The other agency was the Office of Inspection (*Sahŏnbu*) whose primary duty was to investigate and impeach official misconduct. Both were institutional manifestations of the Confucian ideal that genuine loyalty requires officials to continually admonish the ruler and correct his errors. To ensure their independence, officials in the Censorate were given immunity from charges of sedition or *lèse majesté*.[3]

The Office of the Court Historian was also a key institution designed to hold the king accountable according to Confucian ideals. Taking literally a passage in the Confucian classic *Liji* (Records of Ritual), Chosŏn scholar-officials insisted that two historians be always present whenever the king held audience with his ministers. One recorded all the verbal transactions, and the other all physical movements. By recording everything that was said and done by the king, the historians ensured that he would be forever accountable for his deeds. Crucially, their daily records included not only accurate descriptions but also normative commentaries on the king's conduct of state affairs. By law, the king was not allowed to see the historians' daily records or to have any say in their appointments. Upon the king's death, the daily records, including the historians' judgments, were collected and edited into an official 'Veritable Record' of the deceased king's reign.

B. Sources of Confucian Constitutional Norms

Chosŏn's basic law code was the *Kyŏngguk Taejŏn* (Great Canon for Governing the State), which first went into force in 1470. It specified the powers and organisation of all government agencies. It was compiled with the purpose of providing a permanent legal basis for Chosŏn government and as such it was expected to be observed by all succeeding generations, including the king himself. For the king, the Confucian virtue of 'filial piety' (*hyo*) demanded that he respect the code as the embodiment of the wisdom and will of his forebears, particularly the 'dynastic founders'. Any change to existing laws was prima facie suspect as a potentially unfilial act and required special justification.[4] Even when the code was amended or updated, this presumption in favour of older

---

[3] JK Haboush, 'The Confucianization of Korean Society' in G Rozman (ed), *The East Asian Region: Confucian Heritage and Its Modern Adaptation* (Princeton University Press 1991) 96.

[4] C Hahm, 'Ritual and Constitutionalism: Disputing the Ruler's Legitimacy in a Confucian Polity' (2009) 57 *American Journal of Comparative Law* 135, 155.

laws was maintained.[5] New editions of the *Taejŏn* preserved the entire corpus of the original code, while inscribing new laws in smaller types at the end of each article. Even when the meaning of some provisions of the original code became inaccessible, later generations 'dared not alter or change' them.[6]

While the *Kyŏngguk Taejŏn* and its later iterations were accorded the utmost respect, they were not exhaustive of the norms that regulated government conduct, particularly the monarch's. Aside from the dynastic code, the model of ancient sage-kings found in classical Confucian texts as well as historical examples of virtuous kings were considered norms to be followed by the king. When remonstrating with the king or passing judgment on the king's conduct, Confucian scholar-officials referred to both the dynastic code and past examples of kingly virtue. Confucian constitutional discourse was thus a mixture of institutional arrangements and ethical exhortations designed to discipline the ruler. These sources of constitutional norms can be subsumed under the rubric of 'ritual propriety' (*ye*), which refers to not only rules for performing certain ceremonies but also the standard of all civilised behaviour including government. From the Confucian viewpoint, a ruler who relied on physical force or threat of coercion to govern was not civilised and was in violation of the requirements of ritual propriety. Such a ruler could not claim to be virtuous or legitimate and ultimately risked revocation of Heaven's mandate. On this view, even the dynastic code was just an institutional tool for disciplining the ruler according to ritual propriety. Anything that conduced to ensuring that the king was benevolent and virtuous could be mobilised in this Confucian constitutional system. That is why the government had specialised agencies like the Royal Lecture, the Censorate, and Court Historians. That is also why the government expended time and resources to ensure that the king properly observed the requisite state rituals according to Confucian classics. One such effort was the compilation of a separate code called *Kukcho Oryeŭi* (Manual on the Five Rituals of Our Dynasty), which included specific prescriptions on how to perform five categories of rituals requisite for any legitimate Confucian dynasty.[7] This also functioned as a source of constitutional norms in Chosŏn.

---

[5] On the mechanism for updating the codes, see J Bourgon and P-E Roux, 'The Chosŏn Law Codes in an East Asian Perspective' in M S-H Kim (ed), *The Spirit of Korean Law: Korean Legal History in Context* (Brill 2016) 28–30, 34–35.

[6] Hahm (n 4) 156.

[7] The five categories were: offering sacrifice to numerous deities or spirits of the state; observance of state funerals; greeting foreign emissaries; performance of military exercises; and performance of royal weddings and other felicitous events in the royal family.

In sum, in a Confucian state, ritual propriety formed the basis of political legitimacy and provided the means with which to contest the ruler. Policy issues were debated in terms of whether they conformed to ancient models of virtuous rulers and the dynastic codes compiled by the king's forebears. After Chosŏn was invaded by the Japanese (1592–1597) and the Manchus (1636–1637), national reconstruction was also understood as a project of rectifying ritual norms that had been disrupted by war.[8] The last Chosŏn monarch to fully adhere to the ideal of Confucian kingship may have been King Yŏngjo (r 1724–1776), who became so proficient in Confucian learning that he was able to lecture to his Royal Lecturers.

II. ADVENT OF MODERN CONSTITUTIONALISM AND COLONIAL RULE

By the nineteenth century, the dynasty was essentially controlled by a handful of powerful families that had produced queens. Government had become a private enterprise of the king's in-laws. Attempt was made to reassert the king's power and authority under the regent Taewŏngun whose son Kojong acceded to the throne at the age of 12 in 1863. The regent levied new taxes to rebuild the original royal palace that had been destroyed by the Japanese in 1592. Claiming that the numerous Confucian academies throughout the country were the source of factionalism and government stalemate, he shut down most of them and stripped the remaining ones of their financial and tax privileges. He ordered a major update and overhaul of the legal system, including the revision of the *Kyŏngguk Taejŏn*. Taewŏngun adopted a policy of strict isolationism under which all foreigners were to be forcibly repelled and any interaction with them punished as treason.

A. The Ideal of Constitutional Monarchy

Shortly after King Kojong assumed the reins of government in 1873, he departed from his father's policies to conclude treaties of amity and commerce with foreign countries. He even employed foreign advisers in an effort to modernise the country in the hopes of fending off imperialist ambitions of various nations. He undertook far reaching reforms in

[8] Hahm (n 4) 166.

1894 which included the abolition of the traditional civil service examination, which meant that Chosŏn was no longer a Confucian state. Class distinctions were abolished so that, at least in the formal legal sense, all became equal subjects of the king. Government agencies were reorganised along Western models and a state law school was established for training judges and prosecutors.

The initial phase of the reforms was consummated by Kojong's proclamation on 12 December 1894 of a 14-article document called *Hongbŏm*. In it, he vowed to secure the foundation for national independence and to enact a law to clarify the line of succession and to separate palace matters from government affairs. It also stated that the queen, the king's in-laws, and members of the royal clan are to stay out of state matters. In addition to several articles on reforming and modernising the administration of taxes and state finances, the document provided for the clear definition of the powers of government officials at both the central and local levels. It also promised the enactment of clear civil and criminal laws to ensure everyone's life and property, as well as regularisation of both the military and national education. While this document is sometimes considered Korea's first 'modern' constitution, the fact that Kojong announced it at the royal ancestral shrine in the form of an oath to his ancestors' spirits suggests that it might be more accurate to describe it as a last attempt to shore up the dynastic order.

The 1894 reforms produced considerable advances for Korea's law and society. Yet, their significance was undercut by the fact that they were carried out on the 'advice' of the Japanese Empire, which was trying to place Korea under its sphere of influence. This naturally made them quite unpopular among the people who chose to oppose the reforms out of nationalist concerns. Anti-Japanese sentiments in Korea turned decidedly worse when Kojong's wife, Queen Min, was brutally murdered at the hands of Japanese swordsmen who stormed the royal palace at the instruction of Japan's minister in Seoul. In an attempt to ward off Japan's further encroachment on Korea and to ensure his own personal security, Kojong tried relying on the influence of other foreign nations, especially Russia. Taking advantage of a temporary lull in Japan's influence, the king withdrew a few of the previous reforms implemented under Japanese pressure and, in 1897, declared himself an emperor, adopted the reign name of Kwangmu, and changed the dynasty's name to *Taehan Cheguk*, or Great Han Empire.

The emperor's effort to bolster the ruling house's dignity was greeted with approval by many who were apprehensive about the growing threat to national independence posed by the numerous concessions to foreign powers. To fight this trend, various civic organisations, most notably the Independence Club (*Tongnip Hyŏphoe*), campaigned against granting foreign countries control over territories and/or resources in Korea. Led by modernisers who had studied or lived in Japan and the United States, the Independence Club even argued that the nation's independence and wealth could be best preserved by reforming the government to allow for increased input from the people. Through various newspapers and private works, they were instrumental in introducing the ideas of people's rights, popular sovereignty, republicanism, democracy, and political representation to Korea. Leaders of the Independence Club did not advocate a transition to republican form of government but did push for the expansion of people's right to participation and the freedom of speech and assembly.

In October 1898, the Independence Club organised an assembly in the streets of Seoul where debates were held between ordinary citizens and government officials on various issues facing the nation. Among the speakers at the assembly was a young moderniser named Yi Sŭngman, better known as Syngman Rhee, who would later become South Korea's first president.[9] The assembly drew up a 'Six-Article Respectful Recommendations' (*Hŏnŭi Yukcho*) to be submitted to the emperor.[10] This document ostensibly affirmed the emperor's powers, but it also included implicit demands for limiting his personal influence over policy and personnel matters. Kojong initially responded favourably by agreeing to establish a semi-representative body in which half of its members would be nominated by civic groups such as the Independence Club.[11] Ultimately, however, the emperor changed his mind in response to fabricated rumours that the Club's leadership were secretly plotting to overthrow the monarchy and establish a republic. Anyone implicated in the street assembly and the adoption of the Recommendations was arrested and put behind bars.

Having dashed all hopes for a constitutional monarchy, Kojong announced in 1899 a document called *Taehanguk Kukche* (National Polity of the Great Han), which proclaimed that Korea was an autonomous and

[9] Throughout this book, all Korean names will be romanised according to McCune-Reischauer system and will follow the Korean convention of placing the family name before the given name. Syngman Rhee is an exception, as are authors' names where the person's own romanisation is known.

[10] Y-h Ch'oe et al (eds), *Sources of Korean Tradition*, vol II (Columbia University Press 2000) 285.

[11] Suh H-K, *Taehan Minguk Hŏnpŏp ŭi T'ansaeng* [*Birth of the Constitution of Republic of Korea*] (Changbi Publishers 2012).

independent empire recognised by the international community (art 1) and an eternal 'despotic polity' (art 2) ruled by an emperor with unlimited powers (art 3). The nine-article charter was entirely concerned with the emperor's plenary powers with no mention at all of people's rights or any other government agency. The emperor apparently concluded that national sovereignty could only be preserved by strengthening his own powers and by personally superintending every aspect of state affairs. Anyone who dared to intrude on the emperor's powers was deemed to have forfeited their status as the emperor's subject.[12]

Despite Kojong's attempts to strengthen his powers, the Great Han Empire was ultimately too weak – economically, militarily, and diplomatically – to forestall foreign encroachments. Even the modernisers' proposal for a constitutional monarchy, via some form of 'joint rule' between the emperor and the people, had been made in the hopes of strengthening the state and preserving national sovereignty. Under the pretext of protecting Korea from Russia's interference, Japan forced upon Korea a series of treaties which progressively increased its own influence. After acquiring the right to station its troops on Korean soil, and to bring its own military police, Japan gained control of Korea's diplomacy and turned it into its 'protectorate' in 1905. When Kojong tried to resist these intrusions, he was forced to abdicate in 1907. The Japanese resident-general then took control over Korea's domestic affairs including legislation and appointment of officials. After disbanding the remnants of the Great Han Empire's military, Japan consummated its takeover of Korea with the infamous 1910 Treaty of Annexation by which Korea lost its sovereignty and became a colony of Japan.

B. Colonial Subjugation and the Republican Dream

With annexation, Korea was placed under a colonial administration headed by a Japanese governor-general, an imperial appointee. Although Koreans were formally Japanese nationals, they were colonial subjects governed by a separate legal regime, which differed from that for the Japanese.[13] The Constitution of the Japanese Empire (also known as the Meiji Constitution) was not applicable to Koreans.[14] Clearly, colonial

[12] Suh (n 11) 44–48.
[13] E I-t Chen, 'The Attempt to Integrate the Empire: Legal Perspectives' in RH Myers et al (eds), *The Japanese Colonial Empire, 1895–1945* (Princeton University Press 1984).
[14] M S-H Kim, *Law and Custom in Korea: Comparative Legal History* (Cambridge University Press 2012) 153.

subjects were not to avail themselves of the constitution's rights provisions. The governor-general had the power to make laws for Korea and to
decide which laws made by Japan's legislature (Imperial Diet) would be
enforced in Korea. A Japanese-style court system was introduced, whose
judges were appointed by the governor-general. Being accountable only
to the Japanese emperor, the governor-general was essentially beyond the
control of Japan's cabinet and legislature in Tokyo.

While some Koreans utilised the colonial legal system to protect their
economic interests, it was virtually impossible to advance their political status legally.[15] As subjugated people, Koreans had no representatives
either in the colonial government or the Imperial Diet. They were mere
objects of control and surveillance through such institutions as the
household registration system. Under the pretext of 'assimilation', the
Korean language was banned. Toward the end of the colonial occupation, all Koreans were forced to adopt Japanese names so that they could
be conscripted into the Japanese military. Any activity aimed at regaining
independence was harshly punished. Many leaders of the independence
movement thus moved overseas.

Constitutionalist discourse and practices were thus extinguished
in Korea during colonial occupation. Yet, outside Korea, the ideals of
constitutionalism persisted and acquired another layer of meaning and
urgency. A constitution was now perceived to be an essential means not
merely for limiting the ruler's powers, but rather for regaining independence. To become a sovereign nation again, Korea had to go through the
process of constitutional founding. A consensus soon emerged within
the independence movement that the new state to be founded must be
a democratic republic.[16] Instead of a restored monarchy, the renewed
Korea would be governed by the people through their representatives.

The 'Declaration of Harmonious Unity' (*Taedong Tangyŏl ŭi Sŏnŏn*),
issued in 1917 as a vow of unity among various overseas groups fighting
for independence, reveals how the ideals of republicanism and people's
rights were understood in relation to the goal of regaining national
sovereignty. It proclaims that Korea's last emperor's ceding of sovereignty
resulted in the transfer of sovereignty to the Korean people. According to
this document, it has historically been an 'unwritten fundamental state
law' that sovereignty can only be exchanged among members of the same

[15] C Lee, 'Modernity, Legality, and Power in Korea under Japanese Rule' in G-W Shin and
M Robinson (eds), *Colonial Modernity in Korea* (Harvard University Asia Center 1999).
[16] Kim D-H, *Taehan Chegukki ŭi Chŏngch'i Sasang Yŏngu* [*A Study of Political Thought
During Taehan Empire*] (Chisiksanŏpsa 1994) 426–34.

nation. When the Korean monarch surrendered his sovereignty, it was only the people of Korea who could legitimately inherit his awesome prerogatives. No foreign prince could purport to assume sovereignty over Korea.[17] The hour that the emperor's powers were terminated was the hour that the people's powers were born, and the last day of old Korea was the first day of new Korea. In practically the same breath, the document asserted both the legitimacy of the people's assumption of sovereignty and the unlawfulness of Japan's annexation.[18]

It was thus natural that when a historic nationwide peaceful protest against the colonial authorities was convoked in 1919, it started with an invocation of national independence and people's rights. The 'Declaration of Independence' that sparked the March 1st Independence Movement proclaims that 'Korea is an independent state and Koreans are a self-governing people'.[19] Less than a decade after Chosŏn's last emperor ceded sovereignty, support for the monarchy among Koreans had practically evaporated and republicanism became the new *zeitgeist*.

C. Korean Provisional Government and 'Extraterritorial' Constitutionalism

The March 1st Independence Movement, though brutally suppressed by colonial authorities, marked a turning point in Korea's struggle to regain independence and her path toward constitutionalism. The following month, as many as eight different groups, both inside and outside Korea, announced 'constitutions' purporting to set up a government for the Korean people, and all of them claimed to be establishing a republican government based on popular sovereignty. The authors of these charters regarded themselves as implementing and formalising the Korean people's sovereign will expressed so unmistakably through the March 1st Movement. They were executing the people's *pouvoir constituant*, that is, their will to establish a new constitutional republic.

While many of these groups turned out to be 'paper governments', three were genuine organisations with real membership. The one in

[17] C Hahm and SH Kim, *Making We the People: Democratic Constitutional Founding in Postwar Japan and South Korea* (Cambridge University Press 2015) 173.

[18] Suh (n 11) 67–68.

[19] Ch'oe et al (n 10) 337. Rejecting coercive imperialist expansionism as a relic of the blighted past, it justifies independence as a dictate of not only Korea's national will, but also as a means for preserving peace in East Asia and complying with universal norms of justice.

Shanghai was the first to proclaim a 'Provisional Charter of the Republic of Korea' (11 April 1919), consisting of 10 articles, which declared that Korea 'shall be a democratic republic' and affirmed the equality of all people regardless of sex, class, and wealth. The charter also provided for various civil and political rights. It even employed a new Republican Calendar and stated that the constitution was being promulgated in 'Year One of the Republic'. Some commentators regard this document as the starting point of Korea's modern constitutional history.

In late 1919, an agreement was reached to merge the three 'provisional governments' in Seoul, Shanghai, and Vladivostok. A united 'Provisional Government of the Republic of Korea' (KPG) was proclaimed, with its headquarters in Shanghai. A more comprehensive 'Provisional Constitution' was adopted (11 September 1919), consisting of 58 articles, which explicitly stated that sovereignty of Korea resides in the entire people of Korea (art 2). The constitution was the basis of the KPG's claim to act on behalf of all Koreans. While its leadership was constantly plagued with internal discord regarding the best way to regain independence, no one disputed the need for a constitution that set out the powers and organisation of the provisional government. Such dedication to governing according to a constitution persisted throughout the colonial period to form a valuable part of Korea's constitutional history.

The KPG's experience is particularly significant in that it shows how leaders of the independence movement sought to adhere to the principles of constitutionalism and republicanism. For example, the revised Provisional Constitution of 1925 provided that 'activists in the independence movement' (*kwangbok undongja*) shall represent and act on behalf of the entire Korean people (art 3). In the 1927 version, this became more concrete with the statement that 'during the period of struggle for independence, state sovereignty shall reside in the entire independence activists' (art 1). Since elections for the Provisional Legislative Council could not be held inside Korea, independence activists who hailed from electoral districts in Korea and who resided in the site of the KPG were authorised to vote on behalf of their compatriots.

The KPG constitution went through numerous revisions to adapt to changing circumstances both internally and externally. The initial Provisional Constitution of 1919 provided for an awkward power-sharing arrangement between the Provisional President, who was the head of state and overseer of state affairs, and the Prime Minister, who was the chief of the executive branch (State Council). This was probably an attempt to hold together the various factions within the independence movement. When this system proved unstable, the constitution was revised in 1925 to combine the head of state and the chief executive into a new office called the 'Premier'. Two years later, however, this position was abolished, and executive power was placed under the collective leadership of the State Council. The 1927 revision seemed to mandate a system of legislative supremacy by declaring that 'highest state power' resides with the Provisional Legislative Council (art 2). This may have been another attempt at a compromise between numerous 'parties' vying for control of KPG. By 1940, however, the need for effective and energetic leadership dictated another revision to empower the Chairman of the State Council to issue executive orders and even superintend a 'national military' (art 27). In anticipation of the conclusion of the Second World War and the upcoming task of state building, the 1944 revision further strengthened the Chairman's powers.

As an entity consisting of overseas independence activists who had fled Japanese repression, the KPG sometimes appeared less like a 'government' than a group of underground activists planning attacks on Japanese government officials.[20] It never succeeded in attaining recognition from the international community, despite the dedicated efforts of figures such as Kim Kyu-sik and Syngman Rhee. It suffered from a chronic shortage of operating funds and had to constantly relocate within China to flee the advancing Japanese military. However, even when its future seemed uncertain due to internal dissensus and external threats, the KPG leadership made sure that their activities were authorised by the constitution. The numerous revisions show that the principle of governing according to a constitution had become firmly entrenched during the KPG's 27-year history.[21]

Moreover, KPG constitutions enshrined the March 1st Movement as the founding moment of Korea's republicanism. According to another constitutional document called *Kŏnguk Kangnyŏng* (Essential Points for Founding a State), the March 1st Movement was the 'Great Revolution' that simultaneously toppled foreign despotism and destroyed the 'five-thousand year-old encrustation of monarchic rule'. The goal was not just the rejection of foreign domination but also the repudiation of dynastic

---

[20] Oh HM, 'Taehan Minguk Imsi Chŏngbu wa Iphŏnjuŭi: "Hŏnpŏpkukka" rosŏŭi Chŏngdangsŏng Hwakpo wa Tillema [Korean Provisional Government and Constitutionalism: Its Legitimation and Dilemma as Constitutional State]' (2009) 49 *Kukche Chongch'i Nonch'ong* 277, 293–96.

[21] The constitution's official name varied over time to include, *hŏnjang* (charter), *hŏnpŏp* (constitution), and *yakhŏn* (concise constitution).

government.[22] The 1944 Provisional Constitution also recalls, in the preamble, the 'March 1st Great Revolution' and the blood and tears of countless patriots which led to the establishment of the new Republic of Korea. This reference to the March 1st Movement would become an important basis of the legitimacy of South Korea's founding.

III. FROM LIBERATION TO CONSTITUTIONAL FOUNDING

Korea was finally liberated on 15 August 1945 when Japan announced its surrender to the Allied Powers. Yet, liberation was accompanied by national division as the Allies decided to divide the Korean Peninsula in half at the 38th parallel. In the northern part, the Japanese military were to surrender to the Soviet Union's Red Army while those in the south would surrender to the United States Army Forces in the Far East. As soon as Japanese surrender was announced, even before the occupying armies arrived,[23] a group of Koreans launched a 'People's Republic of Korea' in Seoul under the leadership of Yŏ Un-hyŏng, a centre-left politician who had once been a member of KPG. However, neither occupying military authority recognised it as a lawful entity. The Americans in the south set up the US Army Military Government in Korea (USAMGIK) which declared itself the only legal authority in the territory, while the Soviets established a Civil Administration and began organising 'people's committees' at various levels throughout the northern part.

When the two occupation forces came to Korea, the only thing that was clear seems to have been the understanding that there was no sovereign state in Korea. In the words of Ernst Fraenkel, a legal adviser to USAMGIK, they were coming to a 'no man's land'[24] with no governing authority. The KPG's claim to be a 'government' was not recognised. A clearer directive on the Korean question finally came in late December 1945 at the Moscow Conference of Foreign Ministers of US, UK, and the Soviet Union. The stated goal was to place Korea under the United Nations trusteeship, to be overseen by 'four powers' (US, UK, China, and Soviet Union). This was to last up to five years, during which a 'Provisional Korean Democratic Government' would be set up, with the

---

[22] Hahm and Kim (n 17) 174–75.
[23] The Red Army arrived in Pyŏngyang around 24 August 1945 and the US military arrived in Seoul on 6 September.
[24] E Fraenkel, 'The Structure of United States Army Military Government in Korea' (1948), reprinted in (1985) 2 *Journal of Modern Korean Studies* 69.

assistance of a 'US-Soviet Joint Commission' which would consult with local 'democratic parties and social organizations'. As soon as the news of the trusteeship plan was announced, protests erupted throughout Korea. Having been liberated from Japan's occupation just a few months earlier, Koreans were not ready to accept another form of foreign rule. Most activists in the overseas independence movement had returned to Korea by this time[25] and they vehemently argued that the only acceptable solution was immediate and complete independence.[26]

The occupying authorities on both sides nonetheless proceeded to form the US-Soviet Joint Commission, which had its first meeting in March 1946. The proceedings soon got bogged down, however, over the issue of which local groups should be allowed to participate in setting up the Provisional Korean Democratic Government. Whereas the Soviet delegation asserted that anyone who criticised the trusteeship plan should be excluded from the process, their American counterpart argued that a democratic government cannot be established without respecting the people's freedom of expression. This stalemate would essentially continue until November 1947 when the United States finally decided to refer the question of Korean independence to the United Nations. Yet, this was also when various political groups in Korea produced numerous constitutional drafts. When the US-Soviet Joint Commission asked local social organisations to submit outlines for the government of new Korea, over 400 proposals were submitted. Although marked by great uncertainty and volatility, it was a time when people engaged in constitutional politics of the highest sort to debate and argue about the new Korean state's form and principles.

A. Constitutional Debates under the US Military Government

The Soviet occupying forces in the north quickly quelled criticism of the trusteeship plan and set about establishing a separate government. In February 1946 a Provisional People's Committee for North Korea consisting of supporters of the Moscow decision was set up, followed by a permanent People's Committee in 1947, which began preparing a

---

[25] Syngman Rhee and his colleagues returned from the US on 16 October 1945. The first cohort of KPG leaders arrived from China on 1 November 1945, but per USAMGIK's orders not as members of any putative 'government'.

[26] S-Y Choi, 'Trusteeship Debate and the Korean Cold War' in B BC Oh (ed), *Korea under the American Military Government, 1945–1948* (Praeger 2002).

constitution for a separate northern regime. In the southern part under US occupation, anti-trusteeship demonstrations continued, and the US military government wavered between adhering to the trusteeship plan and preparing for a separate, pro-American South Korean government. As its goal was not clear, USAMGIK showed relatively little interest in constitution-making.

For Koreans in the US-zone, however, adopting a constitution and founding a new state was one of the most urgent issues. For example, a group called Emergency National Assembly was formed under Kim Ku, the last Chairman of the KPG, and with the support of the newly formed right-wing Korean Democratic Party, this group in February 1946 appointed a committee to draw up a draft constitution. This group soon merged with another one led by Syngman Rhee, called the National Society for the Rapid Realisation of Korean Independence. The combined group then delegated to Rhee and Kim the power to appoint a 'supreme political commission' – a 28-member body that was renamed the Korean Representative Democratic Council of South Korea (*Nam Chosŏn Taehan Kukmin Taep'yo Minju Uiwŏn*). Clearly not an elected body, this body was not expected to replace the US military government. Regardless, it immediately started acting as if its job was to be a transitional government and appointed a committee to draft a constitution.

Another early attempt to adopt a constitution was made in January 1946 by a group consisting mostly of Koreans who had served in the colonial bureaucracy. Although these individuals feared being branded 'collaborators' in the post-independence context, their experience and expertise were sought out by Shin Ik-hŭi, a former KPG member, who brought them together to form the Administration Research Association (*Haengjŏng Yŏnguhoe*). This group had committees with experts to prepare the basic laws and policies on numerous issues which the new Korean state would be facing. Most significantly, it produced a draft constitution which would later play an important role during the eventual constitution-making process after the UN-sponsored general election of 10 May 1048.

Similarly significant were the efforts by the Korean Interim Legislative Assembly (KILA, *Nam Chosŏn Kwado Ippŏp Uiwŏn*) to adopt a constitution for the new Korean state. Set up in December 1946 as the legislative arm of USAMGIK, KILA was meant to showcase local support for the US occupying authorities. It had 90 members (half elected and half appointed by the US authorities), and its mandate was to formulate policy and legislative bills which would become law upon the US military governor's 'concurrence'. It was clearly not expected to draft a constitution. Regardless, KILA members began drafting a constitution as soon as they convened.

In fact, KILA produced three draft constitutions, although only one was formally adopted by it. First was an 'outline' of a constitution prepared for the purpose of providing a legal basis for the administration of the territory under US control. Despite being labelled a 'transitional' charter, this document provided for a fully fledged government consisting of legislative, executive, and judicial branches as well as local government and a state fiscal system. From USAMGIK's perspective, however, this was clearly beyond the competence of KILA, since no decision had been made to create a separate government in the south. In response, another draft constitution was prepared encompassing the entire Korea, which might later be used when a unified Korean government was established. Yet, this was also problematic for the US occupying authorities because an assembly representing only the southern half had no authority to draft a constitution for the whole of Korea. The third draft was intended to be a compromise between the first two, and was actually passed by the KILA. The 'Temporary Constitution of Korea', however, never went into effect because the US military governor refused to give his concurrence, on the grounds that a constitution should be drafted when a unified Korean government was set up.

B. UN-Authorised General Election and Constituent National Assembly

As mentioned, the meetings at the First Session of the US-Soviet Joint Commission stalled over the issue of whether local groups that opposed the trusteeship plan should be consulted in the process of forming the 'Provisional Korean Democratic Government'. The Second Session of the Joint Commission began in May 1947, but the same issue blocked any progress. With the Cold War already in full gear, the idea of establishing a unified Korean state through US-Soviet cooperation was becoming increasingly unrealistic. In September 1947, the United States referred the 'problem of Korean independence' to the United Nations. In November the UN General Assembly adopted a resolution, over Soviet Union's objections, to send a commission to Korea to 'facilitate and expedite the attainment of the national independence of Korea and withdrawal of occupying forces'.[27] A United Nations Temporary Commission on Korea

---

[27] UNGA Resolution 112(II), 14 Nov 1947.

(UNTCOK) consisting of members from eight member states, arrived in Korea in January 1948, only to find that it was blocked from entering the Soviet zone. Unable to observe and consult with Koreans in the north, UNTCOK asked the Interim Committee of the General Assembly how to proceed. When the Interim Committee responded that they should oversee a general election 'in such parts of Korea as are accessible to the Commission', UNTCOK proceeded to observe and certify a general election held only in southern Korea on 10 May 1948. The following July, it drew up a report submitted to the General Assembly, which said: 'The result of the ballot was a valid expression of the free will of the electorate of those parts of Korea which were accessible to the Commission and in which the inhabitants constituted approximately two-thirds of the people of all Korea.' In terms of legal authorisation, the UN thus played a crucial role in the establishment of Korea's modern constitutional order.

On 31 May 1948, the 198 elected 'representatives of the Korean people' convened for the historic opening ceremony of the National Assembly,[28] whose first order of business was drafting a constitution. In terms of political orientation, the National Assembly was dominated by right-wing politicians who were affiliated with either the Korean Democratic Party, widely seen as representing land-owning interests, or an unofficial group led by Syngman Rhee who was elected the first Speaker of the National Assembly. Leftists had been purged from the political scene by the US authorities, and key centrist figures such as Kim Kyu-sik chose not to participate in the election.[29] On 3 June 1948, a Constitution Drafting Committee was formed comprising 30 Assembly members and 10 'expert advisers'. After 16 meetings, the committee presented a final draft to the plenary session of the National Assembly on 23 June 1948. The entire membership then debated on the draft during which time numerous changes were made. The final bill for the constitution was passed on 12 July and, with the Speaker's signing on 17 July, it was promulgated and went into effect immediately.

[28] According to UNTCOK's scheme, the southern part of the Peninsula was allotted 200 representatives, but two from districts in Cheju Island could not be elected due to interference by leftists who sabotaged the election. For a 2001 case addressing the violent sabotage of the Republic's founding process, known as the 4.3 Incident, see ch 9.

[29] Along with Kim Ku, KPG's last Chairman, Kim Kyu-sik objected that holding a separate election in the south would only make the division of Korea more permanent. Yŏ Un-hyŏng, the other key centrist politician in the south, had been assassinated in July 1947, before the election.

The fact that the constitution was created in only six weeks may be a sign of haste that marked the drafting process.[30] Yet, it also reflects the accumulated experience in constitution-making since the KPG period and under the US military government. Even before the process formally began, numerous draft constitutions were submitted to the National Assembly for consideration. When the drafting committee met, it adopted two pre-existing drafts as 'base texts' to frame the discussions. The 'primary text' is commonly known as the Yu Chin-o Draft after its 'author' who was at the time a law professor at Posŏng College (predecessor of Korea University). A graduate of Keijo Imperial University, the only university in Korea during colonial times, Yu was one of a handful of legal scholars in Korea at the time with some knowledge of public law and was thus appointed one of the expert advisers. According to his memoirs, he had already been commissioned by the US military government's Justice Department in the fall of 1947 to prepare a draft constitution. Around the time Yu completed the draft in early May 1948, Shin Ik-hŭi reportedly asked him to collaborate with the Administration Research Association to draw up a constitution.[31] As mentioned, this group had already prepared a draft constitution in 1946, and so when they met with Yu in May of 1948 both sides already had complete drafts from which to prepare a joint draft. This was finished literally on the eve of the National Assembly's opening. It was this joint draft which came to be known somewhat inaccurately as the 'Yu Chin-o Draft'.[32]

The other base text adopted by the committee as a 'reference text' was known as the 'Kwŏn Sŭng-yŏl Draft'. This draft bears the name of a Korean jurist who at the time was the deputy chief of the US military government's Justice Department and another expert adviser to the Constitution Drafting Committee. This draft is sometimes seen as representing the views of the USAMGIK Justice Department, but there is controversy as to whether this draft was really a separate text from the one that Yu Chin-o had drafted for the US military government.[33]

---

[30] The National Assembly decided early on that 15 August, the anniversary of Japan's surrender, would be the date for the inauguration of the new government of the Republic of Korea. As a result, the Assembly members were under pressure to finish the drafting process and to form the government by that deadline.

[31] Yu Chin-o, *Hŏnpŏp Kich'o Hoegorok* [*Recollections on the Drafting of the Constitution*] (Ilchogak 1980).

[32] Members of the Administration Research Association seem to have preferred not to be identified as the draft constitution's authors due to their previous careers in the colonial government.

[33] Yu claimed that his original draft constitution had been submitted to the Justice Department's Code Drafting Commission and that the Kwŏn Draft was substantially the

Nevertheless, as there were some significant differences, the drafting committee chose to utilise it as a 'reference text'.

IV. MAKING OF THE FOUNDING CONSTITUTION

When Yu first embarked on his drafting project, he decided on four guiding principles for the constitution of the new Korean state: (a) bicameral legislature; (b) parliamentary-cabinet system of government; (c) farmland reform; and (d) state control and/or ownership of major economic enterprises.[34] These were maintained in the so-called 'Yu Draft' jointly prepared with the Administration Research Association members. In the end, only two of them would be retained in the Founding Constitution.

A. Power Structure and Judicial Review

During deliberations in the Constitution Drafting Committee, the legislature was changed to a unicameral system on grounds that electing an upper house would be too costly and time-consuming. Having just gone through a general election, holding another round of elections to create an upper house would cause too much turmoil and delay. One of the more progressive Assembly members also argued that it would end up being the bastion of privileged aristocratic interests. This unicameral system was adopted without much discussion at the plenary deliberations.

The issue that caused the most controversy during the drafting process was the choice between parliamentary and presidential systems. Here, the role of Syngman Rhee was pivotal in the decision to adopt a presidential system. At the time, Rhee's stature and reputation was such that there was near universal agreement that he would become Korea's first head of state. Yet, under the Yu Draft, the office of the president was

---

same as his draft except for some minor alterations. Kwŏn argued, however, that he and his colleagues at the Code Drafting Commission had never heard of Yu's draft. It is conceivable that Yu's original draft submitted to the Justice Department was delivered to Kwŏn and others for further refinement and elaboration. Kim S-y, *Kŏnguk kwa Hŏnpŏp: Hŏnpŏp Nonŭi rŭl t'onghae bon Taehan Minguk Kŏnguksa* [*Founding and the Constitution: History of Korean Founding as Seen Through Constitutional Debates*] (Kyŏngin Munhwasa 2008) 241–42.

[34] Yu (n 31) 19.

merely a figurehead with ceremonial functions.[35] Yu firmly believed that a presidential system was inefficient and prone to gridlocks between the executive and legislative branches and that the case of the United States was an exception. This suited the Korean Democratic Party, which was fast becoming Rhee's primary rival in the National Assembly and which expected that a parliamentary-cabinet system would provide a better chance for it to gain power. By contrast, Rhee, though not a member of the drafting committee, repeatedly expressed his preference for a presidential system. He argued that a parliamentary system would be more inefficient due to endless bickering among different political factions in the legislature and that the head of state should have the proper powers befitting the position, especially in a country like Korea that was facing so many urgent state-building tasks.[36] Ultimately, he prevailed by threatening to withdraw his participation from any government to be established unless the constitution provided for a presidential system. Korean Democratic Party's leadership had to relent because they knew that without Rhee's support, the new government's legitimacy would greatly suffer. Alterations were made to the committee's final draft just before submitting it for plenary deliberations at the National Assembly. Yu Chin-o protested that such a change required much more than the mere deletion and relocation of a few articles, but he had no choice but to acquiesce.[37] The changed government form was adopted with very little modification during plenary deliberations.

The result was a 'hybrid' regime of sorts which provided for a strong presidential system with elements of the parliamentary system. In addition to the president and the vice-president, the constitution provided for a prime minister appointed by the president with the consent of the legislature, who was to 'assist' the president and serve as the vice-chair of the State Council (cabinet). Major decisions of the president had to be approved by the State Council, but all of its members were appointed by the president. And while cabinet members could retain their seats in the legislature, the legislature could not dismiss the prime minister or hold the cabinet accountable. The system inevitably caused confusion as to

[35] In the Kwŏn Draft the baseline was also a parliamentary system, but by comparison it envisioned a stronger executive branch under a president with veto powers over legislation and a stricter separation of powers than in the Yu Draft.

[36] Lew Y-I, 'Yi Sŭngman Kukhoe Uijang kwa Taehan Minguk Hŏnpŏp Chejŏng [Speaker of the National Assembly Syngman Rhee and the Making of the Korean Constitution]' (2006) 189 *Yŏksa Hakpo* 101, 124–25.

[37] Yu (n 31) 74–80.

the locus of real power in the government. In a way, it was also a return
to the familiar attempt, going back to the KPG constitutions, at power-
sharing among different political groups.[38]

The locus of the power of judicial review was also a point of
contention during the drafting process. Even before the constitution
was adopted, a fully operating judiciary was already in place because
the US military government had preserved the colonial court system
by filling the vacancies left by Japanese judges with Korean jurists.
Despite the initial shortage of Koreans with legal training, most courts
were filled by Koreans by the time the National Assembly drafted the
constitution. More importantly, Korean jurists were becoming an
interest group of their own. This was facilitated by the idea, recently
imported from the US, of judicial independence. The Administration
Research Association's draft reflected this by adopting the American
system under which the Supreme Court had the power of judicial
review.

Yu Chin-o, however, was adamant that Korean judges, trained as
they were under the colonial regime, had neither the experience nor
the expertise needed to adjudicate constitutional issues. The rather
tenuous nationalist credentials of judges were another reason why
he thought it politically inadvisable to have them review the constitutionality of laws. When members of the Administration Research
Association insisted on a US-style judicial review system, Yu had to
relent, but he still managed to convey his reservations. So, at the drafting committee, when an Assembly member challenged the wisdom of
granting the Supreme Court the power of judicial review, Yu promptly
agreed that such a system was inadvisable. Other committee members
also agreed that regular judges 'did not have sufficient credibility and
authority' to strike down legislation.[39] In the final draft, the power of
reviewing the constitutionality of laws was given to a special agency
called the Constitution Committee. This would be chaired by the vice-
president and comprise five members each from the Supreme Court and
the National Assembly.[40]

---

[38] Kim SH and Choi S, '1948 nyŏn Kŏnguk Hŏnpŏp e Nat'anan Honhapchŏk Kwŏllyŏkkujo ŭi Kiwŏn [Origins of the Mixed Power Structure of the Founding Constitution]' in Hanguk Mirae Hakhoe (ed), *Chehŏn kwa Kŏnguk* (Nanam, 2010) 13–15, 25–29.

[39] Yu (31) 53.

[40] The same method was to be used to constitute the Impeachment Tribunal, which became necessary because the legislature was changed to a unicameral system.

B. Inheriting and Reimagining the Past

Another interesting aspect of the founding process is the discussion regarding the proper name for the new Korean state. For many, *Chosŏn* was the common denomination for their country, but given that it had been the name of the dynasty responsible for the loss of national sovereignty, it did not have a positive connotation. This was aggravated by the fact that during the colonial period, the word was associated with second-class status within the Japanese Empire. Further, the fact that the communist regime in the north was calling itself Chosŏn People's Democratic Republic caused the Assembly members to be sceptical. As an alternative, some people proposed *Koryŏ* Republic, referencing the dynasty that preceded Chosŏn, and from which the Western name 'Korea' was derived. While it had less political baggage, many found it unsuitable for a democracy. Others preferred the more neutral *Hanguk*. This had been the name used in the Yu Draft. The drafting committee's final choice, however, was *Taehan Minguk* or Republic of *Taehan*. The immediate source was the Kwŏn Draft, but in fact Taehan Minguk had been KPG's official name since its establishment in 1919. It thus had an obvious aura of respectability.

At the plenary deliberations, this choice was retained, but only after some challenges. A few Assembly members pointed out that the term *Taehan* originated from Taehan Cheguk, the name of the ill-fated empire proclaimed by Kojong just before the demise of the Chosŏn Dynasty. One even claimed that this supposed empire was a 'congenital deformity' borne of the 1895 Treaty of Shimonoseki, such that it was never expected to survive.[41] For other Assembly members, however, the reference to the spirit of independence manifested in the March 1st Movement and the KPG was enough to override any negative association with the short-lived empire responsible for the loss of sovereignty.[42]

This association with the March 1st Movement would become the focal point of the South Korean state's claim to legitimacy and autonomy. In the Yu Draft the preamble pledged to commemorate the March 1st Revolution's 'great footsteps and hallowed sacrifices' and to inherit its 'indomitable spirit of independence'. Building on this, Syngman Rhee insisted during plenary deliberations on the inclusion of reference to the

---

[41] This treaty, concluded at the end of the First Sino-Japanese War, gave Japan freedom to interfere in Korean affairs.

[42] Hahm and Kim (n 17) 169–70.

fact that the Republic of Korea was not a new entity created by foreign powers' generosity but rather a continuation, or 'reconstruction', of a democratic state that had already been established via the March 1st Revolution. As a result, the preamble's final version stated that Taehan Minguk had been established and proclaimed throughout the world by the March 1st Movement and that the Korean people were 'presently engaged in the re-establishment of the democratic independent state'. Although no longer labelled a 'revolution,' the March 1st Movement was now clearly indicated as the origin of the Republic of Korea.

This, however, created an interesting tension within the text which reflected the uneasy relationship between the KPG and the new Korean state. Despite the constitution's invocation of the 'Spirit of March 1st' and its claim that a republic had already been proclaimed, the preamble did not mention the KPG. This was likely because Kim Ku, KPG's most emblematic leader, refused to participate in the 10 May general election that created the National Assembly. For many Assembly members, KPG was just one of many political groups. So, the 'Republic of Korea' being re-established connoted a much more ideational entity than the historical group that operated in China under that name. This was evidenced on the floor of the National Assembly when its members summarily rejected the idea of revising or amending the KPG constitutions. They claimed that only the 'spirit' of KPG was being succeeded to, rather than any of its specific charters or institutions.[43] They were enacting a new constitution for a new Republic of Korea.

In order to make a fresh start, the shameful legacy of colonial occupation had to be rejected and that meant that some form of punishment was required for the nation's traitors who had enriched and ennobled themselves under Japanese rule. Lustration was needed to cleanse the nation's soul. Indeed, for many Koreans, that was the most urgent task facing the nation. In the summer of 1947, before the general election, KILA had drafted a bill for the 'Special Act on National Traitors, Pro-Japanese Collaborators, and Crafty Profiteers' but it was vetoed by the US military governor. In the election law for the 10 May general election, however, the KILA bill's definition and classification of collaborators were employed to bar certain individuals from voting or running for office. Collaborators were thus barred from participating in the creation of the 'constituent National Assembly'. When the process of constitution-making began, demands flared up again for

---

[43] Hahm and Kim (n 17) 167–68.

actual punishment of the collaborators. While the Yu Draft contained no provision on this issue, the Kwŏn Draft had a provision for punishing 'traitorous acts committed prior to the enactment of the constitution' and it specifically stated that punishment shall be applied 'retroactively to the time of the acts'. Drawing on this, the final draft prepared by the drafting committee provided: 'The National Assembly which enacted the Constitution may establish a special law dealing with the punishment of malicious anti-national acts committed prior to 15 August 1945' (art 101). After extended discussion on the scope and the cut-off date of anti-national acts, the provision was passed without change.[44]

C. Enshrining a 'Socialistic' Economic Order

Competition with the emerging communist regime in the north could not but leave a mark on the constitution. An example is the provision on land reform and, more generally, the entire chapter on the Republic's economic order. Already in March 1946, farmland was being redistributed to tenant farmers in the north under Soviet supervision. Land reform was an important political issue in the south as well, where peasants comprised most of the population. When the 10 May 1948 general election was scheduled, the US military government hurriedly distributed to farmers land that had been confiscated from the Japanese. It is therefore not surprising that the Constitution Drafting Committee's two base texts both had provisions for farmland redistribution. Land reform had become a constitutional mandate and its importance was not disputed in the National Assembly. Whereas the committee's final draft provided that farmland shall be distributed to farmers 'in principle', debates during the plenary session resulted in deletion of that qualifier (art 86).[45]

Other provisions on ownership and management of economic resources also reflected an awareness of the need to respond to the progressive reforms taking place in the north. Indeed, the Founding Constitution was marked by a heavy dose of 'socialistic' ideas and institutions.[46] Its stated basic economic principle was to realise social justice, meet everyone's basic needs, and develop an 'equitable' economy (art 84). The state was to own most natural resources, which could be licensed to private citizens (art 85). Important enterprises of a 'public nature', such

---

[44] Hahm and Kim (n 17) 175–77.
[45] Hahm and Kim (n 17) 108–11.
[46] PS Dull, 'South Korean Constitution' (1948) 17(7) *Far Eastern Survey* 207.

as transportation, communication, finance, insurance, electricity, water power, and gas, were to be under state or public management (art 87). Even foreign trade was put under state control. In part, this was a legacy of the colonial period during which many Koreans, including Yu Chin-o, had been drawn to socialist ideas in response to the abuses of Japanese imperialism. For them, free market capitalism was a thing of the past that had to be overcome.

It bears noting, though, that such a state-centred economic order was not seen as 'revolutionary', or even leftist, by the founding generation. The *status quo ante* had been one in which the state was in control of virtually all aspects of economic life. By the time of liberation, Japanese authorities had conscripted practically all resources that could be mobilised in the war efforts and there were very few private economic actors.[47] The situation did not change much under the US occupation forces, who had no choice but to continue the colonial rationing system for basic goods such as rice and sugar. Under such conditions, it was only natural to prescribe an economic order in which the state would assume a central role in meeting everyone's basic needs.[48] In introducing the final draft to the plenary session, Sŏ Sang-il, the Constitution Drafting Committee's chair, emphatically stated that the goal was to establish a 'national socialist' system! According to Yu Chin-o, the aim was to realise economic and social democracy. Whatever the label, there was wide agreement that classical free market economy was not an option for the new Korean state.

It was against this background that the constitution came to include a unique provision guaranteeing the workers' 'right to an equal share in the profits of private enterprises' (art 18). Although quite socialistic on surface, it bears noting that in the context of 1948, the provision was in fact a right-wing response to, or a defence against, communist propaganda. By way of deflecting the leftist call for outright state ownership of all economic enterprises, moderate labour groups demanded the inclusion of this right, which made sense only on the presumption of the continued existence of private enterprises.[49] Arguments for such a right had been rejected at the drafting committee, but it was proposed again during plenary deliberations and, after one of the most heated debates on the floor, was finally included in the constitution.

---

[47] Eighty-five per cent of all assets in Korea were in the hands of the colonial government at the time.

[48] Hahm and Kim (n 17) 102.

[49] Hahm and Kim (n 17) 103–05.

D. Protection of Individual Rights

For members of the National Assembly, it was a matter of course that the constitution should have a bill of rights and that it should include not just civil and political rights but also social and economic rights. There were, nonetheless, a few controversies about the content and placement of specific rights. For example, the right to education had been included as a separate chapter in the Kwŏn Draft and the Administration Research Association's original draft. Yu Chin-o, however, insisted on its placement as a single article in the general bill of rights. This attracted much criticism during plenary deliberations to the effect that the importance of education was being neglected. Some Assembly members proposed that the provision specify that not only the tuition but all costs of education shall be borne by the state, while others argued that compulsory education should be extended to secondary schools. The final provision stated that 'at least' elementary education shall be free and compulsory. Regarding the rights of the criminally accused, the Yu Draft had provided that torture and cruel punishment were to be prohibited. This part was taken out by the drafting committee, but when plenary deliberations began, a proposal was made to put it back in. The proposal was defeated on the grounds that such language was not necessary in light of the general provision on 'freedom of the person'.

One interesting feature of the debates on individual rights was the question whether foreigners were entitled to the rights enumerated in the constitution. This was a byproduct of a controversy over the proper term in Korean to refer to the subject of rights. At the plenary session, a proposal was made to change *kukmin* to *inmin* for the bearer of constitutional rights and duties. The former literally meant 'state-people' and thus connoted, it was argued, a person whose interests are always aligned with the state's. By contrast, the latter meant 'human-people' which was more appropriate for signifying the people as understood in the doctrine of popular sovereignty. Indeed, *inmin* had been used in the Yu Draft. During plenary deliberations Yu Chin-o also argued for that term since the rights protected by the constitution were basically human rights (*inkwŏn*). To this Kwŏn Sŭng-yŏl countered that since the constitution was an agreement between the state and its members, it was proper to refer to the rights of *kukmin*. Another Assembly member added that the explicit reference to the state in *kukmin* might even be politically advantageous given the people's decades-long yearning for an independent state of their own.[50] The proposal to change to *inmin* was thus defeated, but that raised the question of the rights of foreigners who were not members of the Korean state. The result was the inclusion of a provision that guaranteed foreigners legal status and protection under international law. Given that the international community was closely watching the process of constitution-making in Korea, it was agreed that having a separate clause for foreigners' rights would be apposite.

V. CONCLUSION

The establishment of the Republic of Korea in 1948 was a milestone in the nation's long history of experimentation with constitutional ideas and institutions. The dream of a modern democratic republic finally became reality through the historic constitution-making by the National Assembly formed via Korea's first general election based on universal franchise. From a longer historical view, the adoption of the Founding Constitution represented a re-entrenchment of the age-old ideal that governments, to be legitimate, must observe constitutional norms. During dynastic times, such norms were derived from Confucian teachings whose concepts and institutions could be mobilised to both empower and discipline the monarch. From the end of nineteenth century onward, these were replaced with norms based on republicanism, popular sovereignty, and a written constitution. The KPG's experimentation with 'extraterritorial' constitutionalism and the constitution-drafting experience after liberation under US military occupation, though frustrating at the time, all provided valuable resources for the project of establishing a modern democratic constitutional system.

Critics may point out that the events of 1948 were marred by national division and the exclusion of some from the founding process. Indeed, the founding will remain incomplete until every member of Korea's sovereign people is brought within the purview of the constitution. One distinctive feature of Korea's modern constitutional identity is this disjunction, or gap, between the normative claim that Republic of Korea is the only legitimate state on the Korean Peninsula and the undeniable existence of a competing regime that is in control of the northern half of its territory.

[50] C Hahm and SH Kim, 'To Make "We the People": Constitutional Founding in Postwar Japan and South Korea' (2010) 8 *International Journal of Constitutional Law* 800, 843.

FURTHER READING

Deuchler M, *The Confucian Transformation of Korea: A Study of Society and Ideology* (Harvard Council on East Asian Studies 1992).

Hahm C, 'Ritual and Constitutionalism: Disputing the Ruler's Legitimacy in a Confucian Polity' (2009) 57 *American Journal of Comparative Law* 135.

Hahm C, 'Conceptualizing Korean Constitutionalism: Foreign Transplant or Indigenous Tradition?' in S Kim (ed), *Confucianism, Law, and Democracy in Contemporary Korea* (Rowman & Littlefield International 2015).

Hahm C, 'Thirty-Years-Old at Birth? The Constitutional Founding of the Republic of Korea' in K Tan & M Ng (eds), *Constitutional Foundings in Northeast Asia* (Hart 2022).

Hahm C and Kim SH, *Making We the People: Democratic Constitutional Founding in Postwar Japan and South Korea* (Cambridge University Press 2015).

Hahm PC, *The Korean Political Tradition and Law: Essays in Korean Law and Legal History* (Hollym Corp, 1967).

Kim M S-H, *Law and Custom in Korea: Comparative Legal History* (Cambridge University Press 2012).

Kokubun N, 'The Rise of Korean Constitutional Thought (1875–1945): An East Asian Perspective' in M S-H Kim (ed), *The Spirit of Korean Law: Korean Legal History in Context* (Brill 2016).

Lee C, 'Modernity, Legality, and Power in Korea under Japanese Rule' in G-W Shin and M Robinson (eds), *Colonial Modernity in Korea* (Harvard University Asia Center 1999).

2

History of
Constitutional Revisions

Legacy of the Founding Constitution – Presidentialism vs Parliamentarism –
Unlawful Revisions – Presidential Term Limits – Ruptures within
Continuity – Democratic Transition

THE KOREAN CONSTITUTION has been changed a total of nine times
since its first adoption in 1948. The last revision took place in 1987,
when Korea transitioned to democracy. This means that during the
first four decades of the Republic, the constitution had an average lifespan
of a little over four years. By contrast, the current constitution has been in
force for more than three decades. The pre-1987 period is often regarded
as a period of 'constitution without constitutionalism'. The constitution
was sometimes changed by authoritarian leaders to prolong their grip on
power. Revisions were also intended to mark a new beginning after military coups. Yet, it is worth noting that even authoritarian leaders sought to
legitimise their rule through the constitution. No one dared to rule without
the constitution.[1] Further, it is notable that the Founding Constitution has
never been formally repudiated. Even when major changes were introduced
to the form of government, the drafters did so with an awareness that
they were revising the Founding Constitution. One constant feature of
the preamble, which itself has had many versions, has been the paragraph
that states that the new constitution is a 'revision' of the constitution first
adopted in 1948. In that sense, the Founding Constitution has acted as the
anchor for constitutional continuity in modern Korea.[2] This chapter will
examine the vicissitudes of the Korean constitutional history with a view
to understanding how and why the current constitution took the shape
that it did.

[1] D-k Choi, 'The State of Fundamental Rights Protection in Korea' in L Mayali and
J Yoo (eds), *Current Issues in Korean Law* (The Robbins Collection 2014) 87, 107–08.
[2] Sung N-I, *Taehanminguk Hŏnpŏpsa* [*History of Korean Constitutional Law*]
(Pŏpmunsa 2012) 44–68.

I. REVISIONS UNDER SYNGMAN RHEE

The adoption of the Korea's Founding Constitution in 1948 was a milestone in Korean legal and political history. Unfortunately, this constitution was never given a chance to function. In less than two years, the Korean War (1950–1953) broke out when the North Korean regime, armed and aided by the Soviet Union and the People's Republic of China, invaded the South in an attempt to unify Korea under communist rule. While the fledgling Republic managed to survive, through military intervention by the United Nations under the command of Douglas MacArthur, the country entered a long period of authoritarian rule.

Even before the war, the Founding Constitution began to show signs of unsustainability. Under this constitution, the president was elected by the National Assembly for a four-year term which could be renewed once. Given his national stature as a near-legendary leader of the independence movement, Syngman Rhee was elected the first president in July 1948 by an overwhelming majority (180 votes out of 198) of the lawmakers. Unfortunately, the amicable relationship between President Rhee and the National Assembly fell apart almost as soon as the government was launched. In large part, this was due to the Founding Constitution's design, which combined elements from both presidential and parliamentary systems. Rhee complained that the National Assembly was interfering with the president's prerogatives, while the lawmakers protested that Rhee was ignoring the constitution and acting like a dictator. The 'hybrid' form of government proved to be a recipe for constant strife between the executive and legislature.

Beginning with the appointment of the very first prime minister and cabinet members, the new republic saw incessant clashes between the president and the legislature.[3] Members of the National Assembly felt entitled to an active role in the formation and operation of the government. After all, the president owed his position to the National Assembly and executive power was to be exercised collectively through the State Council. Lawmakers could become state councillors (and thus cabinet ministers), while the National Assembly could demand the dismissal of individual state councillors. Rhee, by contrast, insisted that the constitution's basic power structure was a presidential system which gave him exclusive control over the formulation and prosecution of state policy. As someone who prided himself on being above party politics, Rhee was

---

[3] Suh H-K, *Hanguk Hŏnjŏngsa 1948–1987* [*The Constitutional History of Korea 1948–1987*] (Tosŏch'ulp'an Porŏm 2020) 46–91.

determined to exclude all partisan interference from the legislature in making government decisions. The rift only got worse with the passage of time. From issues of transitional justice regarding punishment of 'traitors to the nation' under colonial rule[4] to the way that the government responded to leftist insurrections,[5] practically every political issue became an occasion for clash between the president and the National Assembly.

Not surprisingly, calls for changing the constitution emerged from both sides. It was clear that the two sides were operating with drastically different understandings of the government structure ordained by the constitution. The only way to resolve the difference was to remove the ambiguity from the text. In January 1950, a bill for revising the constitution was introduced by Assembly members critical of President Rhee. The bill proposed a full parliamentary system which would reduce the position of the president to a ceremonial figure. It failed, however, to gather the support of the requisite two-thirds of the lawmakers. Rhee and his supporters successfully argued that, in light of the government's paramount task of securing continued economic assistance from the United States, maintaining political stability was of the utmost importance.

A. Revision of 1952: The 'Culled' Revision

In May 1950, barely a month before North Korea's invasion, a second general election was held,[6] in which opponents of Rhee gained more seats in the National Assembly. Whereas Rhee still preferred to cast himself as being above partisan bickering, the opposition had become more organised and expanded its membership. Opposition to Rhee grew even stronger after the outbreak of war, as lawmakers contested the Rhee government's management of the war efforts. Lawmakers criticised him for failing to deal properly with corruption within the Ministry of National Defence and the cover-up by South Korean armed forces after the killing of innocent civilians.[7] For his part, Rhee regarded

---

[4] C Hahm and SH Kim, *Making We the People: Democratic Constitutional Founding in Postwar Japan and South Korea* (Cambridge University Press 2015) 188–93.

[5] Suh (n 3) 107–16.

[6] Since the first National Assembly was not just a regular legislature but also a constituent assembly, its members decided that they should disband after two years so that a regular legislature could be elected which would serve the full four-year term. The Founding Constitution itself embodied this decision (art 102).

[7] Kim M-s, *Chǒnjaeng kwa Pyǒnghwa: 6.25 Chǒnjaeng kwa Chǒngjǒnch'eje ǔi T'ansaeng* [*War and Peace: Korean War and the Birth of the Armistice Regime*] (Sǒgang Taehakkyo Ch'ulp'anbu 2015) 522–24.

such criticism as an annoyance which hampered his determination to use the war as an opportunity to end the nation's division. Convinced that true independence was not possible unless the communists were completely driven out from the Korean Peninsula, he clashed with the US government which wished to reach a truce with North Korea (and China, which had sent thousands of soldiers to counter what they called American imperialism). Rhee resolutely opposed any negotiations for a ceasefire, which would only restore the pre-war division of the Peninsula. He was convinced that the opposition in the National Assembly were being encouraged by the United States, which was trying to undermine his authority.[8] Yet, he also knew that his chances of re-election by the National Assembly would be very slim as long as the opposition controlled the legislature. He thus started cultivating partisan followers among lawmakers as well as appealing directly to supporters outside the legislature with the argument that the people should elect the president.

In November 1951, with negotiations for a ceasefire ongoing, Rhee proposed a constitutional revision for the direct popular election of the president and the creation of an upper chamber in the legislature. Given that his popularity among ordinary citizens was still relatively high, he argued that electing the president was a prerogative of the sovereign people. Creation of another chamber would be a chance to dilute the opposition in the legislature. Not surprisingly, though, the bill was resoundingly defeated in January 1952 by the opposition-controlled National Assembly.

Emboldened by their victory, lawmakers critical of Rhee submitted in April 1952 another revision bill for adopting a parliamentary form of government. Rhee countered in May 1952 by submitting a different revision bill based on the presidential system. With two separate revisions bills presented at the National Assembly, a 'compromise' bill was hastily drafted by the government, in which some provisions were culled from the two previous bills. This new bill would institute direct popular election of the president and create a bicameral legislature, while enhancing the prime minister's power in the formation of the cabinet and enabling the legislature to hold cabinet ministers accountable by a vote of no confidence. Ultimately, this 'culled revision bill' was adopted by the National Assembly, but only after Rhee started resorting to scare tactics.

[8] Kim I-y, *Kŏnguk kwa Puguk: Hyŏndae Hanguk Chŏngch'isa Kangŭi [Founding the State and Enriching the State: Lectures on Modern Korean Political History]* (Saenggak ŭi Namu 2004) 186–91.

Local politicians and civic groups were mobilised to intimidate opposition lawmakers; they claimed that the National Assembly had ceased to represent the sovereign people. On 25 May 1952, Rhee reimposed martial law,[9] alleging that North Korean commandos had been spotted around the temporary capital. Several members of the National Assembly were arrested on charges of having received contributions from the International Communist Party. Rhee threatened to dissolve the National Assembly (although the president had no such power under the constitution) unless the lawmakers cooperated in passing the revision. On 4 July 1952, with the National Assembly building surrounded by military police, and with barely a chance to deliberate on the bill, the lawmakers took a vote and adopted the 'culled revision bill'. A direct presidential election was held on 5 August 1952 according to the new rules and Rhee was re-elected, winning 74.1 per cent of the votes cast. By contrast, the government put off holding the election for the upper chamber. The National Assembly would remain a bicameral institution only on paper until the Second Republic.

B. Revision of 1954: The 'Round Off' Revision

The next revision took place in 1954. The previous year, an armistice agreement had been signed between the UN forces and North Korea (and China).[10] After three years of hostilities, the entire country lay in total ruin. The government's stated objective for the revision was to change the provisions on the Republic's economic order in the direction of a more market-friendly system. Given that the war-torn country was utterly dependent on foreign economic assistance, particularly from the United States, the argument was that the 'socialistic' provisions in the constitution[11] must be changed to assuage any fears on the part of potential foreign lenders and investors. The United States was in fact pressuring the South Korean government to change the economic system to one that would be more hospitable to private businesses and free

[9] Martial law had been declared on 8 July 1950, two weeks after the war broke out. Then, in different parts of the country, it was lifted partially and declared again depending on the war situation. Chang Y-S, *Taehanminguk Hŏnpŏp ŭi Yŏksa* [*History of Korea's Constitution*] (Korea University Press 2018) 182.

[10] Syngman Rhee acquiesced to the armistice only after being promised a mutual defence treaty with the United States. W Stueck, *Rethinking the Korean War: A New Diplomatic and Strategic History* (Princeton, Princeton University Press 2002) 186–93.

[11] See ch 1.

enterprise.[12] As a result, those provisions that mandated state ownership of major economic resources and government management of key financial institutions and utility companies were dropped or significantly watered down.

For most Koreans, however, the 1954 revision is remembered mostly for the provision that allowed Syngman Rhee to stay in power indefinitely. Whereas the Founding Constitution allowed presidents to serve only up to two terms, an article was inserted which made an exception for the president in office at the time of the revision. This provoked much criticism and protests from the opposition. When the vote was taken in the National Assembly, it was first announced that the revision bill received one vote short of the two-thirds majority (136 votes) required for revising the constitution. Two days later, however, the government retracted the announcement and declared that the bill had passed. It invoked a 'mathematical' argument that fractions must be rounded off to the nearest whole number when dealing with humans.[13] The opposition charged that this was unconstitutional, but there was no effectual way of contesting the government's action. A presidential election was held in 1956 under the changed rules and Syngman Rhee was re-elected for a third term in office.

Other features of this revision included the elimination of the position of prime minister, which moved the government structure closer to a typical presidential system. In line with Rhee's predilection for engaging with the people directly, a provision was added which required a national referendum for 'important issues of national security which would entail a restriction on state sovereignty or alteration of territory'. Further, this provision was declared unamendable, as were the articles proclaiming popular sovereignty and democratic republican form of government. With the 1954 revision, the awkward power-sharing arrangement under the Founding Constitution was resolved, for the time being, in the direction of a straightforward presidential system. At the level of political discourse, however, this spawned the popular narrative in which presidentialism was identified with dictatorship and parliamentary system with true democracy.

II. REVISIONS OF 1960: THE 'SECOND REPUBLIC'

On 15 March 1960, Syngman Rhee was elected to the presidency for the fourth time. Immediately following the election, however, protests

---

[12] Hahm and Kim (n 4) 115–25.

[13] Out of 203 members of the National Assembly, 135 had voted in support of the bill. Although two-thirds of 203 is 135⅓, the government argued that since there could not be a third of a person, the fraction must be discarded.

erupted, initially led by university students who claimed that the election had been rigged. Once it was revealed that law enforcement agents had fired into the crowd of protesters and subsequently tried to conceal the dead body of a student protester, demonstrations spread throughout the nation on 19 April 1960. A week later, Rhee resigned from office and went into self-imposed exile in Hawaii. Today, some commentators refer to these events as Korea's first citizens' revolution which put an end to autocracy and corruption.[14]

A. June 1960: Adoption of Parliamentary System

Following Rhee's resignation, the National Assembly decided to revise the constitution. Although some argued that a new general election should be held to form a new National Assembly which would then draft a new constitution, for practical reasons it was decided that the sitting lawmakers should adopt a new constitution and then hold a general election.[15] Procedurally, in other words, revision followed the rules of the existing constitution. The preamble was left intact to signify continuity with the Founding Constitution. Substantively, however, it involved a major overhauling of the main text. The new constitution was referred to as having inaugurated the 'Second Republic' to emphasise discontinuity with the Rhee administration.

Since the presidential form of government was widely seen as the root cause of all evil under the autocratic presidency of Rhee, most lawmakers agreed that the new constitution should adopt a parliamentary system. While the office of the president was retained, its powers were limited to those relating to diplomacy and emergency situations. Moreover, the president would be elected by the combined session of both houses of the legislature. The day-to-day operation of the government would be the responsibility of the prime minister and the cabinet. The lower house could hold the cabinet accountable through a vote of non-confidence, while the cabinet could dissolve the National Assembly in response to a vote of non-confidence. Elections for both chambers were held to finally form the bicameral legislature. Adoption of a parliamentary form of government was widely seen as a victory for democracy.

Other measures to strengthen democracy and prevent dictatorship included the establishment of a constitutional court and a national elections commission. The constitution also mandated political neutrality of

---

[14] Chang (n 9) 146–51.
[15] Suh (n 3) 364–82.

all public officials (especially the police) to prevent the mobilisation of government apparatus by whoever was in power. Political parties, which used to be at the mercy of the government during Rhee's presidency,[16] were given constitutional protection. Parties could not be disbanded unless and until they were pronounced unconstitutional by the constitutional court.

During the revision process, some lawmakers contended that, rather than revising the existing constitution, a new constitution should be adopted. This was needed, they argued, to highlight the illegitimacy and unconstitutionality of the two previous revisions which Rhee had rammed through. At the least, it should be made explicit that they were revising the original Founding Constitution of 1948, not the unlawful versions of 1952 or 1954. The implication was that the revision procedure of the existing constitution need not be followed. If the National Assembly was faithfully to carry out the 'revolutionary will' of the people, lawmakers need not be bound by the rules set by the ousted autocrat. In the end, however, they decided to follow the revision procedure rather than adopt an entirely new constitution. Many expressed doubts as to whether the National Assembly was authorised to pronounce on the constitutionality of previous constitutions. After all, they themselves had been elected under the rules of the 1954 Constitution.[17] Repudiating everything done since 1954 would be to create a vacuum, both legally and politically.

B. November 1960: Constitutionalising Retroactive Punishment

Before the year 1960 was over, the constitution would go through another revision, which undermined the quality of rule of law under the Second Republic. Impatient with the slow pace of reform under the new government, particularly the lukewarm punishment meted out to those responsible for corruption under Rhee's presidency, student protesters stormed the National Assembly building in late fall of 1960. In response, the government pushed through a revision which enabled the enactment of laws specifically designed to meet the protesters' demands. According to the supplemental provisions added to the constitution on 29 November 1960, it was now possible to retroactively punish those responsible for the

---

[16] In 1958, a minor leftist party was disbanded by an order from the Office of Public Information.
[17] Suh (n 3) 402–09.

rigged election of 15 March 1960 as well as those who abused power to accumulate wealth under the previous government. An exception to the rule of law had to be made in the name of carrying out the mandate of 'April Revolution'.

Giving expression to such revolutionary fervour may have been politically unavoidable. Yet, it is doubtless problematic for maintaining stability or fostering social cohesion. It may have contributed to the loss of constitutional legitimacy for the new government.[18] Indeed, the Second Republic is commonly described as a time of extreme political volatility. During the nine months it was in power, the government of Prime Minister Chang Myŏn went through three complete reshufflings of the cabinet, and the average time in office for cabinet ministers was just two months.[19] When Park Chung-hee staged his coup d'état the following year, he cited the political instability caused by the ineffectual government and the danger of North Korean invasion as justifications for his actions.

III. REVISIONS UNDER PARK CHUNG-HEE

On 16 May 1961, a group of soldiers under the leadership of General Park Chung-hee staged a military coup d'état, dissolved the National Assembly, and suspended the constitution. The group established the 'Supreme Council for National Reconstruction' and, on 6 June, issued the 'Special Measures for National Reconstruction'. According to this supra-constitutional law, the Supreme Council, composed of military officers, was to exercise all powers of the government. A new cabinet was composed but it was under the Supreme Council's control. Citizens' constitutional rights would be protected only to the extent consistent with the prosecution of the 'revolutionary objectives'.

A. Third Republic: Back to a Presidential System

From the beginning, the military leaders promised to transfer power back to a civilian government as soon as they had achieved the goals of their intervention. The Special Measures included a procedure for adopting a new constitution. As there was no National Assembly to propose and

---

[18] Suh (n 3) 450–69.
[19] Sung (n 2) 131–34.

deliberate on a revision bill, a new constitution would be drafted by a special 'Constitution Deliberation Committee' and then ratified by the citizens through a national referendum. Following this procedure, the Constitution of the Third Republic was promulgated on 26 December 1962. Yet, it did not enter into force until almost a full year later, when a new National Assembly was finally convened. Two months prior to that, in October 1963, Park Chung-hee, who had retired from the military, was elected president by one of the narrowest of margins.

The new constitution was marked by a return to presidentialism. The parliamentary system was blamed for the political instability under the Second Republic.[20] It was argued that in a country without a mature two-party system, a parliamentary system cannot produce a stable government that can effectively deal with the chaos and turmoil unleashed in the wake of the revolutionary ouster of a dictator. In a poor war-stricken country like Korea, a strong president was needed, who could provide the requisite leadership for spurring economic development and ensuring national security.

To impart democratic legitimacy, the president was to be elected through a direct popular vote. His term would be four years which could be renewed once. The office of prime minister was retained but it was made clear that the position was essentially an assistant to the president. The National Assembly reverted to a unicameral system. It was argued that having two legislative chambers was wasteful and promoted partisan divisiveness. Since Korea was not a federal state, it was also redundant as members of both chambers were essentially regional representatives.[21] The National Assembly had no say in the prime minister's appointment, although it could 'recommend' the removal of the prime minister or other cabinet ministers.

The preamble was redrafted to include references to the 'righteous protest' (*ŭigŏ*) of 19 April 1960 that brought down the Rhee government and to Park's own May 16th 'revolution' (*hyŏngmyŏng*) that established the new government.[22] New articles were included which guaranteed the citizens' dignity and worth as human beings, the right to choose one's profession, and the right to lead a life worthy of human beings. The Supreme Court was given the power of judicial review as well as the power to decide on dissolution of political parties. Impeachment cases were to be decided by a special tribunal composed of Supreme Court justices

---

[20] Suh (n 3).

[21] Suh (n 3).

[22] At this point, Park claimed that his coup was a continuation of the April 1960 revolution that brought down the Rhee administration.

and National Assembly members. Articles on the economic order were also revised to make it clear that the individual's freedom and creativity formed the basis of Korea's economy. Revising the Constitution now required a national referendum and the president was not empowered to propose a revision. Aside from the National Assembly, citizens could propose a revision by gathering the signature of 500,000 voters.

The adoption of the 1962 Constitution was marked by a fairly thorough drafting process of over three months with input and debates from leading legal scholars, political scientists, and economists. The process also included public hearings. This was a result of the military government's decision to exclude professional politicians, whom they regarded as corrupt and responsible for the chaos and instability under the Second Republic.[23] To be sure, every step was closely watched by the Supreme Council and the deliberations could not exceed the bounds set by its leaders. It is, however, noteworthy that critics of the military government felt free to engage in discussions regarding the propriety of bypassing the constitution of the Second Republic.[24] The claim was that a general election should be held first, to form a new National Assembly which would then be entrusted with the task of revising the constitution, in accordance with the rules of the 1960 Constitution. They argued that a constitution drafted by the military government, after having unlawfully dissolved the National Assembly, lacked legitimacy. The Supreme Council, however, insisted that a new constitution must be adopted without the participation of the inept and partisan politicians and that democratic legitimacy can be supplied by the approval of the sovereign people, ie, via national referendum. One positive outcome of the military government's involvement in constitutional revision may have been the heightened sense of popular sovereignty.[25] It is also noteworthy that the new constitution adopted through this procedure was eventually billed as a 'revision' of the Founding Constitution.

B. Revision of 1969: Third Term for President

In 1967, Park Chung-hee was re-elected president, thanks to the success of economic development undertaken under his government but also in

---

[23] One commentator asserts that this produced a process untainted by partisan interests, which has provided a model for later constitutional revisions. Shin W-C, 'Taehanminguk Hŏnpŏp ŭi Sŏngnip kwa Pyŏn'gyŏng [Creation and Transformation of the Korean Constitution]' (2018) 42(3) *Pŏphak Nonmunjip* 5, 30.

[24] Suh (n 3) 623–40.

[25] Chang (n 9) 202.

part to the failure of the opposition to unite under a single candidate. His ruling party performed very well in the National Assembly election held the same year. Soon thereafter, its leadership started floating the argument that Park should be allowed to serve a third term to provide stable leadership needed for economic development and national defence. This provoked criticism from not only the opposition, but also several ruling party members, who warned Park not to repeat the mistake of Syngman Rhee.[26] In September 1969, however, the ruling party succeeded in passing a revision bill which allowed the president to serve three consecutive terms. The process was marred by irregularities such as intimidation and coercion against members of the National Assembly. The vote was taken in the dead of night, in an annex building of the National Assembly, with only the members of the ruling party in attendance. The bill was then approved by a national referendum. Under the revised constitution, the number of lawmakers in the National Assembly was increased, as was the quorum required to pass an impeachment bill against the president.

In terms of regional geopolitics, the years 1968 and 1969 saw a dramatic rise of tensions on the Korean Peninsula due to a series of provocation by North Korea, including an attempted assassination of the president by armed commandos; the capture of a US Navy intelligence vessel (USS *Pueblo*); over 120 armed guerillas' infiltration into coastal cities; and the shootdown of a US reconnaissance aircraft (EC-121).[27] The announcement of the Nixon Doctrine in July 1969, in which the United States urged its Asian allies to tend to their own military defence, added to the sense of crisis on the part of South Korean government.[28] The Park regime thus started putting more emphasis on the importance of national security and anti-communism. For example, air-raid drills were reintroduced to enhance defence readiness. At the same time, it sought to ease tensions with North Korea by initiating peace talks through the Red Cross. For its part, North Korea also had incentives to improve relations with the South. The progress of détente among the superpowers signalled that the People's Republic of China and the Soviet Union might no longer support its belligerent stance. The result was the 7.4 Joint Communiqué of 1972, announced simultaneously in both Seoul and Pyongyang, which proclaimed that unification was to be sought through peaceful means without interference from external forces.[29]

---

[26] Suh (n 3) 731.
[27] Kim (n 8) 392.
[28] B Cumings, *Korea's Place in the Sun* (WW Norton 2005) 363–66.
[29] D Oberdorfer, *The Two Koreas: A Contemporary History* (Basic Books 2001).

Both sides agreed to continue talks through a South-North Coordination Committee and to establish a hotline between the two governments. For Park's government, every effort had to be expended to avoid another invasion from the North and to safeguard the fledgling economy which was about to enter its 'take off' stage. Stress continued to be laid on the need for strong and stable leadership.

C. Revision of 1972: The *Yushin* Constitution and the Fourth Republic

In April 1971, Park Chung-hee succeeded in being re-elected for the third time, after a very close race against Kim Dae-jung. In the general election held the following month, however, the opposition gained enough seats to block a constitutional revision, possibly reflecting people's disapproval of Park's increasingly heavy-handed approach. In December 1971, the government declared a state of emergency claiming that confrontations in the National Assembly was hindering the peace talks with North Korea. A 'Law on Special Measures for Safeguarding the State' was enacted, which enabled the president to take emergency measures such as controlling the economy, limiting the freedoms of the press and of assembly, and restricting labourers' right to collective action. For Park, opposition politicians had clearly become a nuisance impeding the energetic pursuit of economic development and national security.

On 17 October 1972, Park Chung-hee announced another emergency measure suspending parts of the constitution 'for about two months' for the purpose of overhauling the state system so as to 'better deal with developments in negotiations with North Korea and the rapidly changing geopolitical situation in East Asia'. Under this extra-constitutional measure, the National Assembly was dissolved and all political activities suspended. Legislative power was to be exercised by an 'emergency cabinet' which was mandated to publish a draft constitution in 10 days, which would then be put to a referendum for approval by the people within a month. On 21 November the national referendum was held, with 91.9 per cent of all eligible voters participating and 95.5 per cent of the actual voters approving the new constitution. Once again, the rules for constitutional revision were circumvented in preference for legitimisation through the sovereign people's approval.

Widely known as the *Yushin* (Revitalisation) Constitution, the new constitution was controversial from the beginning and has become synonymous with Park's authoritarian rule.[30] With no term limits for the President, Park was practically ensured of re-election, through an electoral body called the 'National Congress for Unification'. Described as an 'institution of sovereign delegation', this body was placed at the centre of government structure and was supposedly the most immediate expression of the supreme 'overall will' (*ch'ong'ŭi*) of the people. In addition to electing the president, it was also empowered to select, at the recommendation of the president, one-third of the National Assembly members. As a conduit for the people's sovereign will, the National Congress also had the final say in constitutional revisions proposed by members of the National Assembly. The president was also empowered to propose revision bills, which would be approved by a national referendum, without being voted on by either the National Assembly or the National Congress. The powers of the president were strengthened to include dissolving the National Assembly and appointing all judges, thereby clearly signalling his superiority over the other two branches of the government. Many individual rights were subject to 'statutory reservation' and the general provision prohibiting restrictions on the 'essential contents' of individual rights was deleted. The power of judicial review was stripped from the courts and given to a new organ called the Constitutional Committee. The judiciary was specifically barred from reviewing emergency decrees issued by the president.[31]

Although the *Yushin* Constitution was adopted via an extremely high approval rate at the national referendum, it was clear that democracy and human rights were to be postponed until Korea achieved economic development under Park's strong leadership. The National Assembly and all professional politicians, including the ruling party, were practically shut out from important policy decisions. The government became thoroughly depoliticised to enable the president to personally oversee the implementation of a 'heavy and chemical industrialisation' policy.[32] This laid the foundation for the development of South Korea's economy, but it obviously came at the expense of political freedom and constitutional politics. Through a series of emergency decrees, Park essentially banned any talk of reform from politicians, students, and labourers. The United States, under the Jimmy Carter administration, tried to pressure South Korea to improve its human rights record. Park's government responded

---

[30] HB Im, 'The Origins of the *Yushin* Regime: Machiavelli Unveiled' in B-K Kim and E.F Vogel (eds), *The Park Chung Hee Era: The Transformation of South Korea* (Harvard University Press 2013).

[31] Some *Yushin* era emergency decrees were later declared unconstitutional. See ch 9.

[32] Kim (n 8) 422–24.

with the idea of 'Korean-style democracy', ie, Korea's democracy should not be judged according to Western yardsticks. Park also resisted America's seemingly inconsistent demand to increase Korea's military budget. Whereas Carter wished to withdraw US troops stationed in Korea, Park contended that increased military spending would put an intolerable strain on Korea's weak economy.[33]

IV. REVISION OF 1980: THE 'FIFTH REPUBLIC'

The *Yushin* era ended abruptly when Park Chung-hee was assassinated on 26 October 1979 by his own chief intelligence officer, who held a grudge against Park and his head security guard.[34] While the government declared martial law (except for Cheju Island) to guard against any possible incursion from North Korea, many were hopeful for a chance to embark on a process of democratisation. Work began in both the National Assembly and the government (under an 'interim' president) to revise the *Yushin* Constitution to introduce democratic reforms and better respect for human rights.[35] These, however, were cut short by another military coup led by General Chun Doo-hwan, then-head of the military intelligence, and his Korea Military Academy classmate Roh Tae-woo, then-commander of the 9th Infantry Division, stationed on the border with North Korea.

On 12 December 1979, Chun and Roh staged a mutiny and took control of the military by arresting, on trumped-up charges, the martial law commander-in-chief.[36] The following April, Chun made himself the acting head of the Korea Central Intelligence Agency to take charge of the entire state apparatus. Then, on 17 May 1980, he forced the interim government to place the entire nation under martial law, banned all political activities, including all assemblies or demonstrations, and

---

[33] H-A Kim, 'Heavy and Chemical Industrialization, 1973–1979: South Korea's Homeland Security Measures' in H-A Kim and CW Sorensen (eds), *Reassessing the Park Chung Hee Era, 1961–1979: Development, Political Thought, Democracy, and Cultural Influence* (University of Washington Press 2011) 19, 34–36.

[34] Park's assassin, Kim Chae-kyu, was swiftly prosecuted and convicted of 'murder with intent of insurrection' and 'attempted insurrection' by a court martial. His death sentence was carried out in May 1980, four days after the Supreme Court affirmed the conviction. M S-H Kim, *Constitutional Transition and the Travail of Judges: The Courts of South Korea* (Cambridge University Press 2019) 244–45, 249–62.

[35] Suh (n 3).

[36] In carrying out the mutiny, soldiers under Chun and Roh's command stormed the martial law commander's headquarters, during which three servicemen guarding the headquarters were killed. Later, victims of the coup sought legal redress. See ch 9.

suspended all university classes. Numerous politicians and civic leaders were arrested on charges of fomenting social disorder and stoking
student protests. When a massive civilian protest broke out the next
day in the southwestern city of Kwangju, the leaders of the coup sent
army special forces and paratroopers, which resulted in the 'bloodiest
massacre openly perpetrated as a full-scale military operation'.[37] Next,
Chun created an extra-constitutional body called 'Emergency Council
for Safeguarding the State' (later renamed 'Legislative Council for
Safeguarding the State') which took over all powers of the government.
In August 1980, Chun was elected president by the National Congress
for Unification under the *Yushin* Constitution which was still in force
at the time. Yet, in September 1980, the 'Legislative Council' unveiled a
new constitution which was adopted through a national referendum on
22 October 1980. Another presidential election followed on 25 February
1981 under the new constitution, which established Chun as the president of the 'Fifth Republic'.

Overall, the 1980 Constitution sought to mitigate some of *Yushin*
Constitution's excesses while maintaining a strong presidency. It stipulated that the president could only serve a single seven-year term and
even provided that any change to the president's term of office shall
not apply to the incumbent president at the time of the revision. The
National Congress for Unification was abolished, and the power structure was returned to a more conventional presidential system based on
separation of powers. Yet, as with the *Yushin* Constitution, the president
was elected by an electoral body, rather than by direct popular election.
Requirements for issuing emergency decrees were more stringent and the
courts were no longer barred from reviewing emergency decrees. Efforts
were made to enhance the oversight function of the National Assembly,
but the president still had the power to dissolve the National Assembly.

Protection for basic rights was enhanced with the elimination of
'statutory reservations' attached to individual rights provisions and
the restoration of the general provision prohibiting restrictions on
the essential contents of basic rights. Better protection for criminal
defendants was sought by including provisions that made explicit
the principle of 'innocent until proven guilty', prohibition of 'guilt
by association', and the exclusionary rule for confessions. The 1980
Constitution also introduced for the first time in Korean history the

---

[37] J K-c Oh, *Korean Politics: The Quest for Democratization and Economic Development*
(Cornell University Press 1999) 83. The exact number of casualties, as well as who ordered
the troops to fire into the crowd, is the subject of continuing controversy.

concept of environmental rights and even declared that all citizens have the 'right to pursue happiness'.

Such improvements, however, could not erase the fact that the Fifth Republic itself was an authoritarian regime borne of an unlawful military coup. Although Korea's economy charted some of the most impressive growth during the period, constitutionalism and the rule of law remained largely stagnant. Aside from the government's repressive policies, this was also because the 1980 Constitution retained the system of judicial review which the *Yushin* Constitution had created. The Constitutional Committee had the power to review the constitutionality of statutes enacted by the National Assembly.[38] In reality, however, no case was ever filed at the Constitutional Committee, primarily because any request for constitutionality review of statutes had to be first certified by the Supreme Court. With the entire judiciary under the tight control of the president, it was practically impossible to obtain the Court's certification.[39] The constitution itself precluded any challenges to laws passed by the Legislative Council for Safeguarding the State, the extra-constitutional governing body Chun had established following the military coup.

V. REVISION OF 1987: TRANSITION TO DEMOCRACY

During his presidency, Chun Doo-hwan repeatedly pledged that he would leave office at the end of his seven-year term, thereby achieving a peaceful transfer of power for the first time in modern Korean history. It was widely known, however, that he would be succeeded by his comrade-in-arms Roh Tae-woo under the 1980 Constitution's system of indirect presidential election. Many opposition politicians and university students thus began demanding constitutional reforms to allow for direct election of the president. Chun responded by declaring that he would 'uphold' the constitution and banned all discussions of constitutional revision. This provoked several weeks of nationwide protests during June 1987. Now called the 'June Uprising', these protests were joined by ordinary citizens, including office workers, shopkeepers, teachers, and even some law enforcement officers.[40] On 29 June, Roh, the ruling

---

[38] In addition, the Constitutional Committee had the power to decide on impeachment cases and to dissolve unconstitutional political parties.

[39] Kim (n 34) 266.

[40] Oh (n 37) 91–93.

party's presidential candidate, finally announced that he would agree to constitutional reforms including direct presidential elections and better protection of civil and political rights.[41]

A special committee was set up in the National Assembly to deliberate on a draft constitution. For the first time in Korean modern history, negotiations took place among representatives of the ruling party and the opposition parties.[42] On 18 September 1987, a draft constitution was presented to the National Assembly, which approved it on 12 October. The constitution of the Sixth Republic was promulgated on 29 October 1987 following a national referendum which had taken place two days previously.

Aside from providing for direct election of the president, the 1987 Constitution shortened the president's term of office to five years, while retaining the ban on re-election. Also preserved was the provision precluding the application of any revised rule on term limits to the incumbent president. The president's power to dissolve the National Assembly was eliminated, while the National Assembly was granted the power to 'inspect affairs of the state'. Protection of basic rights was enhanced by, *inter alia*, including a specific ban on censorship regarding freedom of the press; declaring it a state duty to protect the physically infirm and the socially disadvantaged; and obliging the state to adopt a system of minimum wage. In the General Provisions chapter, a provision was inserted which made it a state duty to 'pursue peaceful unification on the basis of free democratic basic order'. The preamble was revised to refer to the Provisional Government of the Republic of Korea established in 1919 as the source of legitimacy for the modern Korean state.

Perhaps the most significant result of the 1987 revision for the development of Korea's constitutionalism was the establishment of a separate Constitutional Court. When negotiations began in 1987 for revising the constitution, however, creating a separate court for constitutional questions was not a foregone conclusion. The issue of judicial review and constitutional adjudication was not a high priority agenda. Neither the ruling party of Chun and Roh nor the three opposition parties showed much interest in the issue, most likely because constitutional adjudication had never been activated under previous constitutions.

For negotiators from opposition parties, there was agreement that reviewing the constitutionality of laws should be the job of the Supreme

---

[41] JM West and EJ Baker, 'The 1987 Constitutional Reforms in South Korea: Electoral Processes and Judicial Independence' (1988) 1 *Harvard Human Rights Yearbook* 135, 146–50.
[42] Chang (n 9) 272.

Court. This was part of their demands for enhancing judicial independence, along with the idea of taking away the power of judicial appointment from the president and giving it to a new 'Judicial Officer Recommendation Committee'. The ruling party also recognised that the previous Constitutional Committee must be replaced, but it opted to create a separate court for constitutional issues. It was apprehensive of embroiling the judiciary in political issues, especially if the Supreme Court was also empowered to disband unconstitutional political parties. The opposition parties agreed to the idea of creating a separate court, on condition that it would also have jurisdiction over 'constitutional complaints' similar to the *Verfassungsbeschwerde* adjudicated by the German Federal Constitutional Court. The ruling party agreed to that condition, in return for the opposition dropping the demand for the Judicial Officer Recommendation Committee.[43]

As for the Supreme Court, the idea of creating a separate court appears to have elicited two conflicting responses. On the one hand, it was wary of having to contend with a new competitor for judicial authority. On the other, it was relieved at the prospect of not having to deal with highly political issues which might jeopardise its independence. More senior judges generally took the latter view, while younger judges tended to take the former, who preferred to have the power of judicial review.[44] In the event, a separate court was created without clearly delineating the jurisdictional boundary between it and the Supreme Court.

The adoption of the 1987 Constitution marked the beginning of Korea's transition to democracy. Yet, some commentators claim that transition was significantly hampered even after the new constitution was adopted. As the new electoral system did not include a runoff vote, a candidate could become president with only a plurality of the electorate's votes. The failure of the opposition to unite under a single candidate ensured the election of Roh Tae-woo even though he received a mere 36.6 per cent of the popular vote. An unintended consequence of this may have been the more negotiated or 'pacted' transition to democracy.[45] For some, this meant that democracy was introduced in

---

[43] J Guichard, *Regime Transition and the Judicial Politics of Enmity: Democratic Inclusion and Exclusion in South Korean Constitutional Justice* (Palgrave Macmillan 2016) 33–36.

[44] 'Taedam: 6 Wŏl Minjuhwaundong 30 Chunyŏn: Tong Asia ŭi Minjuhwa wa Hŏnpŏp [Colloquy: Thirtieth Anniversary of the June Democratization Movement: Democratization in East Asia and the Constitution]' (2017) 23(3) *Hŏnpŏphak Yŏngu* 125, 172.

[45] C Hahm, 'South Korea's Miraculous Democracy' (2008) 19 *Journal of Democracy* 128, 134–36.

a more peaceful and orderly fashion; for others it meant the delay of democratic transition and obstruction of efforts to root out the legacy of the authoritarian era.

VI. CONCLUSION

It may be an exaggeration to describe Korea's history of constitutional revisions as an instance of 'hyper-constitution-making'.[46] Nevertheless, nine revisions between 1952 and 1987 suggest that for a long time the constitution failed to become a norm that regulated state power. Aside from authoritarian rulers who disregarded the constitution, this was also due to the structural instability built into the Founding Constitution with its hybrid power structure.

With the adoption of the 1987 Constitution, it may appear that this instability has been resolved in favour of presidentialism. This is rather ironic because, during the period of authoritarian governments, the parliamentary form of government used to be touted by many as the pathway to democracy. Presidentialism was blamed for all the political ills plaguing Korea. After the democratic transition in 1987, however, a special connection emerged between presidentialism and democracy. At the end of the Fifth Republic, changing the constitution to allow for citizens' direct election of the president was the most critical item on the agenda for democratic reform. The people's right to pick the highest leader of the nation with their own hands was the most important trophy of the June Uprising of 1987.

That is not to say that there is universal approval for the presidential system. Critics argue that too much power is concentrated in the office of the president. The National Assembly is constantly trying to rein in the president's powers. Korea's history of constitutional revision has been marked by the ongoing tension between the call for an effective government under a strong president and the demand for greater democratic accountability to the people's representatives. As will be seen, the current constitution also contains attempts to blend elements of presidentialism and parliamentarism. The Founding Constitution's attempt at hybridity may be shaping the path of Korea's constitutional development.

---

[46] A Harding and P Leyland, *The Constitutional System of Thailand: A Contextual Analysis* (Hart Publishing 2011) 1.

FURTHER READING

Brazinsky G, *Nation Building in South Korea: Koreans, Americans, and the Making of a Democracy* (University of North Carolina Press 2007).

Kim H-A and Sorensen CW (eds), *Reassessing the Park Chung Hee Era, 1961–1979: Development, Political Thought, Democracy, and Cultural Influence* (University of Washington Press 2011).

Kim SH, 'Constitutional Revolution Redux: Postwar Japan and South Korea' (2020) 10 *Yonsei Law Journal* 83.

Oh JK, *Korean Politics: The Quest for Democratization and Economic Development* (Cornell University Press 1999).

West JM and Baker EJ, 'The 1987 Constitutional Reforms in South Korea: Electoral Processes and Judicial Independence' (1988) 1 *Harvard Human Rights Yearbook* 135.

3

The 1987 Constitution and its Basic Features

Popular Sovereignty – Representative Democracy – Rule of Law – Separation of Powers – Protection of Basic Rights – Economic Order and the Welfare State – Dual Nature of the North Korean Regime – Free Democratic Basic Order

THE 1987 REVISION that produced the current constitution was the result of the citizens' 'June Uprising' whose primary goal was the direct popular election of the president. It was the first time that the constitution was revised through negotiation between the government and the opposition. Aside from empowering the people to choose the president, the revision's focus was on strengthening the level of protection for individual rights and on better implementing the separation of powers and the rule of law. Efforts were also made to empower regional and local governments as a way to reduce the powers of the central government. This chapter will examine the major principles of the current constitution such as popular sovereignty, representative democracy, the rule of law, separation of powers, and protection of basic rights. It will also look at the principle governing the economic order. In theory, all previous constitutions had been based on the same principles, but under the current system the Constitutional Court has accumulated a sizeable jurisprudence on their concrete meaning, which deserves elucidation. The chapter will also discuss constitutional issues relating to the goal of national unification and the security threat posed by the North Korean regime.

I. A DEMOCRATIC REPUBLIC

Article 1(1) of South Korea's constitution proclaims: 'The Republic of Korea shall be a democratic republic.' This is followed by article 1(2): 'The sovereignty of the Republic of Korea resides in the people, and all state power derives from the people.' These two statements have been a fixture of the Korean constitution ever since the Founding Constitution. In other words, being a democratic republic based on popular sovereignty has always been the governing ideal of the modern Korean state. Yu Chin-o, one of the drafters of the Founding Constitution, thought that although the term 'republic' signified a democratic state, the qualifier 'democratic' was needed because many putative republics turned out to be dictatorships (eg, Nazi Germany) or totalitarian states (eg, Soviet regimes). Put differently, 'democratic' in article 1 signified that the South Korean state was a republic based on the principle of separation of powers.[1] In the context of South Korea's founding, this was especially important because of the need to distinguish itself from the communist regime being created in the north on the principle of 'dictatorship of the proletariat'. In short, 'democratic republic' denoted the rejection of North Korea's 'people's republic'.

A. Popular Sovereignty

The principle of popular sovereignty means, at a minimum, the rejection of a monarchy. The people are the source of all power and, as indicated by the preamble, the constitution is a fundamental law given by the people to themselves. Among commentators, there is some discussion as to whether sovereignty is a power that can actually be exercised by the people. While some understand sovereignty as the highest decision-making power within a state, others argue that sovereignty should be understood as the ultimate ground of legitimacy. Those taking the former view tend to regard the constitution-making process as an exercise of the people's sovereign power, which is distinguished from inferior 'constituted' powers exercised by various organs of the state (ie, legislature, executive, and judiciary). When the constitution proclaims that sovereignty resides in the people of Korea, that means that the people are making the most fundamental decision regarding their political life. Those of the latter view, however, stress that the people cannot exercise any power or make any decisions directly. Popular sovereignty must be understood as a principle of legitimation in the sense that all exercise of state power must be justified by reference to the people. The Constitutional Court seems to assume that sovereignty is a power that

---

[1] Yu Chin-o, *Shin'go Hŏnpŏp Haeŭi* [*Constitutional Law Explained, Revised Edition*] (Ilchogak 1953) 45.

can be exercised. It has stated that in practice 'sovereignty is exercised through the exercise of voting rights at elections' and that a democratic electoral system must be established, so as to enable the proper exercise of the people's sovereignty.[2]

A related discussion has to do with how to understand the term 'people'. A distinction is often made between the people as an 'ideational unity' who possesses sovereignty and the people as the 'totality of voters' who actually exercise sovereignty. In this context, many commentators introduce the conceptual distinction that supposedly came out of the French Revolution between *le peuple* and *la nation*. The common explanation is that the former refers to the entirety of actual citizens who can exercise sovereignty, while the latter indicates an abstract conceptual unit which is unable to make any decisions directly.[3] It is doubtful if this distinction is applicable to modern Korea. More importantly, discussion tends to become confused because many still employ terms like the people's 'sovereign will', which suggests an agent that can exercise its will and make decisions, while claiming that the popular sovereignty must be regarded as an abstract principle of legitimation, which suggests that people are unable in reality to have a unified will. The Constitutional Court also uses the idiom of the people 'exercising' sovereignty through elections and national referendums.[4] Yet, even if the people is an agent with a unified will that can be embodied in the constitution, the sovereign people whose fundamental decision establishes the constitutional order cannot be the same as the electorate whose rights and status are determined by the constitution and statutes. The Court, however, seems to equate the exercise of voting rights, which may be regulated by statutes, with the exercise of sovereignty.[5]

In the Korean context, the confusion is in part aggravated by the fact that the constitution uses the same term (*kukmin*) to refer to the collective sovereign agent (art 1) and the individual bearer of constitutional rights and duties (arts 10 to 37). One is the maker of the constitutional order, whereas the other is the recipient of the protection provided by the constitution. Further, the same term is also used for 'Korean nationals' whose status is to be prescribed by legislative enactment (art 2(1)).[6] This may be why many commentators define the sovereign people as the

---

[2] Const Ct 88 Hun-Ka 6 (8 September 1989).

[3] This difference is then often related to the debate on the permissibility of 'binding mandates' for elected representatives of the people.

[4] Const Ct 2002 Hun-Ma106 (25 September 2003).

[5] Const Ct 93 Hun-Ka 4 (consolidated) (29 July 1994).

[6] C Lee, *Report on Citizenship Law: The Republic of Korea* (European University Institute 2019).

entirety of the holders of Korean nationality. Yet, if the rights and duties of Korean nationals may be defined and altered by the legislature, they should be conceptually distinguished from the sovereign people who determine the competence of the legislature.[7]

B. Representative Democracy

According to the Constitutional Court, the Korean constitution mandates that the people's sovereignty be exercised through representation, while also providing for occasional, supplemental use of direct participatory procedures.[8] 'Indirect democracy' is the default, whereas 'direct democracy' is ancillary. Regarding representation, a question often raised is: who is being represented? Is it the individual voters who elect the representatives, the constituency of a given electoral district, or the whole sovereign people of Korea? The constitution states that 'all public officials shall be servants of the entire people' (art 7(1)). In relation to individual lawmakers, it also provides that 'members of the National Assembly shall give preference to national interests' (art 46(2)). Based on these provisions it is widely agreed that it is the entire people that is being represented rather than any subpart of it.

A related issue is whether elected representatives have an obligation to implement the specific wishes of the electorate. Are members of the legislature given a 'free mandate' or 'imperative mandate'? Since their constitutional duty is to give preference to national interests, lawmakers must be free to ignore specific instructions from the voters. The constitution also provides that they must 'perform their duties in accordance with their conscience' rather than following anyone's directive. The Constitutional Court has also stated that the relationship between the voters and the National Assembly is based on a 'free mandate'.[9] While the representatives should heed the people's demands and opinions, the 'people's will' that must be obeyed is ultimately something that should be constructed through the representatives' deliberation. Some commentators thus insist that there is no pre-existing object or entity that must be represented by the representatives.[10] Chronologically speaking, that

---

[7] For example, it is constitutional to statutorily deprive a person of Korean nationality upon voluntary acquisition of another state's nationality. Const Ct 2011 Hun-Ma 502 (26 June 2014).

[8] Const Ct 2007 Hun-Ma 843 (26 March 2009).

[9] Const Ct 96 Hun-Ma 186 (29 October 1998).

[10] Chong J-s, *Hŏnpŏp Yŏn'gu (1)* [*A Study of Constitutional Law (1)*] (Ch'ŏlhak kwa Hyŏnsil Sa 1994) 275–76.

may be true, but from a normative standpoint, the 'people's will' must be assumed to be pre-existing, as the representatives' legitimacy will suffer once they are perceived to be ignoring the 'people's will'.

The system of electing representatives will be seen as less than legitimate if some voters have more say than others. In a democracy, every citizen's vote should carry the same weight. Yet, inequality in the worth of citizens' votes may be unavoidable unless every electoral district has the exact same number of voters. In a series of cases, the Constitutional Court has dealt with this issue. In 1995, it held that the population of the most densely inhabited district must not be greater than four times the population of the least populous district.[11] In a 2001 decision, it mandated the ratio of 3 to 1 as the upper limit for constitutionally tolerable population disparity.[12] Then, in 2014, the Court specified the ratio of 2 to 1 as the tolerable level of disparity of the value of votes.[13] This means that, in sparsely populated rural areas, several counties with few common interests might have to be joined to form an electoral district whose population is at least half the size of the most densely populated urban district. For the Court, this was unavoidable to maintain the parity of the value of votes.

To allow for increased diversity of viewpoints in the legislative process, the constitution provides that proportional representation is to be used as part of the process of forming the National Assembly (art 41(3)). In addition to those elected from electoral districts, some lawmakers are chosen through a party-list proportional representation system. The precise manner of structuring the system is left to the legislature. As will be seen below, the latest change in the rules for electing proportional representatives actually made it more difficult for smaller parties to be represented in the National Assembly.

Under exceptional circumstances, the Korean constitution permits the people's direct participation in political affairs via national referendums. There are two instances in which a national referendum may be called. One is to ratify a bill for constitutional revision after the National Assembly has approved it (art 130(2)). The other is when the president deems it necessary to decide on 'important policies relating to foreign relations, national defence, unification and other matters' (art 72). While this grants to the president the discretion to decide whether to call a referendum, the Constitutional Court has stated that the range of issues to be decided by a referendum must be narrowly construed. Specifically, it held

---

[11] Const Ct 95 Hun-Ma 224 (consolidated) (27 December 1995).
[12] Const Ct 2000 Hun-Ma 92 (consolidated) (25 October 2001).
[13] Const Ct 2012 Hun-Ma 190 (consolidated) (30 October 2014).

that a referendum cannot be called for the purpose of asking the people's confidence in the sitting president because such use does not constitute submitting 'important policies' within the meaning of article 72.[14] Other forms of 'direct democracy' such as popular initiatives or popular recall are not recognised under the Korean constitution.

C. 'Party State'

Given that political parties decide on the list of candidates from which lawmakers will be chosen in proportion to votes received, parties play a critical role in the Korean system of representation. The constitution guarantees a multi-party system and state protection for parties. The state is even allowed to provide operational funds to parties (art 8). That is why Korea is commonly referred to by courts and commentators as a 'party state' (*Parteienstaat*).

The phenomenon of a 'party state' means that political parties are increasingly taking on an active role as intermediaries between the citizens and the state. Particularly, the growth of party discipline over its member lawmakers has raised concerns that the dominance of parties is undermining individual lawmakers' right and duty to decide 'in accordance with their conscience'. So far, the Constitutional Court has held that no constitutional problem arises even if a party disciplines (or even expels from the party) a member who went against the party line.[15] Critics point out, however, that under the constitution, members of the National Assembly are individually organs of the state, whereas political parties are mere private associations that happen to receive heightened protection from the state, and that such a private body should not be allowed to infringe upon the autonomy and independence of an organ of the state.[16]

II. GOVERNMENT UNDER LAW

The Korean constitution adopts several principles and mechanisms designed to ensure that the elected political leaders do not abuse their powers. While they may not be explicitly provided for in the text, there is universal agreement that they form part of the constitutional order.

[14] Const Ct 2004 Hun-Na 1 (14 May 2004).
[15] Const Ct 2002 Hun-Ra 1 (30 October 2003).
[16] Const Ct 2019 Hun-Ra 1 (27 May 2020) (dissenting opinion).

A. Rule of Law

The Constitutional Court has declared that the rule of law is a 'leading principle of our constitution'. This principle demands that, in order to ensure predictability in the exercise of state power, the agent, manner, and scope of the exercise of power must be prescribed by a statute enacted by the National Assembly. In addition, even when delegation of authority to an executive agency is necessary, the delegating statute must be sufficiently clear as to enable citizens to predict the general contours of the delegated lawmaking power.[17] Included in this demand is a ban on open-ended delegation of lawmaking powers as well as the limitation on discretionary powers.

These requirements are deemed to follow from several constitutional provisions. Article 37(2) declares: '[t]he freedom and rights of citizens may be restricted by statute only when necessary for national security, for the maintenance of law and order, or for public welfare'. A more specific articulation in the context of criminal justice is found in article 12(1) which requires statutory authorisation for all arrests, detentions, searches, seizures, and interrogations, as well as prohibiting all forms of punishment without due process of law. The rule against retroactivity is enshrined in article 13(1) which declares that no one may be prosecuted for acts that did not constitute a crime when they were committed, as well as article 13(2) which prohibits retroactive legislation that limits political rights or deprives property rights.[18] Articles 75 and 95, which authorise government officials to issue regulations upon delegation by statute, are commonly interpreted to include a mandate against comprehensive delegation of legislative authority to the executive.[19]

In sum, the rule of law demands that the exercise of state power must be authorised by formal laws (ie, 'statutes') enacted by the National Assembly, and that such laws be prospective (not retroactive), general, and clear, so as to provide predictability to citizens in making plans for their own lives. But, it is generally agreed that the rule of law is not limited to such formal requirements. Many commentators discuss the historical evolution of the German concept of *Rechtsstaat* in response to the Nazi regime's 'legal' atrocities to stress that the rule of law is a rejection of arbitrary power even when it is exercised under legal guise. It must be distinguished from 'rule by law' or *Gesetzesstaat*. Put differently, the rule

---

[17] Const Ct 92 Hun-Ma 80 (13 May 1993).

[18] For constitutional exceptions to this general rule against retroactivity, see ch 2.

[19] Const Ct 2006 Hun-Ka 4 (26 July 2007).

of law requires not only that the law exhibit certain formal qualities but also that the law-making process itself be democratic. More expansive readings of the concept include the requirement that the law be oriented toward the achievement of substantive justice by safeguarding the human dignity and basic rights of the individual.

The Korean Constitutional Court appears to adopt such an expansive approach. In numerous decisions, it has stressed that the rule of law is more than a demand that regulation of citizens' rights and duties take the form of legislation. The concept must be understood in a substantive manner to include the mandate that the purpose and content of such legislation be consistent with the constitution's ideal of protecting basic rights.[20] The Court even employs the term 'substantive due process of law' to explain its understanding of rule of law. The Court has also stated that a sub-level principle of 'protection of (legitimate) expectations' should be recognised, as a corollary of the principle of rule of law. If individual citizens have formed legal relations based on a reasonable expectation that certain legal norms or institutions will endure into the future, then the legislature should honour such expectations to the extent possible.[21] This idea of protecting citizens' legitimate expectations may be deemed an expression, at a higher level of generality, of the same values that are served by the rule against retroactivity.

B. Separation of Powers

As seen above, 'democratic republic' has been understood in South Korea as mandating a commitment to the principle of separation of powers. For the founding generation, this was what distinguished the Republic of Korea from the communist North Korean regime based on so-called 'democratic centralism'. Popular sovereignty, in other words, did not mean entrusting the exercise of all state power in the hands of a single unitary agency. On the contrary, popular sovereignty could only be realised by ensuring that no one actor or institution be allowed to speak for the entire people.

According to the 1987 Constitution, legislative power is vested in the National Assembly (art 40), executive power in the 'Government headed by the President' (art 66(4)), and judicial power in the 'Courts composed of judges' (art 101(1)). A chapter of the constitution is devoted to each

---

[20] Eg, Const Ct 92 Hun-Ba 27 (consolidated) (21 July 1995).
[21] Const Ct 97 Hun-Ma 38 (6 July 1997).

of these branches. In addition, the Constitutional Court is provided for in a separate chapter.[22] These four institutions are then expected to check and balance one another through a complex system of mutual restraint and interdependence.

One way in which the National Assembly acts as a check on the Government is through the appointment process. The president is required to obtain the National Assembly's consent when appointing the prime minister, the chief justice and other justices of the Supreme Court, the head of the Constitutional Court, and the chair of the Board of Audit and Inspection. It also has the power to pass a bill of impeachment against the president and other high-level public officials. It may 'recommend' the dismissal of the prime minister and other members of the State Council (ie, cabinet ministers). By way of checking the conduct of the Government, the National Assembly is empowered, *inter alia*, to inspect and investigate state affairs, to demand the presence of the prime minister and other members of the State Council for questioning, to withhold approval for emergency orders issued by the president, and to demand the lifting of martial law.

In return, the president may act as a check on the National Assembly through the powers to veto bills passed by the National Assembly, to request the convening of an extraordinary session of the National Assembly, to attend and address the National Assembly in person or via written message, to issue emergency orders having the same force as statutes passed by the National Assembly, and to call a national referendum on policy issues of national importance.

The president and the Government may act as a check on the courts through the powers to appoint the chief justice and other justices of the Supreme Court, to formulate the courts' budget, and to pardon, commute sentences, and restore rights of persons convicted by a court. The courts have the power to review the legality and constitutionality of orders, regulations and measures issued by the executive branch.

Toward the courts, the National Assembly may exert restraint through its power to offer or withhold consent on the appointment of the chief justice and other justices of the Supreme Court, to enact statutes on the organisation of the courts, to approve the courts' budget, and to impeach judges. The courts in return may check the National Assembly through their power to request review on the constitutionality of statutes passed by the National Assembly.

---

[22] The National Election Commission is also allotted a separate chapter in the constitution and is thus regarded as having a status co-equal to other branches of the government.

Lastly, the Constitutional Court may limit the powers of the Government and the National Assembly through its powers to review the constitutionality of statutes, to adjudicate constitutional complaints, to settle competence disputes, to decide impeachment cases, and to dissolve unconstitutional political parties. The National Assembly may act as a check on the Constitutional Court through its powers to nominate justices of the Constitutional Court, to offer or withhold consent on the appointment of the head of the Constitutional Court, to enact statutes regarding the Constitutional Court, to approve the Constitutional Court's budget, and to impeach justices of the Constitutional Court. The president and the Government may restrain the Constitutional Court through the power to appoint the justices of the Constitutional Court, and to formulate the Constitutional Court's budget.

Despite these mechanisms, it is difficult to deny that the relationship between the president and the other branches is not exactly 'balanced'. This can be seen from the fact that the president may declare martial law which may suspend parts of the constitution, issue emergency orders having the same force as statutes enacted by the National Assembly, propose a legislative bill to the National Assembly, call a national referendum on important policy issues, or propose a bill for revising the constitution. Such powers go beyond what is granted, for example, to the President of the United States. Furthermore, that the president may dominate the conduct of state affairs may be seen from the array of appointment powers which include the chief justice and other justices of the Supreme Court, the head of the Constitutional Court, the chair of the Board of Audit and Inspection, and the prosecutor general. Even though reducing the power of the presidency was a key aim during the process of constitutional revision in 1987, it is apparent that more could have been done to achieve that goal.

C. Basic Rights

Understood as the project of preventing arbitrary use of state power, constitutionalism predates the idea of individual rights. A variety of resources – philosophical, religious, and institutional – can be, and have been, marshalled to serve the goal of restraining state power and averting tyrannical governments.[23] In the modern period, however, the idea of

---

[23] S Gordon, *Controlling the State: Constitutionalism from Ancient Athens to Today* (Harvard University Press 2002).

rights which individuals possess even before the creation of the state has become the instrument of choice in pursuing the objective of restraining state power. Protection of individual rights has become so important that it is widely regarded as the *raison d'être* of the state and its constitutional order.

In the Korean context, the experience of Japanese colonial occupation and the series of authoritarian governments understandably strengthened the demand for enshrining basic rights in the constitution. The Founding Constitution even made it explicit that citizens have rights and liberties beyond those enumerated in the text of the constitution. This commitment to protect unenumerated rights has remained constant despite the numerous changes to the constitution. This may suggest dedication to the idea of 'certain unalienable rights'[24] or 'the natural and imprescriptible rights of man'[25] extolled by liberal thinkers and revolutionaries of the eighteenth century. Yet, drafters of the Korean Founding Constitution were also aware that with the advent of the welfare state, so-called social rights unknown to the liberal social contract theorists have emerged and been given recognition in modern constitutions.[26] It is thus not necessary to ascribe natural rights theory to the constitution. The Constitutional Court has also refrained from characterising constitutionally protected rights as natural rights. It has read article 37(1) of the current constitution, which mandates respect for unenumerated rights, primarily as a source for recognising new basic rights,[27] without necessarily invoking the theory of natural rights.

It bears noting that the constitution's commitment to protect unenumerated rights has generally been invoked with caution. It is generally understood that the provision's role is supplementary. Given that the Korean constitution contains an extensive catalogue of basic rights, protection of rights should be sought by invoking the various enumerated rights rather than the general pronouncement on unenumerated rights.

Indeed, except for the *Yushin* Constitution, each revision of the constitution represented an attempt to improve on the catalogue of basic rights. For example, with the 1960 Constitution adopted after the ouster of Syngman Rhee, the formulation of the rights provisions was changed to remove the possibility of constitutionally sanctioned 'legal'

---

[24] US Declaration of Independence, para 2 (1776).
[25] French Declaration of the Rights of Man and of the Citizen, art 2 (1789).
[26] Eg, Yu (n 1) 56–61.
[27] Const Ct 2007 Hun-Ma 369 (28 May 2009).

restrictions on basic rights. Previously, under the Founding Constitution, many articles had taken the form: 'the right to X shall not be infringed unless through legislation'. It had become clear that this formulation (often called a 'statutory reservation') could allow for restriction of basic rights if it was done through a legislative enactment. The June 1960 revision thus eliminated the qualifier 'unless through legislation' from most rights provisions. Also, a provision was added which prohibited restrictions on the 'essential content' of a right even if restrictions could be justified for reasons of public welfare or maintenance of order.

Even the 1962 Constitution adopted after Park Chung-hee's coup d'état saw improvements in rights protection. A provision was added which declared that all citizens have 'dignity and worth as a human being' and that the state has the duty to protect the basic human rights of the citizens. This provision has remained part of the constitution ever since. The 1980 Constitution also made advancements in basic rights protection by undoing the harms wrought by the 1972 *Yushin* Constitution. Most significantly, it took out most of the statutory reservations that had been reintroduced in 1972. Similarly, it reinstated the ban on restriction of essential content of rights, which had been eliminated by the *Yushin* Constitution. The 1980 revision also strengthened the right to personal freedom by enshrining *habeas corpus* rights, the principle of 'innocent until proven guilty', and the ban on 'guilt by association'. New rights were also introduced such as the right to pursue happiness, the right to privacy, and the right to live in a clean environment.

The 1987 Constitution resulted in a more dramatic expansion of rights protection by further elaborating upon due process rights relating to personal freedom. It also introduced the victim's right to receive state assistance for injury resulting from another person's crime and made it the state's duty to implement a system of minimum wage and to endeavour to ensure comfortable housing for all citizens. In addition, existing rights such as the freedom of expression, labour rights, right to property, and the autonomy of universities were given stronger and clearer expression in the text.

To be sure, these textual changes would have little meaning unless they resulted in tangible change and improved protection of basic rights. In this regard, the creation of the Constitutional Court was without doubt one of the most significant contributions of the 1987 Constitution. The introduction of constitutional complaints in particular has empowered ordinary citizens to seek better protection and enforcement of their basic rights. The Court's adoption of the principle of proportionality in reviewing claims of rights infringement may also be seen as an attempt to give real meaning to the improved rights protection found in the text. The proportionality test has been applied to evaluate the propriety of even the Court's own exercise of coercive power. It reasoned that the dissolution of a political party by an order of the Court must be justifiable under a proportionality analysis.[28]

III. WELFARE STATE AND THE ECONOMIC ORDER

Courts and commentators often employ the German term 'social state' (*Sozialstaat*; in Korean, *sahoe kukka*) principle to express the idea that Korea's constitutional order is committed to realising justice throughout the fields of society, economy, and culture. The term is used to describe a basic constitutional principle which authorises a proactive role for the state in realising social justice and in coordinating social relationships among individual citizens.[29] The Constitutional Court has stated that the social state principle has been incorporated into Korea's constitutional order via the preamble,[30] the provisions on social rights, and the provisions on the economy which make it a state duty to take an active role through planning, guiding, and redistribution.[31] According to a more expansive reading, this principle affords a separate constitutional basis for limiting individual freedom in order to realise public welfare.[32]

Many commentators, however, are sceptical as to the propriety of using a term that is so laden with the historical and political experience of a particular country.[33] This is so not only because in the Korean language, the meaning of 'social state' (*sahoe kukka*) is not immediately obvious to ordinary citizens. In a state that has had to wean its constitution of the 'socialistic' elements to ensure its very survival after the devastation wrought by war, 'social state' is liable to cause needless

---

[28] Const Ct 2013 Hun-Da 1 (19 December 2014).

[29] The *Grundgesetz* describes the Federal Republic of Germany as a 'democratic and social federal state'. Basic Law, art 20(1) and 28(1). See W Heun, *The Constitution of Germany* (Hart Publishing 2011) 44–46.

[30] The reference seems to be the preamble's passage on the constitution's commitment to 'afford equal opportunities to every person in all fields, including political, economic, social and cultural life' and to 'elevate the quality of life for all citizens'.

[31] Const Ct 2002 Hun-Ma 52 (18 December 2002).

[32] Han S-W, *Hŏnpŏphak* [*Constitutional Law*] (6th edn, Pŏpmunsa 2016) 315–16.

[33] Chong J-s, *Hŏnpŏphak Wŏllon* [*Principles of Constitutional Law*] (11th edn, Pakyŏngsa 2016) 238–39. The German Federal Constitutional Court has even described the social state as an essential part of Germany's unique 'constitutional identity'. DP Kommers and RA Miller, *The Constitutional Jurisprudence of the Federal Republic of Germany* (Duke University Press 2012) 50.

confusion. If the point is to highlight the fact that modern states must assume a proactive role in providing such basic services as education, health care, and social insurance, then a more general term like 'welfare state' (*pokchi kukka*) may be more appropriate.

Further, in adjudicating actual cases, the so-called 'social state principle' has not always been useful in protecting individual rights or finding state actions unconstitutional.[34] In one case, the Constitutional Court even invoked the idea to justify unequal treatment of individuals and restrictions on rights.[35] Compared to the German constitution, which contains no provision on social rights and therefore needs to rely on the terse reference to the 'social state', the Korean constitution features numerous articles geared toward promoting public welfare and protecting the disadvantaged members of the society. It states, for example, that property rights must be exercised within the bounds of public welfare (art 23(2)) and authorises special protection for working women and working minors (art 32(4) and (5)) and for motherhood (art 36(2)). It also guarantees 'the right to a life worthy of human beings' and requires the state to promote the welfare of women, senior citizens, and the physically disabled, among others (art 34). The right to receive education (art 31(1)) and the right to work (art 32(1)) are specifically provided for in the constitution's text. It also lists 'public welfare' as one of the legitimate grounds for restricting citizens' basic rights (art 37(2)). In sum, it will be better to rely on these concrete provisions than to invoke an abstract and ambiguous term like the 'social state'.

A. 'Social Market Economy'

All South Korean constitutions since 1948 included a separate chapter called 'Economy'. The Founding Constitution originally provided for what was deemed a 'socialistic' economic order under which most economic resources and enterprises were placed under government control. This was revised in 1954 in the direction of a more market-friendly system. To reconstruct the economy and social infrastructure after the Korean War, attracting foreign aid and investment was imperative, and the constitution had to be changed to facilitate this process.

---

[34] In Germany, too, 'the social state principle has never been held to invalidate governmental action or inaction'. Heun (n 29) 45.

[35] Const Ct 99 Hun-Ma 289 (29 June 2000) (invoking 'social state' to justify a social insurance scheme that charged different premiums depending on income level, even for persons with the same risk level).

Most provisions mandating state ownership or public management of economic entities were dropped, although the Economy chapter still opened with a proclamation that the goal was to realise 'social justice under which all citizens' basic needs for living can be satisfied' and to achieve 'balanced development of the nation's economy'. After the 1962 revision, this statement was preceded by a declaration that Korea's economic order is founded on 'respect for the economic freedom and creativity of the individual'. The intent was evidently to stress that the market is primary and government intervention secondary. With the 1987 revision, the subject of 'economic freedom and creativity' has been expanded to 'the individual and firms' (art 119(1)).

Despite this shift toward a more market-oriented economy, the South Korean constitution has never abandoned the founding era's commitment toward achieving an equitable and balanced economic order. During the 1954 revision, it was taken for granted that the purpose was not to adopt the classical liberal *laissez-faire* economy. During the 1987 revision, the earlier language of satisfying everyone's basic material needs was deleted, but it was replaced with the mandate for maintaining 'balanced growth and stability of the nation's economy' and for pursuing 'proper distribution of income', as well as preventing 'market domination and abuse of economic power' (art 119(2)). The directive for equitable and balanced economic order was given more concrete and specific expression.

The constitution's mandate to temper the market led by private initiatives with the ideal of an equitable and balanced economic order is often expressed via the term 'social market economy'. The Constitutional Court routinely uses the term, which it explains as 'an economy that takes as its basis a free market economy based on respect for private property and free competition, but which also permits state regulation and coordination for eliminating the various attendant contradictions and realising social welfare and social justice'.[36] This is often presented as an interpretation of article 119 which mandates in section (1) the 'rule' of free market economy, but then authorises in section (2) the 'exception' of state intervention to correct the excesses of the market.

Another instance of the German influence on Korean law, the term 'social market economy' is a translation of *soziale Marktwirtschaft*, which was an economic slogan promoted in post-war West Germany by the Adenauer administration.[37] A specific economic policy of Germany has apparently been elevated to the status of a constitutional principle

---

[36] Const Ct 92 Hun-Ba 47 (25 April 1996).
[37] Heun (n 29) 112.

in Korea.[38] Yet, it is doubtful if that term is needed to properly interpret the Korean constitution. Not only is the term itself subject to multiple definitions, all that can be said about article 119 is that that it mandates some form of a 'mixed economy'. It is up to the legislature and policymakers to decide on the specifics regarding the type and duration of policy tools to be adopted in light of the ever-changing economic situations.[39] Even the view that article 119 mandates free market economy as the 'rule' and state intervention as the 'exception' (sometimes called the principle of subsidiarity) reflects a very simplistic understanding of market–state relationship, as 'free market' does not mean the absence of state intervention. Proactive state intervention is sometimes needed to maintain an economic order dedicated to the freedom and creativity of individuals and private enterprises.

A more practical issue is whether article 119 may be used as a yardstick for reviewing the constitutionality of legislation or economic policies. If the 'social market economy' is a constitutional principle, then presumably the state has a duty to realise it. Further, it should function as a criterion for assessing government action. It is, however, unclear what the normative import of such a 'principle' might be. It is also doubtful what added benefit can be derived from using such a principle as a standard of review, which could not be derived from using the more conventional standards such as basic economic rights and the proportionality principle.[40] The Constitutional Court has not been consistent on this point. In some of its decisions, it stated that article 119 is a statement of a constitutional guideline and that 'economic freedom and creativity' mentioned in it should be understood as having been given concrete protection through the various specific provisions on economic rights and the principle of proportionality.[41] The implication seems to be that the abstract guideline contained in article 119 need not be invoked in constitutionality review of statutes. Yet, in other cases, the Court has in fact engaged in a separate analysis to determine whether a given legislation violated article 119.[42]

---

[38] The German Federal Constitutional Court has said that the German Basic Law does not guarantee a 'social market economy'. Heun (n 29) 213.

[39] Cheon K-s, *Hanguk Hŏnpŏpnon* [*Treatise on Korean Constitution*] (Chiphyŏnje 2016) 876–77.

[40] Han (n 32) 318–19.

[41] Eg Const Ct 99 Hun-Ba 76 (31 October 2002); Const Ct 2015 Hun-Ba 371 (consolidated) (30 June 2016).

[42] Eg Const Ct 99 Hun-Ma 365 (22 February 2001) (compulsory participation in national pension held not in violation of art 119).

IV. THE NORTH KOREAN QUESTION

As seen in Chapter 1, the constitution of Korea was adopted, revised, and applied under conditions of national division, which has inevitably coloured its implementation. Even after democratisation, South Korea's constitutional order continues to be impacted to a significant degree by issues arising from national division and the existence of a competitor regime in the north. It is worth noting, however, that the Founding Constitution was not intended as an interim measure designed to be in force until unification. It was designed as a complete and permanent constitution for the unified Korean state. In this regard, the drafters of Korea's first constitution took a different approach from their counterparts in West Germany, where the Basic Law (*Grundgesetz*) of 1949 was drafted to be a temporary law until unification with East Germany, when a permanent constitution would be formally adopted. The label 'Basic Law' was deliberately chosen to avoid calling it a constitution (*Verfassung*) and provisions were made for the process by which the two Germanys would become unified. By contrast, in the text of Korea's Founding Constitution, there was no recognition of the fact of national division. Since the Republic of Korea was the only legitimate state for the entire Korean nation, its constitution could not contain any affirmation of a competing government or regime exercising effective control over even a part of its territory.

The most dramatic statement reflecting this self-understanding is the territory provision of the Founding Constitution, which states: 'The territory of the Republic of Korea shall consist of the Korean Peninsula and its adjacent islands.'[43] Throughout all the subsequent revisions of the constitution, this provision has never been changed and is preserved as article 3 of the current constitution. This means that as a matter of constitutional law the North Korean regime is merely an unlawful entity that is forcefully and illegitimately occupying the northern territory. This outlook was further fortified by the enactment in December 1948 of the National Security Law which, without specifically referring to North Korea, prohibits and punishes activities carried out on behalf of an 'anti-state organisation' (*pan'gukka tanch'e*), a term defined as any group that 'fraudulently uses the title of a government' in violation of the constitution.[44] Indeed, the only status which North Korea could

---

[43] 1948 Constitution, art 4.
[44] National Security Law, art 2 (Law No 13722, 6 January 2016). The exact definition of anti-state organisation has gone through several mutations, but the phrase 'fraudulently uses the title of a government' has never been altered since the law was first adopted.

possibly have within the South Korean legal system was that of 'enemy' which needed to be vanquished and obliterated. This hostile attitude would be maintained throughout the early years of the Republic when the trauma from the North's invasion was still acutely felt. Put differently, matters relating to North Korea were questions of fact and force, which lay outside the purview of the constitution.

This began to change in the early 1970s, when the two Koreas started engaging in peace talks. As regards the constitutional text, it was the 1972 *Yushin* Constitution which first enunciated the principle of 'peaceful unification' in the preamble. South Korea started utilising the rhetoric of 'peaceful coexistence' and even began suggesting that the two Koreas simultaneously become members of the United Nations so as to reduce tension on the Korean Peninsula.[45] Aside from the reference in the preamble, the pledge to 'work faithfully toward peaceful unification of the homeland' became part of the constitutionally prescribed oath taken by presidents upon inauguration.[46] South Korea's constitution, in other words, began to acknowledge the fact of national division and to mandate peaceful unification as a national goal. During the 1987 revision, a provision was added, which proclaimed that the Republic of Korea shall pursue unification and implement 'policy of peaceful unification based on free democratic basic order' (art 4).[47] This in part reflects the growing confidence on the part of South Korea that it has clearly won the competition for 'regime legitimacy', particularly in the global arena and in terms of economic performance.

It may thus appear that the Korean constitution is no longer intended as a complete and final constitution for the entire Korean nation, but rather as a temporary one applicable only to the southern part until unification. One might conclude that it has changed its character to become similar to the German Basic Law. This, however, would not be entirely correct insofar as these changes exist side by side with the territory provision which still proclaims that the territory of the Republic is the entire Korean Peninsula and its adjacent islands. There has been no change in the official stance that the Republic of Korea is the only lawful authority in the territory. Although revised several times, the National Security Law

[45] The two Koreas eventually joined the United Nations simultaneously in 1991.

[46] 1972 Constitution, art 46. Although the exact wording of the president's inaugural oath has changed, working toward peaceful unification remains a part of it. 1987 Constitution, art 69.

[47] For an account of the insertion of art 4 following democratisation in 1987, see D-K Yoon, *Law and Democracy in South Korea: Democratic Development Since 1987* (Kyungnam University Press 2010) 259–60.

still remains in force, which defines North Korea as an 'anti-state organisation'. As a result, the current constitutional order of South Korea is characterised by an uneasy coexistence of, on the one hand, provisions that reveal a clear awareness of the need to achieve unification with the North in the future[48] with, on the other, those that seem to be based on a refusal to accept the fact of national division.

A. The 'Dual Nature' of North Korea

For some commentators, this indicates that the Korean constitutional order contains certain tension, if not outright contradiction. The argument is that the territory provision is premised on the view that North Korea is an unlawful and illegitimate entity which must be obliterated from the face of the earth, whereas the provisions on peaceful unification require a recognition of the North Korean regime as a legitimate dialogue partner entitled to peaceful coexistence. On this view, the numerous laws enacted to promote and support dialogue and exchange with the North, as well as the many inter-Korean agreements aimed at the same end, must be seen as unconstitutional because they are inconsistent with the premise of the territory provision. Alternatively, these laws and agreements are evidence that the territory provision is no longer relevant and therefore cannot be taken literally.

According to the Constitutional Court, however, this is not a contradiction but merely a reflection of the 'dual nature' of North Korea. Responding to the claim that the enactment in 1990 of the 'Law on South-North Exchange and Cooperation' was inconsistent with the National Security Law, the Court stated that the two laws have different goals and regulate different conducts, and that there was no irreconcilable tension between them. It specifically pointed out that North Korea is at once a partner in the negotiations toward peaceful unification and an 'anti-state organisation' still dedicated to the destruction and communisation of the South.[49] In another case, the Court held that defining North Korea as an anti-state organisation within the meaning of the National Security

---

[48] For example, article 66(3) specifically mentions the pursuit of peaceful unification as one of the duties of the president and article 92 authorises the establishment of a 'National Unification Advisory Council' under the president.

[49] Const Ct 92 Hun-Ba 6 (consolidated) (16 January 1992). The Court also stated that the simultaneous accession to the United Nations by the two Koreas does not necessarily mean the recognition of North Korea as a state by the South.

Law and sanctioning anti-state activities that support the North is not a violation of the principle of peaceful unification enshrined in the constitution. Here, too, the Court pointed to the 'undeniable fact' that North Korea continues to engage in provocations aimed at subverting the free democracy of the South – even after the simultaneous accession to the United Nations and the signing and entering into force of the so-called 'South-North Basic Agreement'.[50] It is not necessarily a contradiction, in other words, for the constitution to embody different attitudes toward North Korea. The constitution is simultaneously a normative expression of South Korea's self-understanding as the only legitimate state on the Korean Peninsula as well as a practical document that seeks to provide a realistic and historically grounded roadmap for the future.

Nevertheless, the 'dual nature' of the North Korean regime can be a source of some confusion. For example, there is uncertainty regarding the legal nature of the South-North Basic Agreement. Signed by the prime ministers of South and North in 1991, this is the basic framework for the inter-Korean relationship and as such may be likened to a treaty between the two countries. Yet, since both Koreas refuse to recognise the other side as an independent state, questions remain as to whether the Basic Agreement can be analogised to an international treaty. If such an analogy were valid, the consent of the National Assembly would be required, per article 60(1) of the constitution, in order for it to become legally effective. Pointing to the absence of such consent from the legislature, the Constitutional Court has concluded that the Basic Agreement is essentially a non-binding gentlemen's agreement.[51] According to the preamble of the Basic Agreement, the two Koreas in fact recognised that their relationship was not a relationship between states, but 'a special interim relationship stemming from the process towards reunification'. This same language was later included almost verbatim in the 'Law on the Development of the South-North Relationship' enacted by South Korea's National Assembly in 2005.[52] This intent to differentiate inter-Korean relationship from international relationships is actually discernible from the fact that the document was titled 'agreement' (*hapŭi*) rather than 'treaty' (*choyak*). At the same time, the Law on South-North Exchange and Cooperation provides that economic transactions such

---

[50] Const Ct 89 Hun-Ma 240 (16 January 1997). The full name for the Basic Agreement is 'Agreement on Reconciliation, Non-aggression and Exchanges and Cooperation between the South and the North' (effective 19 February 1992).
[51] Const Ct 92 Hun-Ba 6 (16 January 1997).
[52] Law No 7763 (enacted 29 December 2005).

as investments and transfer of goods between the two Koreas shall be regulated *mutatis mutandis* by the Foreign Exchange Transactions Act, thereby analogising North Koreans, in effect, to 'foreigners' (or 'non-residents') under limited circumstances.[53] According to the Constitutional Court, however, this should not be construed as recognition of North Korea as a 'foreign state'.[54]

B. Territory Provision and Nationality

By virtue of the territory provision, all who reside on the Korean Peninsula, including North Korea, are in principle citizens of the Republic of Korea. This principle applies even to individuals who were born before the establishment of the Republic of Korea in 1948 and who have been subsequently issued a nationality card by North Korean authorities.[55] As such, North Korean 'escapees' who succeed in finding their way to South Korea need not go through the process of naturalisation because they are already holders of South Korean nationality. Indeed, up until the early 1990s, individuals who defected from the North were greeted as freedom fighters and were given a sizeable amount of settlement funds.

With the dramatic rise, however, in the number of persons claiming to be North Korean defectors, there emerged a need for some mechanism to distinguish between residents of North Korea, who have a *prima facie* right to enter and settle in South Korea, and genuine foreigners, such as ethnic Korean-Chinese, who must first be naturalised or become permanent residents in order to acquire such rights. The result was the enactment of the 'Law on the Protection and Settlement Support of North Korean Escapees'.[56] As is indicated by the title, this allows individuals who have escaped from North Korea into a third country to seek 'protection' at a diplomatic mission of the Republic of Korea. According to the law, the ultimate decision-making authority lies with the Minister of National Unification, but in cases where there is a higher likelihood that national security may be affected, the Director of the National

---

[53] Law on South-North Exchange and Cooperation, art 26(3) (Law No 4239, 1 August 1990). This provision also lists other statutes applicable to inter-Korean relationship, which were enacted to regulate 'international' economic transactions, namely, the Foreign Investment Promotion Act, the Export–Import Bank of Korea Act, and the Foreign Economic Cooperation Fund Act.

[54] Const Ct 2003 Hun-Ba 114 (30 June 2005).

[55] Sup Ct 96 Nu 1221 (12 November 1996).

[56] Law No 5259 (enacted 13 January 1997).

Intelligence Service makes the final determination. A decision to offer protection constitutes a determination that the applicant is a national of the Republic of Korea. If it is found, however, that the applicant misrepresented his/her identity, upon a thorough screening after the person's admission into South Korea, the decision may be revoked.[57]

Another route by which an individual may be recognised as a North Korean, and thus a national of the Republic of Korea, is a procedure called 'nationality determination' provided for by the Nationality Act. This allows a person who is already in South Korea (eg, under a Chinese passport) to seek a determination that he/she is actually from North Korea, and thus already holds South Korean nationality. This is done by obtaining a decision of 'possession' (of Korean nationality) from the Minister of Justice. Nationality determination might even be used by persons who have been refused the above-mentioned 'protection' from the Ministry of National Unification, even though it was not designed to serve as a means for appealing the non-protection decision.

What these mechanisms reveal is that the institutional procedures for making sure that a person is from North Korea have in fact evolved to resemble the process of naturalisation. Even though, in theory, the task is one of merely ascertaining a pre-existing fact (of having Korean nationality), in practice, the government agencies have a wide range of discretion in making these determinations, which means that it has become difficult to tell them apart from decisions to grant Korean nationality to foreigners. In case of 'protection' decisions, the law even provides for certain categories of persons to whom protection may be refused. These include perpetrators of serious crimes like murder or international crimes such as 'aircraft hijacking, drug trafficking, terrorism or genocide'; those suspected of having staged their escape from North Korea; and those who have earned a living for 10 or more years in the state where application for protection is made.[58] In other words, the mere fact that the person has escaped from North Korea may not be sufficient grounds on which to be recognised as a national of the Republic of Korea. Even if an individual is bona fide from the northern part, that person could be denied Korean nationality if the decision-making agency has reason to think that the person will not be a good citizen of South Korea.[59]

---

[57] C Lee, 'The Law and Politics of Citizenship in Divided Korea' (2015) 6 *Yonsei Law Journal* 27.

[58] Law on the Protection and Settlement Support of North Korean Escapees, art 9(1), items (i) to (iv).

[59] According to Chulwoo Lee, the 'nationality determination' procedure results in 'performative' decisions that have 'the effect of realizing the state's desire to create a citizen'. Lee (n 57) 28.

Ultimately, this may be a reflection of the dual nature of the North Korean regime noted above. Given that North Korea is still sending spies to subvert and overthrow the Republic of Korea, there is an ever-present need to be vigilant in deciding whom to admit into the South Korean society. The constitutional principle that all residents of the territory north of the DMZ are *de jure* nationals of the Republic of Korea cannot but be refracted in the process of dealing with the *de facto* division of the nation.

C. Free Democratic Basic Order

Article 4 of the Korean constitution mandates that the state shall pursue peaceful unification based on 'free democratic basic order' (*chayuminjujŏk kibonjilsŏ*). The preamble of the constitution also mentions that 'We, the People of Korea' are committed to further strengthening the free democratic basic order. In terms of its provenance, this phrase is a direct translation of the German term *freiheitliche demokratische Grundordnung*, which is enshrined in the German Basic Law. In the German context, it is seen as an expression of the idea of 'militant democracy' (*streitbare Demokratie*) which holds that democracy cannot be based on value relativism or be neutral toward forces that seek to destroy democracy by gaining power through the electoral process. Widely seen as a response to Germany's painful experience under the Weimar Republic when Hitler was able to rise to power via democratic means, militant democracy allows for pre-emptive actions against enemies of democracy and relies on the idea of 'free democratic basic order' as the yardstick. A political party, for example, that seeks to destroy free democratic basic order may be dissolved.[60]

By inscribing 'free democratic basic order' in the constitution, Korea is widely regarded as having adopted this principle of militant democracy. What is distinctive, however, about the Korean appropriation is that this concept has become tightly wound up with the North Korean issue, whereas in the German context it was more geared toward preventing the re-emergence of fascism and totalitarianism.[61] This is no doubt due to the fact that in the Korean constitution the phrase appears in a provision

---

[60] Basic Law, art 21. Also, article 18 provides that if an individual abuses certain basic rights to combat the free democratic basic order, those rights may be forfeited by a declaration from the Federal Constitutional Court.

[61] HB Mosler, 'Decoding the "Free Democratic Basic Order" for the Unification of Korea' (2017) 57(2) *Korea Journal* 5.

specifically on the issue of unification. To be sure, commentators and the courts often hold up 'free democratic basic order' as the highest ideal of the Korean constitutional order, without necessarily relating it to unification. Yet, most attempts to give substance to the term and to apply it to concrete situations have taken place in connection to the threat posed by North Korea.

For example, the Constitutional Court offered one of its earliest interpretations of free democratic basic order in a case involving the constitutionality of the National Security Law. The claim was that article 7(1) of that statute was void because it prescribed punishment for such vague and imprecise behaviours as 'praising, encouraging, or sympathising with' the activities of an anti-state organisation, it members, or anyone following its directives. Also challenged for the same reason was the phrase 'otherwise benefit an anti-state organisation'.[62] The Court's decision started out by agreeing that such unclear standards may have a chilling effect on the exercise of the freedom of speech and the press and the freedom of learning and the arts, and thus can be inconsistent with the principle of *nulla poena sine lege*. Rather than striking down the provision, however, the Court rendered a decision of 'limited constitutionality' and held that the law shall be constitutional so long as it is applied only to cases where those proscribed acts 'threaten the existence/security of the state or pose a clear danger to the free democratic basic order'. The Court then elaborated on what it meant by free democratic basic order:

> [A] governing order based on self-government of the people through majority-rule and the rule of law according to the basic principles of freedom and equality, which precludes all violent and arbitrary government such as the anti-state organisation's one-person or one-party dictatorship ...; to be more specific, [it includes] respect for basic human rights, separation of powers, parliamentary process, multiparty system, electoral institutions, economic order based on private property and market economy, and judicial independence.[63]

The principle of free democratic basic order became even more closely associated with North Korean issues when the National Assembly amended the National Security Law by essentially inserting the Constitutional Court's interpretation into the text of the law. Now, it is

---

[62] Similarly at issue was article 7(5) of the National Security Law which made it a crime to 'manufacture, import, reproduce, possess, transport, distribute, sell, or acquire' any expressive materials, with the intention of praising, encouraging, or sympathising with, or otherwise benefitting an anti-state organisation.

[63] Const Ct 89 Hun-Ka 113 (2 April 1990). This definition is substantially based on the German Federal Constitutional Court's decisions. For a comparison, see Mosler (n 61).

a crime to praise, encourage and sympathise with an anti-state organisation only when it is done 'with the knowledge that it may threaten the existence/security of the state or free democratic basic order'.[64] Even after the amendment, however, several challenges have been made that the law is still too vague and prone to abuse by the law enforcement and intelligence agencies. The Court has maintained the position that, as amended, the law no longer contains unclear or imprecise language serious enough to impair its constitutionality.

The idea that free democratic basic order refers to the core of South Korea's constitutional identity (in contradistinction to North Korea) was reinforced with the case against the Unified Progressive Party (UPP), decided by the Constitutional Court in 2014. Originally formed through a merger of various fringe leftist groups, UPP had managed to win 13 seats in the National Assembly (out of 300) at the 2012 general election. By the time the case was filed by the government, however, internal conflict had caused some of its members to leave and form another party, leaving UPP with only five National Assembly members. Also, one of the remaining five was being prosecuted for plotting to overthrow the government through an underground group called 'RO' (Revolutionary Organization). The government's case against UPP was that the party itself was responsible for these alleged criminal acts and was therefore an unconstitutional party that needed to be disbanded under article 8(4).

In an 8-to-1 decision, issued even before the conclusion of the criminal proceedings against the UPP Assembly member, the Constitutional Court ordered the dissolution of the party and stripped all five UPP lawmakers of their seats in the National Assembly.[65] The decision declared that UPP posed a 'concrete danger of causing substantial harm' to the constitutional order because its stated goal of realising so-called 'progressive democracy' was basically indistinguishable from North Korea's 'revolutionary strategy', which is ultimately geared toward the establishment of North Korean-style socialist regime in the South. According to the Court, this directly contravenes South Korea's democratic basic order because the North's system is based on blind acceptance of the North Korean Workers' Party's platform as absolute truth. It also pointed out that at the basis of North Korea's government is the class-based notion of 'dictatorship of people's democracy' and the theory of 'great leader' which is used to justify one-person autocracy.

[64] During this amendment, the phrase 'otherwise benefit an anti-state organisation' was deleted.
[65] Const Ct 2013 Hun-Da 1 (19 December 2014).

The Court took pains to emphasise that democracy requires a pluralistic worldview based on value relativism, which recognises the relative truth and rationality of all political viewpoints. By contrast, North Korea's ideology, which UPP sought to implement, rejected such pluralism and value relativism, which is why it was inconsistent with democracy. Militant democracy, which originated in Germany as a criticism of, and an alternative to, the Weimar Constitution's value relativism (for its failure to prevent the rise of Nazism), has ironically been interpreted and justified in the South Korean context as a means to safeguard value relativism.

Article 8(4) of the constitution states that a political party may be disbanded if its goals or activities violate 'democratic basic order'. Note that 'free' is missing from the phrase. In the UPP decision, however, the Constitutional Court defined the phrase by invoking almost the same language as that used to define 'free democratic basic order'. The only difference was that free market economy was missing in the definition of 'democratic basic order'. Apparently, political parties need not advocate free market economy to be tolerated under the South Korean constitution.

V. CONCLUSION

Most of the principles described in this chapter can be found in the constitutions of other democratic countries. Yet, the specific way in which they are put into practice and given concrete meaning in Korea is unavoidably coloured by the nation's constitutional history and political realities. For example, the ideal of 'free democratic basic order' was imported from German constitutional jurisprudence, but it has been interpreted in a way that reflects South Korea's unique geopolitical environment. That environment has also coloured the way the ideal of 'democratic republic' is understood in South Korea to mean the rejection of the North's 'people's democracy'.

More recently, the term 'democratic republic' may have become more indigenised by entering South Korea's popular culture. A common protest song sung at rallies has lyrics taken verbatim from article 1 of the constitution: 'Republic of Korea is a democratic republic. All power derives from the people.' The apparent intent is to remind government officials to heed the sovereign people's will. To be sure, there may be a gap between what is demanded on the streets and how these principles are implemented through the constitutional institutions. Yet, it is undeniable that whatever progress South Korea has made toward constitutional democracy has been due in large part to a contentious, rights-conscious citizenry which has shown remarkable eagerness in invoking the principles of the constitution.

FURTHER READING

Chubb DL, 'Statist Nationalism and South Korea's National Security Law' in J-H Kwak and K Matsuda (eds), *Patriotism in East Asia* (Routledge 2014).

Guichard J, *Regime Transition and the Judicial Politics of Enmity: Democratic Inclusion and Exclusion in South Korean Constitutional Justice* (Palgrave Macmillan 2016).

Hahm C, 'Uneasy about the Rule of Law: Reconciling Constitutionalism and "Participatory Democracy"' in J Mo and DW Brady (eds), *The Rule of Law in South Korea* (Hoover Institution Press 2009).

Mosler H, 'Translating Constitutional Norms and Ideas: Genesis and Change of the German "Free Democratic Basic Order" in Korea' (2019) 52 *Verfassung in Recht und Übersee* 195.

Yoon D-K, *Law and Democracy in South Korea: Democratic Development Since 1987* (Kyungnam University Press 2010).

4

President and the Government

Head of State – Legislative Powers – Appointment Powers – Emergency
Powers – Martial Law Powers – Prime Minister and the State Council –
Administrative Ministers – Board of Audit and Inspection – Holding the
President Accountable

T HE KOREAN GOVERNMENT'S power structure is commonly described
as a 'modified' or 'hybrid' presidential system, because there are
some elements drawn from the parliamentary form of government. This hybridity seems to have been intended to prevent an overbearing presidency. For example, the constitution states that executive power
is vested in 'the Government headed by the President' (art 66(4)). It also
provides that the State Council, whose membership includes the president,
the prime minister, and state councillors, 'shall deliberate on important
policies that fall within the power of the Government' (art 88(1)). This
implies that the president is not a unitary executive, and that important
government decisions must be made collectively by the State Council.
Further, the prime minister is authorised to 'direct the Administrative
Ministries under order of the President' (art 86(2)). Some commentators
read these provisions as mandating a quasi-dual executive system in which
the president takes a more political role while the prime minister oversees the government administration. The constitution, however, makes it
clear that the prime minister is institutionally dependent on the president
and has little autonomous power. It also declares the president to be the
'head of state' who represents the state vis-à-vis foreign states (art 66(1)).
Moreover, the president is endowed with an array of substantial powers
that enables the president to act as not just the 'head of government' (chief
executive) but the shaper of the nation's future in very many aspects.
This chapter will examine the powers of the president within the Korean
constitutional system. It will be noted that despite, or perhaps due to, the
so-called hybrid features of the government, the powers of the president
remain quite strong, such that the term 'imperial presidency' is often
invoked by the opposition.

I. IMPERIAL PRESIDENCY AND ITS DISCONTENTS

The president is elected by the people for a non-renewable five-year term (arts 67(1) and 70). To be elected, a candidate does not need to win a majority of the votes cast. As there is no provision in the constitution for a runoff election, a candidate may become president on a mere plurality of the votes. Of the eight presidents elected to date under the current constitution, seven of them received less than half of the votes cast. The only one to win by a majority (51.6 per cent) was Park Geun-hye, who ironically was the only president to be removed from office via impeachment. This means that most presidents come into office with less than a clear mandate from the people. This in turn fuels the complaint that the powers wielded by presidents are disproportionate to their democratic legitimacy.

The president holds a dual status: as the head of state, the president is responsible for overseeing affairs of the entire state, and as the head of government, the president is in charge of administration of the executive branch. The term 'head of state' was first introduced in the 1960 Constitution of the Second Republic. It was omitted during the revision of 1962 (Third Republic) and then reintroduced in 1972 (Fourth Republic under *Yushin* Constitution) and has remained ever since. Even without the label, presidents are prone to exercise their authority in an expansive manner. As seen below, even some powers that ostensibly belong to the 'head of the government' (rather than the head of state) tend to elevate the office of president above the other branches.

A. Superintendent of State Affairs

The president has the duty to uphold the constitution and safeguard the 'nation's independence, state's territorial integrity, and continuity of the state' (art 66(2)). The oath of office taken upon inauguration includes the pledge to 'defend the state' and to 'advance national culture' (art 69).[1] Clearly, the president is expected to be the guardian of the Republic and superintendent of state affairs.

As the head of state, the president has the authority to conclude and ratify treaties with other states, to send and receive diplomatic missions,

---

[1] The reference to advancement of national culture was added with the 1980 revision, along with an article making it a state duty to 'advance national culture' and to sustain and develop traditional culture.

and to declare war and conclude peace (art 73). For the conclusion of certain treaties and declaration of war, the National Assembly's consent is required (art 60). The president is also the commander-in-chief of the nation's armed forces (art 74). This power to command the military is, however, restrained by the constitutional principle on the renunciation of all wars of aggression and the maintenance of the military's political neutrality (art 5). The clause on political neutrality of the armed forces was inserted during the last constitutional revision in 1987 as a repudiation of past military governments.

The president cannot be criminally prosecuted for ordinary crimes while in office (art 84). This privilege also stems from the president's status as the head of state and the need to ensure the smooth execution of the president's duties. The Constitutional Court has interpreted this to mean that the statute of limitations is suspended during the term of office such that prosecutors may bring an indictment after the president leaves office, which is when the statute of limitations starts to run.[2] Article 84 specifically excludes the crimes of insurrection and treason from this privilege, thus allowing prosecution of the president even while in office. This implies that the statute of limitations is not suspended during the term of office, which in practice has the effect of reducing the time within which the president can be charged for insurrection and treason after leaving office. Given that it is very difficult to indict a sitting president, this makes it harder to prosecute the president for heavier crimes.

B. Power to Call Referendums

The president is accorded a range of powers on the premise that the president must manage and steer the overall direction of state affairs. For example, the president may, 'when he deems it necessary', call a national referendum to decide on important policy issues 'related to foreign relations, national defence, unification, and other matters of state integrity' (art 72). Although allowing the people to decide on momentous matters may be desirable from the perspective of popular sovereignty, such a mechanism can be an invitation to would-be neo-Bonapartist leaders who might resort to referendums to disregard parliamentary procedures. Indeed, for critics, this provision is an unwelcome remnant from

[2] Const Ct 94 Hun-Ma 246 (20 January 1995).

the period of authoritarian regimes. Under the *Yushin* Constitution, the president had been empowered to submit any important policy issue to a national referendum. In 1975, Park Chung-hee called a referendum to ascertain the people's support for the *Yushin* Constitution and for his performance as president. Of the votes cast, 73.1 per cent agreed with his argument that the *Yushin* system be maintained to deal with the threat of North Korean invasion. In the 1980 Constitution, the scope of issues for which a referendum could be called was narrowed to those relating to 'foreign relations, national defence, unification, and other matters of state integrity'. The same provision was retained in the 1987 Constitution.

While no referendum has been held under the current constitution, the Constitutional Court has stated that a referendum may not be used for a confidence vote. In one case, involving Roh Moo-hyun's proposal in 2003 to call a referendum to verify the electorate's confidence in him, the Court warned that using the process for such plebiscitarian purpose is dangerous and inconsistent with Korea's constitutional order.[3] The Court revisited the same issue when Roh was impeached by the National Assembly in 2004. It concluded that his proposal to call a referendum as a plebiscite on his performance was a violation of the president's duty to respect and uphold the constitution.[4] While the Court ultimately declined to dismiss Roh from office, it evidently regarded the plebiscitarian use of article 72 as sufficiently dangerous to merit an official negative pronouncement.

C. Proposing Constitutional Revisions

Another aspect of the president's status as the superintendent of state affairs is the power to propose a bill for revising the constitution. In addition to the lawmakers in the National Assembly, that is, the president may initiate the process of revision by sending a bill to the National Assembly. Throughout Korea's constitutional history, the only time that the president could not initiate a revision was under the 1962 Constitution of the Third Republic, adopted after Park's coup. Yet, even without the formal power to initiate revision, Park was able to change the constitution in 1969 by directing ruling party lawmakers to initiate and pass a revision bill that allowed him to serve a third term as president. With the 1972

---

[3] Const Ct 2003 Hun-Ma 694, 700 and 742 (consolidated) (27 November 2003).
[4] Const Ct 2004 Hun-Na 1 (14 May 2004).

revision that produced the *Yushin* Constitution, the president was once again empowered to introduce constitutional revision bills.

The 1980 Constitution retained the same system, but with an interesting innovation. Any revision for extending the president's term of office or for eliminating the ban on re-election would not apply to the sitting president at the time of the revision. A president, in other words, may propose a revision to lengthen the president's term of office or to allow for re-election, but that president cannot benefit from the new rule. The same is true even if the revision is proposed by the National Assembly. This was Chun Doo-hwan's way of showing his intent to serve only one term and to effect a peaceful transfer of power. After democratic transition in 1987, this provision was retained verbatim in the current constitution (art 128(2)). The fact that South Korea has not seen any constitutional change since 1987 and was able to consolidate its democracy may be attributable in no small part to this innovation.

D. Powers Relating to the Legislature

Another power accorded the Korean president, which may not be the norm for presidential systems, is the power to introduce legislative bills. Article 52 provides: 'Bills may be introduced by members of the National Assembly or by the Government', thereby formally recognising the executive branch as a rightful initiator of the law-making process. This is commonly explained as an example of the 'hybrid' nature of the Korean constitutional system. To be sure, even in the United States, where the constitution does not allow the president to initiate legislation, the president is in practice able to do so informally through 'executive communication' to the Congress. The Korean constitution, by contrast, presupposes that the Government will routinely introduce legislative bills. The Government is even required by law to submit an annual plan for all the legislative bills that it intends to send to the National Assembly.[5]

The president has the power to veto bills passed by the National Assembly. Article 53(2) provides that the president may return bills and request reconsideration by the National Assembly. When exercising this power, the president must return the bill within 15 days and request the legislature's reconsideration by attaching a written explanation of the objections. The president also has the right to express views to the legislature either by writing or by attending and addressing a session of the

---

[5] National Assembly Act, art 5-3 (Law No 15620, 17 April 2018).

National Assembly (art 81). There is no corresponding right on the part of the National Assembly to demand the president's attendance to direct questions at the president or listen to the president's opinions.

According to critics, one institutional cause of the imperial presidency is the fact that the power of the purse is divided between the executive and the legislative branches. The Government is officially in charge of preparing the budget, and the National Assembly's role is limited to approving it. The constitution specifically prohibits the National Assembly from increasing the amount of any expenditure item or introducing new items in the budget, without the consent of the Government (art 57). Although this is intended to prevent individual lawmakers from engaging in 'pork-barrelling' (ie, allocating funds to local projects in an attempt to secure support and votes from constituents), it may have the negative effect of limiting the role of the National Assembly to a secondary actor, while giving the Government the primary initiative for planning the nation's budget. When combined with the fact, noted below, that the job of auditing the budget is also under the president's control, this ends up concentrating the powers of the purse in the hands of the executive despite the nominal division of labour with the legislature.

Under the current constitution, the president has no power to dissolve the National Assembly. This is a conscious departure from the previous constitutions of the Fourth and Fifth Republic. During the transition to democracy in 1987, an important goal was to strengthen the power and status of the legislature vis-à-vis the executive branch. Authorising the president to dissolve the National Assembly was an obvious expression of the president's superiority over the legislature and was therefore considered unsuitable for a democratic constitution.

E. Powers of Appointment

Even without the power to dissolve the legislature, the president is still able to influence other branches through powers of appointment. This allows the president not only to oversee state affairs but also to shape the future of the nation by participating in the formation of constitutional bodies.

i. *The Supreme Court*

The president appoints the chief justice of the Supreme Court (art 104(1)), who then recommends other justices to the president for appointment (art 104(2)). In other words, all members of the Supreme Court, the highest organ of a co-equal branch, are appointed by the president. Given that Supreme Court justices serve for the relatively short term of six years (art 105), and that they are subject to a mandatory retirement age of 70,[6] it is possible for a sitting president to appoint quite a few new justices, thereby changing not only the personal composition of the Court, but also its ideological outlook. For example, during Roh Moo-hyun's term (2003–2008), 13 out of 14 justices were replaced. His successor Lee Myung-bak appointed all 14 justices. To be sure, the president's appointment of Supreme Court justices requires the consent of the National Assembly, and to that extent, the president may not be free to appoint whomever he wishes. This mechanism, however, will not be so effective if the National Assembly is controlled by the government party, as was the case during the presidency of Moon Jae-in, who also appointed 13 justices. It is thus unsurprising to hear criticism that this system for judicial appointment undermines the independence of the judiciary and the rule of law. At the least, it does provide opportunity for the president to exercise undue influence over, and even mould in his image, a co-equal branch of government.

ii. The Constitutional Court

The president is also able to influence the composition of the Constitutional Court. According to the constitution, the president is authorised to appoint three of the nine justices of the Constitutional Court. In addition, the president of the Constitutional Court is also appointed by the president (of the Republic) from among the justices, with the consent of the National Assembly (art 111). As for the other six seats on the Court, they too are nominally 'appointed' by the president, but the president does not have the freedom to choose them. The president must appoint whomever is nominated by the National Assembly (three seats) or designated by the chief justice of the Supreme Court (three seats). Thus, aside from the nominal power to confer the letter of appointment, the president's influence in relation to the Constitutional Court is limited, in theory, to only a third of its personnel.

In reality, the president exerts much greater influence. This is due in part to the fact, mentioned above, that the Supreme Court chief justice is appointed by the president. It is thus plausible to assume that the political outlook (and judicial philosophy) of the three justices designated by the chief justice will tend to be close to, or at least not inconsistent with,

---

[6] Court Organisation Act, art 45(4) (Law No 15490, 20 March 2018).

that of the president. Beyond that, even the justices nominated by the National Assembly are indirectly influenced by the president because, by convention, one of the three seats is allotted to the government party within the National Assembly. Another seat is given to the opposition, while the third is filled by a 'compromise' candidate. This means that the president's ideological orientation may be reflected in at least seven justices, if not more. In other words, although the appointment system for the Constitutional Court envisions a 'division of labour' among the three government branches, in practice, the president can have much more sway on the Court's composition. The president's ability to mould the Constitutional Court is further strengthened by the fact that the justices of this Court also serve for the relatively short term of six years. As in the case of Supreme Court justices, a sitting president may have the opportunity to replace nearly all justices of the Constitutional Court. During Lee Myung-bak's presidency, he appointed seven new justices. Less than two years into his five-year term, Moon Jae-in appointed eight new justices.[7] The fact that these justices are not reappointed at the end of their terms may mitigate the danger that they will curry favour with the president through their decisions. Nevertheless, the fact that presidents can replace the justices so frequently is dangerous to the independence and stability of the Court. Such a 'formative' influence on the Constitutional Court is another factor contributing to the charge that the Korean president occupies an imperial position.

iii. National Election Commission

Provisions for administration of elections first entered the constitution with the 1960 Constitution. This was a reaction to the rigged presidential election of 15 March 1960, which triggered the nationwide protest that brought down the Syngman Rhee regime. Fair and independent administration of elections was deemed to be of paramount importance for a democracy, deserving separate mention in the constitution. Under the current constitution, the National Election Commission is co-equal in status with the executive, legislative, and judicial branches, and the Constitutional Court. In light of the appointment procedure, however, there is an ever-present danger that the president may unduly influence its composition and operation.

---

[7] This was partly due to the fact that Moon's predecessor Park Geun-hye was not able to finish her term in office due to dismissal following impeachment. Had she finished her term, she might have appointed three new justices, which might have reduced Moon's influence on the Constitutional Court.

Members of the National Election Commission are appointed through the same 'division of labour' scheme as that for the Constitutional Court (art 114(2)). The president, the National Assembly, and the chief justice each choose three members of the Commission. A minor difference is that there is no formal process of 'appointment' of all nine members by the president. Also, the Commission's chairperson is elected among the members themselves, rather than being appointed by the president. By custom, the chairperson is also a Supreme Court justice and is chosen from the chief justice's designees.[8] Of the nine members, however, eight, including the chairperson, are non-standing members who hold other professions. The sole standing member of the Commission is an appointee of the president.[9] This is why the president's influence can go far beyond the three seats allotted to the president.

Indeed, Moon Jae-in caused a row in 2019 when he appointed as the standing member a person who had been a special assistant to Moon's campaign when he was running for president in 2017. While the government party explained that his name was included in the party publication 'by mistake' and that he had never participated in the campaign, the opposition denounced the appointment as an attempt to manipulate the upcoming general election of 2020 and the presidential election of 2022. Even the appearance of partiality, the opposition claimed, was enough to disqualify him from the momentous role of ensuring fair elections. Although the opposition refused even to hold a confirmation hearing for the candidate, the president went ahead with the appointment.[10]

iv. Prime Minister and State Councillors: Subordination of National Assembly

In his capacity as the head of government, the president is authorised to appoint members of his Administration, which include the prime minister and state councillors. The constitution envisions the State Council as a deliberative body that collectively makes executive decisions on

---

[8] This is a holdover from the constitution of the Second Republic, which sought to ensure the National Election Commission's neutrality by providing that its chairman be chosen from among the justices of the Supreme Court. Even though that provision has been removed, the practice still remains, which to critics is a potential violation of the separation of powers.

[9] Election Commission Act, art 6 (Law No 13756, 15 January 2016). Although art 6(2) of this law provides that the standing member shall be elected among the members themselves, one of the presidential appointees has always taken up the position.

[10] On confirmation hearings by the National Assembly for candidates for official positions, see ch 5.

important matters. The reality, however, is that the president's dominance is nearly absolute because the members of the State Council, including the prime minister, serve at the president's pleasure. The State Council therefore is less a collective decision-making body than a 'cabinet' of ministers who owe their position and loyalty to the president. Even the prime minister is appointed by, and thus accountable only to, the president. The constitutional job description of the prime minister is to 'assist the President' and to direct the administrative ministries 'at the order of the President' (art 86(2)). The prime minister is authorised to recommend to the president the appointment and removal of state councillors (art 87(1) and (3)). The prime minister also recommends, from among the state councillors, heads of administrative ministries (art 94). Yet, this recommendation is merely a formality since the president has sole authority regarding the appointment and removal of state councillors and administrative ministers.

This power to appoint members of the Administration is technically an incident of the president's position as the head of the executive branch. Due to a unique feature of the Korean constitution, however, this power has the effect of elevating the president far above the National Assembly and even subordinating the legislature to the executive. The president is free to appoint members of the National Assembly as prime minister or state councillors. Although Assembly members are constitutionally forbidden to hold concurrent offices (art 43), the statute which defines the range of prohibited offices specifically excludes the offices of prime minister and state councillors.[11] This is another example of the so-called 'hybrid' nature of the Korean constitutional system, which goes back to the Founding Constitution of 1948. During the drafting process, one of the authors of the draft constitution Yu Chin-o defended the possibility of appointing Assembly members as heads of administrative ministries on the grounds that it will conduce to a more cooperative relationship between the legislature and the executive.[12] The idea was that having an administrative minister who is also a member of the National Assembly will allow for better communication between the two branches and enable the government to pursue its goals more effectively by making it easier to put its policy initiatives into legislations.

The reality, however, is that the system undermines the principle of separation of powers by according the executive, particularly the

---

[11] National Assembly Act, art 29(1).

[12] Proceedings of the Plenary Meeting of the Constituent National Assembly, 18th Meeting of the First Session (26 June 1948) 26–27. Yu acknowledged that the Korean system would be different from the American constitution in that regard.

president, a dominant position vis-à-vis the National Assembly. This is particularly so given that the National Assembly has no power to hold the prime minister or state councillors accountable. It may only make a non-binding recommendation for their dismissal to the president (art 63). The Korean Constitutional Court has in fact warned that concurrent office-holding is inconsistent with separation of powers because, whereas the role of the legislature is to be a watchdog over the executive, this ends up making an executive public official a watchdog over himself/herself.[13] The case in which the Court elucidated this reasoning, however, only addressed the question whether an employee of an enterprise partially owned by the state may run in elections for local (legislative) councils. In a constitutional complaint which directly challenged the constitutionality of the provision in the National Assembly Act that permits appointment of Assembly members as state councillors/administrative ministers, the Court dismissed the case for lack of standing, ie, that no constitutional rights of the complainant were affected by the concurrent office-holding as permitted under the said provision.[14] Given that the only persons who are directly affected by the provision are Assembly members who actually benefit from this system, it is unlikely to be challenged in the future.

Indeed, many commentators and pundits complain that Assembly members regard it as a 'promotion' or an advancement in their political careers to be called by the president to join the administration as a state councillor. Such holders of concurrent offices are often criticised by the press for continuing to receive compensation for both positions while being fully dedicated to neither. However, each time a proposal was made in the National Assembly to forbid concurrent office-holding, it was defeated. This is natural given that many Assembly members hope to be appointed as a state councillor by the president. That so many lawmakers have accepted the president's offer with alacrity naturally contributes to the public perception that members of the National Assembly are lower in rank to the president. This was only reinforced in 2020 when a former Speaker of the National Assembly, Chung Sye-kyun, accepted President Moon Jae-in's invitation to become his prime minister. Due to the so-called hybrid element of the Korean constitution, the head of the executive branch is able to enjoy a status far above the heads of all the other branches.

---

[13] Const Ct 91 Hun-Ma 67 (25 May 1995).
[14] Const Ct 2013 Hun-Ma 701 (5 November 2013).

F. Emergency Legislative Powers

The Korean constitution endows the president with the power to tempo-rarily exercise the legislative powers of the National Assembly during times of emergency. Under this power, the president is authorised to issue (administrative) dispositions even without legislative authorisation or to issue orders having the same force as statutes enacted by the legisla-ture. A crucial condition is the National Assembly's inability to provide proper legislative responses in a timely manner.

Article 76 provides the basis for this type of emergency power, of which there are two sub-types. According to article 76(1), the president may issue emergency (administrative) dispositions or emergency orders having the force of law regarding financial and economic matters in order to preserve national security or public welfare and order, in the face of a grave national crisis. Such dispositions or orders can be issued only when 'there is no time to await the convocation of the National Assembly'. According to article 76(2), the president is authorised to issue emergency orders having the force of law when necessary to safeguard the state in times of national emergency involving grave armed conflicts. This power can be invoked only when 'the convocation of the National Assembly is impossible'.

The current constitution's scheme of distinguishing between emer-gency dispositions and orders addressing financial or economic matters, on the one hand, and a more general emergency order designed to safe-guard the nation in the face of armed conflicts, on the other, marks a return to the 1962 Constitution of the Third Republic. The *Yushin* Constitution of 1972 made no such distinction and recognised a compre-hensive power to issue 'emergency measures' that addressed 'all aspects of state affairs including domestic politics, foreign relations, national defence, economy, finance, and judicial system' when, according to the president's assessment, national security or public welfare was, or might be, endangered. Through these emergency measures, the president was authorised to 'temporarily suspend the freedom and rights of the citi-zens provided for in the constitution' and to take actions 'regarding the powers of the government and the judiciary'.[15] Between January 1974 and May 1975, Park Chung-hee issued nine emergency measures, which essentially became supra-constitutional law through which he silenced the opposition and students critical of his autocratic ways. To be sure, not all emergency measures were intended to stifle criticism – one was

---

[15] 1972 Constitution, art 53(1) and (2).

intended to alleviate economic hardship brought on by the oil crisis and three were issued to repeal previous decrees. Others, however, banned criticism of the *Yushin* Constitution as well as any calls for its revision, made it a crime to criticise the government (triable by court martial), allowed for arrest of violators without warrants, outlawed all forms of student protests (including boycott of classes or exams), banned the reporting of any protests or criticism of the government, and allowed the military to be called to preserve order in major cities. A couple of emergency measures even made it a crime to criticise the emergency measures themselves. Moreover, the *Yushin* Constitution provided that the president's emergency measures could not become the object of judicial review.[16]

When the 1980 Constitution of the Fifth Republic was adopted, the same scheme was retained by and large. A few improvements included the deletion of the section precluding judicial review and enhancement of the National Assembly's monitoring role.[17] After issuing emergency measures, the president was required to seek the National Assembly's approval and if no approval was forthcoming, then the measures lost effect. Also, if the National Assembly requested the repeal of emergency measures, the president was required to comply,[18] whereas under the *Yushin* Constitution, the president could refuse if there were 'special circumstances'. Despite such mechanisms to prevent the president's abuse, the basic scope of the power and the conditions under which it could be invoked remained essentially unchanged.

With democratic transition in 1987, the drafters of the current constitution decided to narrow the scope of emergency powers and limit the conditions under which they could be invoked, while retaining the enhanced monitoring role of the National Assembly. The result was the return to the scheme laid out in the 1962 Constitution, with its distinction, mentioned above, between two different powers for addressing different types of crises, under different conditions.

Thus far, only the power to issue emergency financial-economic order has ever been invoked. In 1993, President Kim Young-sam issued the 'Emergency Financial-Economic Order on Real-Name Financial

---

[16] 1972 Constitution, art 53(4).

[17] The label for the emergency action also underwent change. The *Yushin* Constitution referred to it as 'emergency measure' (*kin'gŭp choch'i*) (more often rendered 'emergency decree'), whereas the 1980 Constitution called it 'extraordinary measure' (*pisang choch'i*). Since 1987, 'emergency order' (*pisang myŏngnyŏng*) and 'emergency financial/economic disposition' (*pisang chaejŏng kyŏngje ch'ŏbun*) have been in use.

[18] 1980 Constitution, art 51.

Transactions and Confidentiality' which banned the use of false or borrowed names in financial transactions. The purpose was to introduce transparency into the financial system in order to prevent corruption, tax evasion, and the accumulation of secret 'slush funds' by politicians and businessmen. The use, however, of false and borrowed names was not new. Indeed, it went back several decades. It could thus be disputed whether the existing financial system constituted an 'emergency' within the meaning of article 76(1), which lists as examples 'internal turmoil, external menace, natural calamity or grave financial or economic crisis'. In response, the Constitutional Court held that the requirements for invoking this power had been met. It pointed to the fact that the use of false and borrowed names had been damaging the nation's economy for a long time, causing numerous scandals that shook the whole society, as well as the fact that at least two previous attempts to pass legislation requiring the use of real names had been frustrated in the National Assembly by politicians benefitting from the old system.[19]

In the same decision, the Court rejected the government's argument that the president's invocation of emergency powers cannot be the object of judicial review. Specifically, it reasoned that in a democratic constitutional order there is no room for the category of a non-reviewable 'act of state' (*t'ongch'ihaengwi*). While conceding the need for a category of acts requiring high degree of political judgment by the president and which deserve judicial deference, the Court stated that even such 'acts of state' cannot be exempt from the general principle that all state functions must serve to realise the basic rights of the citizens. Besides, since the president's emergency financial-economic orders have the force of statutory law, it was only natural for the Court to review their constitutionality.

Applying similar logic, the Constitutional Court declared unconstitutional a statute that had been enacted under President Park Chung-hee in the lead-up to the adoption of the *Yushin* Constitution. In December 1971, Park declared a state of emergency and pushed through the National Assembly the 'Law on Special Measures for Safeguarding the State' which granted *ex post facto* the president the power to declare a state of emergency 'when necessary to take swift preventive measures' to safeguard the state against serious threat to national security. In a 2015 decision arising from a retrial of a criminal case, the Constitutional Court held that this statutory grant of emergency power to the president was unconstitutional because it went beyond the conditions specified in the

---

[19] Const Ct 93 Hun-Ma 186 (29 February 1996).

constitution. It pointed out that the only emergency power recognised by the constitution was the power to issue 'emergency financial-economic disposition or order' or the more general 'emergency order', and that this new statutory power to declare state of emergency could be subsumed under neither. Also, whereas the constitution mandated the subsequent approval of the National Assembly, this statutory declaration of state of emergency was subject to no such democratic control.[20]

G. Power to Declare Martial Law

A second type of emergency power is the power to declare martial law in case of emergencies requiring the deployment of the military. In a sense, this is an even broader and potentially more dangerous power because the president is permitted to go beyond assuming the role of the legislature. The president is authorised to interrupt the normal operation of the executive and judicial branches as well as suspend certain constitutional guarantees.

According to article 77, the president may choose between two types of martial law: precautionary and extraordinary. Under extraordinary martial law, the constitution permits 'special measures' on the system of warrants (*habeas corpus*), freedoms of speech, the press, assembly and association, and on the authority of the government and the judiciary. After declaring martial law, the president must notify the National Assembly. When the National Assembly demands the lifting of martial law by a majority of its total membership, the president is required to comply.

Korea's political history has shown that the constitution's provisions may be of little effect when martial law is actually declared. Indeed, the text itself has changed very little since the 1962 Constitution. To be sure, the 1948 Founding Constitution only had a very terse provision authorising the president to declare martial law 'as prescribed by statute'[21] and that may have allowed Syngman Rhee to use martial law in 1952 as a means of forcing a constitutional revision. Yet, even after the text became more detailed, martial law has been declared numerous times by presidents to repress political opposition. It was even used by military

---

[20] Const Ct 2014 Hun-Ka 5 (26 March 2015).
[21] 1948 Constitution, art 64.

leaders (Park Chung-hee and Chun Doo-hwan) to gain political power, ie, before they became presidents.

As for the judiciary, it has maintained a deferential attitude toward the declaration of martial law. While the number of cases that dealt with martial law is very small, the Supreme Court has basically maintained that whether to declare martial law is a decision requiring highly political and military judgment and that it is beyond the competence of courts to review the propriety of such decisions.[22] In fairness, though, all of these cases predate the adoption of the current constitution and the Constitutional Court's decision which proclaimed that even highly political 'acts of state' are reviewable. It remains to be seen how either court will decide, if and when it is asked in the future to review the legality or constitutionality of a declaration of martial law.

II. THE ADMINISTRATION

The constitution's chapter on the Government comprises two sections – one on the president and the other on the 'Administration'. The administration is essentially the entire executive branch minus the president. Yet, the section on the administration includes only general provisions, leaving the specifics to other statutes such as the Government Organisation Act and other legislation on individual administrative agencies.

A. Prime Minister and the State Council

Given that the prime minister is appointed by, and is an assistant to, the president, the title 'Prime Minister' may be misleading. The prime minister is not the leader of the governing party in the legislature, nor the head of the government. This office is also a result of mixing parliamentary and presidential forms of government.[23] As the second highest official in the executive branch, the prime minister is the vice-chair of the State Council (art 88(3)) and is authorised to exercise the powers of the president when the president is unable to perform official duties (art 71).

The office of the prime minister is often occupied by a career politician (sometimes even a member of the National Assembly), but it has also been filled by career civil servants, scholars, diplomats, and even former

[22] Eg, Sup Ct 79 Ch'o 70 (7 December 1979).
[23] See ch 1.

military personnel. Presidents tend to appoint someone with national reputation, who can command the respect of the public as well as the bureaucrats in the various administrative ministries. In practice, this has the effect of providing someone to take the blame when the government, for whatever reason, comes under criticism, thereby shielding the president from public censure.[24] When there is a scandal or some embarrassing event, in other words, the president can fire the prime minister and appoint someone else, allowing the president to go on with little accountability. This is another way in which the so-called hybrid nature of the Korean constitution has contributed to the imperial presidency.

The State Council was originally conceived as a collective decision-making body for the executive branch. Under the 1948 Founding Constitution, it was authorised to make binding decisions on important policy matters under the jurisdiction of the president. This, too, was a result of the mixing of different forms of government. What was originally the executive cabinet in the parliamentary system was retained even after the presidential system based on separation of powers was introduced, in the hope that it might restrain the president. This hope was supported at the time by the fact that the president was elected by the National Assembly and that the prime minister and state councillors all had to resign upon the National Assembly's vote of non-confidence. With the constitutional revision in 1952, which introduced direct popular election of the president, Rhee was no longer dependent on the National Assembly. Then, through the 1954 revision, the office of the prime minister was abolished and the National Assembly's powers regarding the State Council were substantially reduced. After the short interlude with parliamentary system under the Second Republic, the position of prime minister was revived under a presidential system in the 1962 Constitution of the Third Republic, to be the 'civilian' face of the military regime.[25] The State Council was reduced from a decision-making institution to a deliberative body, whose decisions are not binding on the president. The current constitution enumerates 16 matters pertaining to the powers of the president, which must be referred to the State Council for deliberation (art 89). It is unclear whether the president's decision on these matters would be valid if they were not deliberated upon by the State

---

[24] This has created the term 'bullet-proof prime minister' (*pangt'an ch'ongri*), referring to the fact that many prime ministers have functioned as a bullet-proof vest or a 'fall guy' for the president.

[25] Under the 1962 Constitution, a provision was added, which still remains, stipulating that no active member of the military could become a prime minister or a state councillor.

Council. Technically, there may be procedural issues, but it is widely recognised that the State Council's 'decision' is essentially *pro forma*.

B. Administrative Ministries and the Civil Service

The constitution provides that the heads of administrative ministries shall be appointed by the president 'from among state councillors' (art 94).[26] In practice, upon appointment as head of an administrative ministry, that person automatically becomes a state councillor. Given that the State Council's deliberation and decision are formalities, the status of heading a ministry is seen as weightier than that of being a state councillor. Also, even though the prime minister is to recommend the ministers to the president (art 94), the recommendation is a formality, and the president essentially appoints whomever the president wishes. Although not prescribed by the constitution, candidates for the heads of administrative ministries are required to undergo confirmation hearings before the relevant standing committee of the National Assembly. The National Assembly's consent, however, is not a precondition for appointment. Appointing a minister without the legislature's approval may be politically difficult but is legally possible.

The number of administrative ministries has fluctuated over the years. Since the last revision of the Government Organisation Act in 2023, there are 19 administrative ministries. These comprise the main body of the central state bureaucracy. In addition, there are several agencies that are directly under the president, such as the Board of Audit and Inspection and the National Intelligence Service, as well as those under the prime minister, such as the Ministry of Personnel Management, the Ministry of Government Legislation, the Fair Trade Commission, and the Anticorruption and Civil Rights Commission.

State agencies are staffed with professional bureaucrats who are selected through a competitive civil service exam. In the past, partly due to the relative underdevelopment of the private sector, the central bureaucracy used to attract the nation's best and brightest.[27] The civil service was regarded as independent and largely apolitical. The heads of administrative ministries were often chosen from such technocrats.

---

[26] In the past, a few state councillors existed who were not administrative ministers (minister without portfolio), but the system has ceased.

[27] S-Y Lee and S Lee, 'Civil Service Reforms and the Development of Korea' (2014) 29(1) *Korean Journal of Policy Studies* 47.

With democratisation, demand has been increasing for more democratic oversight of the bureaucracy and for reforming its hierarchical culture. More ministers are political appointees or external experts who have no prior experience in the ministries. At the same time, the blanket ban on public servants' political activity, intended to ensure their neutrality, is being challenged as overly stringent and infringing on individual freedom. This in turn is raising questions about the neutrality, independence, and professionalism of the civil service.[28]

III. HOLDING EXECUTIVE POWER ACCOUNTABLE

Given the powers at the president's disposal, preventing the return of authoritarian rule is a perennial concern. In principle, the constitution is premised on the idea of checks and balances through separation of powers, but when put into practice, power tends to be concentrated in the executive. As noted, the so-called hybrid approach was intended to restrain the president, but it may be having the opposite effect.

A. Duties of the President

The constitution imposes several duties on the president. At the most general level, article 66 declares that the president has the duty to safeguard the nation's independence, the state's territorial integrity, and the continuity of the state as well as upholding the constitution. Article 69 on the president's oath of office also includes the duty to 'faithfully execute the office of the President' by, *inter alia*, observing the constitution. In the impeachment case against the former President Roh Moo-hyun, the Constitutional Court addressed whether these duties were legal in nature and if so whether they could function as a yardstick for impeaching the president. It began by finding that the duty to faithfully execute the office of the president as well as most of the duties in article 66 were essentially political in nature and therefore did not provide useable legal criteria for the Court. The duty to 'uphold and observe the constitution', however, was a legal duty that was amenable for the Court's assessment.[29] On

---

[28] PS Kim, 'The Civil Service System in the Republic of Korea' in EM Berman et al (eds), *Public Administration in East Asia* (CRC Press 2010).

[29] Y Lee, 'Law, Politics, and Impeachment: The Impeachment of Roh Moo-Hyun from a Comparative Constitutional Perspective' (2005) 53 *American Journal of Comparative Law* 403.

that basis, it pronounced that the president's violation of election laws – including the provision that requires the president to maintain political neutrality in electoral matters – constitutes a violation of this duty to uphold and observe the constitution.[30] Having found a violation of this constitutional duty, the Court nevertheless concluded that it did not amount to a grave enough violation that merited conviction, ie, dismissal from office.[31]

In a later case, the Constitutional Court revisited the issue of the duty of public officials to maintain neutrality in electoral matters. When the National Election Commission in 2007 issued a warning against President Roh to refrain from criticising the opposition party's candidates or expressing partisan support for his own party, he filed a constitutional complaint claiming violation of his right to free speech. The Commission's action was based on article 9 of the Public Official Elections Act, which prohibited all action by public officials that could unduly influence the outcome of elections, and article 65 of the National Public Officials Act, which prohibited public officials from joining any political organisations or expressing support or opposition for a particular party or candidate. Such broad ban on political activity by public officials is a response to Korea's chequered political past, during which the government apparatus was mobilised to ensure favourable results for the ruling party.[32] The Court acknowledged that the president is by law permitted to be a member of a political party and that as an individual citizen, the president's freedom of speech should be honoured and protected. Nevertheless, given the responsibility of the president to ensure fair and impartial elections as well as the overwhelming influence he may exert on the electoral process, the Court concluded that the restrictions on his free speech were within constitutionally tolerable bounds.[33] Between the president's status as a politician and his role as the highest public official in charge of elections, the latter had to be given priority.

B. Board of Audit and Inspection

Under the current constitution, the primary watchdog agency over the executive branch is the Board of Audit and Inspection (BAI). Its

---

[30] Const Ct 2004 Hun-Na 1 (14 May 2004).

[31] For more on impeachment proceedings, see ch 7.

[32] The ban on public officials' political activity was first mandated in 1963, whereas the election law's mandate on neutrality goes back to 1994.

[33] Const Ct 2007 Hun-Ma 700 (17 January 2008).

constitutional mandate is 'to audit the settlement of accounts of the revenues and expenditures of the State' and 'to inspect the performance of duties of administrative agencies and public officials' (art 97).[34] On the one hand, it is entrusted with oversight of public revenue and expenditure by assessing the accuracy of public entities' financial reporting. On the other, it is authorised to call out wrongdoings and irregularities of agencies and officials within the executive branch.

Under the Founding Constitution, a predecessor organisation to the BAI was an independent entity not affiliated with any branch of the government. Yet, since the 1962 Constitution, the BAI has been a part of the administration, located 'under the President'. To be sure, as a constitutional entity, it cannot be statutorily abolished, but its status is clearly subordinate to the president. This raises the question whether the BAI is endowed with the requisite independence for discharging its mandate, especially when it needs to audit or inspect the president or members of the president's office. Can it be a 'supreme audit institution' when it is institutionally subordinated to the president's office? Sceptics point out that the president has the power to appoint the chair of the BAI, with the consent of the National Assembly (art 98(2)). The chair in turn recommends the other members of the Board for appointment by the president (art 98(3)). In other words, the appointment system is the same as that for the Supreme Court and the State Council. The law establishing the BAI is quite frank about its ambivalent status: 'The Board of Audit and Inspection shall be established under the President, but shall retain an independent status in regard to its duties.'[35] Under such institutional constraints, the BAI inevitably faces structural obstacles when auditing and inspecting the president's major policy initiatives.

There is continuing debate whether its mission should be limited to ensuring compliance with governing authorities (legality review), or include reviewing not only the effectiveness, efficiency and economy of government policies and programmes (performance review) but also their propriety and even legitimacy (policy review). The BAI's internal regulation explicitly states that 'major policy decisions of the government' as well as 'the propriety of policy goals' are outside the purview of its inspection.[36] Yet, critics point out that reviewing the effectiveness

---

[34] On the National Assembly's similar but broader power to 'inspect affairs of the state or investigate a specific aspect of state affairs' (art 61), see ch 5.

[35] Board of Audit and Inspection Act, art 2(1) (Law No 17560, 20 October 2020).

[36] Regulations on Inspection of Official Duties, art 4(2)(iv) (BAI Regulation No 304, 12 April 2018).

or economy of policies almost always entails reviewing the propriety of the policy goals as well.

The problem is compounded by the fact that presidents often use the BAI as a political tool to undermine and discredit policies of previous administrations. Park Geun-hye, for example, requested the BAI to audit and inspect again the Four Major Rivers Project, a pet project of her predecessor, Lee Myung-bak, after the Board had initially cleared it of any irregularities. When the BAI is perceived as questioning the sitting president's policy goals, it is likely to be severely attacked for overstepping its competence and questioning the soundness of the president's judgment. For example, when it pointed out that the Moon Jae-in administration's decision to shut down a nuclear power plant was based on faulty assessment of its economic viability, the Board was condemned for challenging the propriety of the president's policy to phase out nuclear power. Many are therefore advocating the creation of a totally independent watchdog agency that will not be subordinated to the president's office. Others argue for the relocation of the BAI under the National Assembly. Either solution, however, would require a constitutional revision.

C. Independent Agencies

In an attempt to address the issue of institutional independence of entities charged with the role of monitoring and keep in check the power of the executive (as well as other branches), several agencies have been established at various stages with slightly different mandates. These institutions inevitably raise the question of their constitutional authorisation. Since they are not specifically provided for in the text of the constitution, they attract criticism that their functions are redundant or that their structure violates the principle of separation of powers. One example might be the National Human Rights Commission, which was established following the recommendation of the 1993 World Conference on Human Rights in Vienna. By design, the Commission is attached to no existing branch of government so as to be an independent watchdog over all state institutions. Given its mission of criticising other state agencies' human rights practices, it frequently attracts criticism that it violates the separation of powers. While it does not belong to the executive branch, it is regarded as exercising power akin to administrative agencies.

Similar concern was raised regarding the recently created Corruption Investigation Office for High-ranking Officials. Even though investigating and prosecuting criminal violations are essentially executive powers, the agency is located outside the existing organisation of the executive branch to ensure its independence even from the president. This raises the question whether such a *sui generis* office violates the principle of separation of powers. The Constitutional Court has held that the need for independence and neutrality justifies the Office's placement outside the ordinary government bureaucracy and that this does not violate the separation of powers.[37] It rejected the argument that the Office's power to investigate alleged wrongdoings of judges could possibly undermine judicial independence.

From time to time, a special prosecutor is appointed to investigate and prosecute violations of the law by high government officials. The goal is to ensure impartiality and objectivity in situations where regular prosecutors would not be able to perform the task due to conflict of interest or external pressure. The specific manner of appointing the special prosecutor has varied depending on the nature of the alleged violation. One appointment method that was challenged for violation of separation of powers was one in which the chief justice of the Supreme Court recommended two candidates among whom the president chose one. The Constitutional Court held that the chief justice's role did not entail improper entanglement of the judiciary with the exercise of executive power.[38]

D. Single-term Presidency and *Ex Post Facto* Control

As seen, the power structure as it exists in Korea makes it difficult to exert meaningful restraint on the president while in office. This creates a pattern whereby the president's transgressions, both legal and ethical, tend to be suppressed during the president's term, only to be revealed toward the end of the term and prosecuted after the president leaves office. As is well known, hardly any president of Korea has had a peaceful post-retirement life. At the start of their terms, each one enjoyed high popularity, but toward the end of their terms, their approval ratings invariably hit rock bottom. As a result, the incoming presidents have an incentive to distance themselves from their predecessor. This is often done by initiating investigation into some form of corruption or abuse

---

[37] Const Ct 2020 Hun-Ma 264 (28 January 2021).
[38] Const Ct 2007 Hun-Ma 1468 (10 January 2008).

of power committed under the previous president. Counting from 1987, when the current constitution was adopted, practically all seven former presidents have been investigated or accused of wrongdoing.

Some contend that due to the imperial powers enjoyed by the president and the lack of meaningful restraint, the president feels free to disregard the law while in office and those with knowledge of the transgression rarely feel safe to come forward with accusation. By the end of the term, however, such inhibition is lifted because everybody knows that the president is constitutionally prohibited from seeking re-election. Accusations start flying against the lame-duck president. After the former president has left office, the new president is under immense pressure to verify the accusations, if only to maintain their own popularity. Hence, the familiar spectacle in Korea of former presidents being brought in for interrogation and examination. And it is at this juncture that the institutions and mechanism noted above are mobilised to carry out the investigation. As mentioned, Park Geun-hye repeatedly instructed the Board of Audit and Inspection to revisit her predecessor Lee Myung-bak's Four Major Rivers Project. During Roh Moo-hyun's presidency, a special prosecutor was appointed to investigate the claim that his predecessor Kim Dae-jung had illegally sent five billion dollars to the North Korean regime as a 'price' for the historic summit meeting between leaders of North and South Koreas. In other words, the institutions for controlling the executive power tend to be utilised only in an *ex post facto* manner, rather than at the time the alleged wrongdoings were being committed. As one commentator observes, the Korean system is one of 'imperial but imperiled presidency'.[39]

IV. CONCLUSION

The constitution endows the president of Korea with a dual status. As the head of state, the president represents the entire state toward other states. As the head of the executive branch, the president is on equal footing with the heads of other branches. Although the president is the chief executive, the constitution vests executive power in the State Council, of which the president is just one member. In practice, however, the president

---

[39] H Jaung, 'The Two Tales of the Korean Presidency: Imperial but Imperiled Presidency' in J Mo and DW Brady (eds), *The Rule of Law in South Korea* (Hoover Institution Press 2009).

is clearly above not only other members of the State Council but also the heads of other branches. The constitution's attempt to combine a collective decision-making system with a single executive agent may have been intended to restrain an overbearing president through some form of collective leadership system. Similarly, elements of parliamentary form of government, such as permitting legislators to become state councillors or allowing the National Assembly to recommend the resignation of state councillors, may have been included to hold the president accountable to the legislature. Yet, it must be admitted that the practice over the years has been rather disappointing. One scholar has observed that presidents still enjoy 'almost the same power exercised by the authoritarian rulers' such that they are 'reminiscent of the latter-day Kings in realizing their desire for power'.[40] Even though the constitutional revision of 1987 sought to reduce the powers of the president, it has evidently not succeeded in eliminating the imperial presidency. It has been suggested that the ambitions of political leaders in 1987 who wished to become presidents worked against the adoption of a more decentralised system. Whatever the cause, there is no denying that the current system concentrates wide-ranging powers in hands of the president. In particular, the panoply of appointment powers and the power of the purse that comes with the office tend to render ineffectual many mechanisms for reining in the president's powers. This may be fuelling the confrontational stance often taken by the opposition in the National Assembly, as well as the constant emphasis on the president's duty to be neutral and impartial, as seen during the impeachment of Roh Moo-hyun and Park Geun-hye.[41] Indeed, the National Assembly's utilisation of the impeachment process against two different presidents, within the span of 12 years, may reflect the fact that the system lacks a more regularised, less drastic, means for restraining the president's powers.

FURTHER READING

Choi J-J, 'Korean Democracy in a Hyper-Centralized State' in H Mosler, E-J Lee and H-J Kim (eds), *The Quality of Democracy in Korea: Three Decades After Democratization* (Palgrave Macmillan 2018).

[40] J-s Chong, 'Political Power and Constitutionalism' in D-K Yoon (ed), *Recent Transformations in Korean Law and Society* (Seoul National University Press 2000) 16.
[41] C Hahm, 'Constitutional Court of Korea: Guardian of the Constitution or Mouthpiece of the Government?' in A HY Chen and A Harding (eds), *Constitutional Courts in Asia: A Comparative Perspective* (Cambridge University Press 2018) 158–63.

Chong J-s, 'Political Power and Constitutionalism' in D-K Yoon (ed), *Recent Trans-formations in Korean Law and Society* (Seoul National University Press 2000).

Jaung H, 'The Two Tales of the Korean Presidency: Imperial but Imperiled Presi-dency' in J Mo and DW Brady (eds), *The Rule of Law in South Korea* (Hoover Institution Press 2009).

Rhyu S-Y, 'Political Leadership' in C-I Moon and MJ Moon (eds), *Routledge Handbook of Korean Politics and Public Administration* (Routledge 2020).

5

National Assembly and its Powers

Proportional Representation and Electoral System – Role of Political Parties – Tyranny of Majority and Legislative Deadlock – Appointment Powers – Impeachment Powers – Inspection and Investigation of State Affairs – Approval of Budget

THE NATIONAL ASSEMBLY is the unicameral legislature of the Republic of Korea, which currently has 300 lawmakers who serve for a four-year, renewable term. It has exclusive powers to pass legislative enactments, ie, statutes. The Government may also propose bills, but only the National Assembly can enact them into law. In its capacity as representatives of the people, it is authorised to give consent to important international treaties and diplomatic matters involving the armed forces (art 60). A bill for revising the constitution must first pass the National Assembly before being put to a referendum (art 130). To underscore its role as the people's representative, the current constitution placed the chapter on National Assembly before the chapters on other state agencies. Yet, it is doubtful if the people's regard for the National Assembly matches the central role entrusted to it by the constitution. In recent years, it has consistently scored the lowest in surveys on the trustworthiness of major state agencies. For many, the privileges, immunities, and remuneration the lawmakers are entitled to are not commensurate with the actual work they perform. Assembly members are often seen castigating government officials without the requisite background knowledge, while automatically voting according to party line rather than engaging in genuine deliberation. The unfortunate perception is widespread that they are aggravating social polarisation with behaviour aimed at stoking the electorate's anger and hatred. This may be a symptom of a larger, more structural, problem about the party system and the legislature's weak position relative to the executive. This chapter will examine these causes as well as some attempts to improve the quality of the legislative process and to win back the people's trust.

I. COMPOSITION OF THE NATIONAL ASSEMBLY

The National Assembly's structure has gone through several changes and distortions over the years. It began as a single-chamber legislature under the Founding Constitution. The constitutional revision in 1952 changed it to a bicameral body, but elections for the upper chamber were never held until 1960 when the Second Republic was inaugurated. It was turned back to a unicameral legislature with the revision in 1962 and has remained so ever since.

The Founding Constitution did not have any provision on the number of legislators. It was up to the National Assembly to specify through election laws how many members it would have. This meant that the number of seats in the National Assembly would change through negotiations and strategic calculations among the members themselves. With the revision of 1962, a provision specifying the upper and lower limits of the number of Assembly members was inserted, as was a requirement that candidates for the National Assembly must receive a party's endorsement. These provisions were removed in the 1972 *Yushin* Constitution, likely reflecting the near irrelevance of the legislative branch under that system. The 1980 Constitution restored only the lower limit of legislative seats (200) in the National Assembly. This has been retained in the current constitution.

According to the National Assembly Act, there are currently 300 seats, of which 47 are filled by proportional representatives from party lists, and the rest from single member districts. Textual basis for proportional representation was introduced in the 1980 Constitution, although the first election that included party list representatives was held in 1963. These 'national constituency' seats were distributed among the parties according to the ratio of support they received in the electoral districts. A major change was then introduced in 2004 regarding the method of electing proportional representatives. This was mandated by the Constitutional Court's 2001 decision which said that a ballot cast by voters in electoral districts cannot be used for two different purposes.[1] The Court reasoned that the voter's preference for a candidate in the district does not necessarily indicate support for that candidate's party. Given that smaller parties cannot field candidates in all electoral districts, a voter who supports a smaller party may not be able express such support if there are no candidates from that party in the voter's district. In such cases, the fact that the voter had chosen a candidate from one party as the

---

[1] Const Ct 2000 Hun-Ma 91 (consolidated) (19 July 2001).

voter's district's representative cannot be interpreted as support for that party. In order accurately to gauge the electorate's support for political parties, each voter must cast two votes – one for choosing the district's representative and another expressing preference for a specific party. The 2004 general election was held under this 'one person – two votes' system. This is commonly seen as a step toward correcting the system that favoured larger parties.

The next major overhaul of the proportional representation system took place in 2020. The goal was to further enhance the smaller parties' chances of gaining seats in the National Assembly and to better reflect the diversity of political outlook among the electorate. The centrepiece of the change was the introduction of a combination of a parallel vote system and a modified mixed-member proportional system for allotting 47 proportional seats (out of 300) among the political parties. According to this two-track approach, 17 of the proportional seats are distributed according to the previous method of following the percentage of the electorates' support as shown in the party preference vote. The remaining 30 proportional seats are allotted through a complex mathematical formula that supposedly benefits smaller parties which garner high support in the party preference vote, but perform relatively poorly in the electoral districts. By using the percentage of support a party receives in the party preference vote as a notional target, the goal is to divide up the 30 proportional seats in such a way as to compensate those parties which failed to reach the target at the district elections. If, by contrast, the number of seats a party wins in the electoral districts reaches or surpasses the notional target (ie, support received in the party preference vote), then no proportional seats (from the 30) are given to that party.

Despite good intentions, the new proportional representation system backfired spectacularly at the actual election. Rather than increasing the presence of smaller parties in the National Assembly, it contributed to expanding the larger parties' share of seats. This happened mainly because the two larger parties engaged in the devious practice of creating a sister, or 'satellite', political party which deliberately chose not to field any candidates in the electoral districts. Instead, these satellite parties only created a list of candidates who would be granted proportional seats according to the mathematical formula designed to benefit smaller parties. This practice was initiated by the largest opposition (conservative) party, which had objected to the adoption of the new proportional representation system. It claimed that it had to protect itself under a system designed to weaken its power in the National Assembly and challenged the legitimacy of election rules adopted without its consent.[2] Indeed, the new system had been adopted under the leadership of the then-ruling party which persuaded other smaller left-leaning parties with the argument that they would be the primary beneficiaries.[3] Having pushed through the new rules, however, the ruling party also created a satellite party to ensure that it would likewise gain proportional seats. After the election, the satellite parties of the two major parties disbanded, with their proportional representatives joining the larger sister parties to increase their seats in the National Assembly. In the end, by gaining 180 seats, the ruling party was the greatest beneficiary of the new rules. Having cooperated with the ruling party in adopting the new proportional system, the smaller parties' voice in the legislature did not increase at all.

II. WEAK PARTY SYSTEM AND STRONG PARTY DISCIPLINE

According to most commentators, Korea is a 'party state'. Article 8 provides for the freedom to establish political parties and guarantees a multi-party system. It also states that parties are protected by state law, while mandating that the goal, organisation, and activities of a party must be democratic. The German concept of 'institutional guarantee' (*institutionelle Garantie*) is often invoked to convey the idea that political parties are constitutionally protected institutions.

Historically, however, parties did not always enjoy such protection. The Founding Constitution contained no mention of political parties. The 1960 Constitution of the Second Republic was the first to provide that political parties are legally protected by the state and that they can only be disbanded by a judgment of the constitutional court. The 1962 Constitution of the Third Republic added the clause on the freedom to establish a political party and the guarantee of multi-party system, as well as the requirement that a party's organisation and activities be democratic. Since the 1980 revision, parties are also entitled to financial support from the state.

---

[2] This opposition party, called Mirae T'onghap-dang (United Future Party) had 112 seats at the time, which was reduced to 103 after the election.

[3] The government party, called Tŏburŏ Minju-dang (Together Democratic Party), utilised a relatively new process called the 'fast track' legislation which allowed them to adopt the new election rules without having to consult the largest opposition party. More on this process below.

A. Weak Party System

Even after transition to democracy in 1987, a strong party system has yet to emerge in Korea. Political parties tend to be formed around particular individuals rather than a coherent ideology or policy platforms. They are rather short-lived, with frequent name changes as well as constant splintering and mergers among transient factions. Some observers attribute this to political culture, especially the influence of Confucian tradition, with its emphasis on personal relationship, regional ties, and respect for authority.[4] Others point to the experience of military government and the way in which democratic transition took place in Korea: the party was not an important basis for the military rulers in their endeavour to wield uninhibited power, nor for the forces of democratisation in their effort to bring down authoritarian regimes.[5] Whatever the cause, the party system remains rather underdeveloped. Without a firm ideological core, parties often pursue policies at variance with their erstwhile identities and form alliances of convenience with former opponents. Despite the deep polarisation that characterises Korean society, this has not translated into stable party loyalty among the electorate.

The political parties' inability to develop into stable institutions with strong voter support based on identifiable policy preference may be related to the treatment they have been accorded by the law. For a long time, a major concern for both lawmakers and judges has been the avoidance of political instability caused by the chaotic sprouting of minor parties with only local or regional support. This may have further weakened the party's ability to connect with the local voters and to cultivate support at the grassroots level.

When a provision in the Political Parties Act was challenged which required that a party must have at least 1,000 members in at least five different cities or provinces, the Constitutional Court held that, although this requirement may limit the freedom to create political parties, preventing an inordinate number of minor parties is a legitimate purpose.[6] Aside from citing the fact that a stable majority within the

---

[4] B-K Kim, 'Party Politics in South Korea's Democracy: The Crisis of Success' in L Diamond and B-K Kim (eds), *Consolidating Democracy in South Korea* (Lynne Rienner 2000).

[5] J Wong, 'South Korea's Weakly Institutionalized Party System' in A Hicken and EM Kuhonta (eds), *Party System Institutionalization in Asia: Democracies, Autocracies, and the Shadows of the Past* (Cambridge University Press 2015).

[6] Const Ct 2004 Hun-Ma 246 (30 March 2006).

legislature is a prerequisite for a working representative democracy, the Court pointed to the need to overcome the deep-rooted regionalism that has long plagued Korean politics.

The demand that political parties have a 'national' character was also manifest in another provision that mandated the automatic cancellation of a party's registration if that party failed to receive 2 per cent of all the votes cast in the preceding general election. The Constitutional Court struck down this clause on grounds that expulsion of a party from the political arena based on its performance in just one election was excessive.[7]

By contrast, the Court upheld a 2004 amendment to the Political Parties Act which abolished parties' local chapters (below the level of cities and provinces).[8] The amendment was in large part a hasty response to a scandal that revealed local chapters as channels for illegal donations to political parties, and as such was passed by a large majority. The lawmakers felt they needed go along with the reformist agenda of rooting out corruption which allegedly arose from the cost of maintaining local chapters. The amendment was challenged in the Constitutional Court on the grounds that abolition of local chapters violated not only the freedom to establish political parties but also the constitutional mandate that parties 'must have the necessary organisation to participate in the formation of the political will of the people' (art 8(2)). In a unanimous decision, the Court held that eliminating local chapters did not impede the functioning of parties and that local chapters were less essential today due to the development of various means of communication and transportation. It reasoned that it was a matter of legislative discretion whether to maintain parties' local chapters, and that political parties can function without any organisation for directly engaging the electorate at the grassroots level. This stance was maintained in a later decision which upheld a ban on 'party-members' council' below the level of cities and provinces.[9] Despite these cases, discussion continues among politicians on the need to revive local chapters.

B. Strong Party Discipline

One result of the emphasis on political parties' 'national' character may be that they are becoming more centralised organisations with little

---

[7] Const Ct 2012 Hun-Ma 431 (28 January 2014).
[8] Const Ct 2004 Hun-Ma 456 (16 December 2004).
[9] Const Ct 2013 Hun-Ka 22 (31 March 2016).

tolerance for intra-party diversity of viewpoints. Rather than providing a forum of debate, parties increasingly expect their members to carry out the central leadership's decisions and vote according to party line. This is due partly to a system whereby the party leadership essentially decides who shall be a candidate in elections. Assembly members who do not follow the party line risk not being selected as their party's candidate in the next election. Also, the fact that parties are in practice incorporated into the National Assembly's organisation tends to enhance the parties' ability to enforce its position among its member legislators. By statute, any party that has 20 or more seats in the National Assembly may form an official 'negotiation group'[10] whose head acts as the floor leader to ensure that its members adhere to the party line.

The Constitutional Court's recent jurisprudence may be encouraging this trend as well. In a couple of decisions, it affirmed a political party's authority to discipline its member who went against the party line. These cases raised the issue of how far 'party discipline' may encroach upon the principle of free representational mandate. Article 46(2) of the Constitution is universally understood as a firm rejection of imperative mandate for Assembly members.[11] As such, lawmakers are in principle representatives of the entire people and not bound by directives or instructions from their constituents or anyone else. The National Assembly Act makes this more specific and provides that lawmakers are not bound by the will of their parties.[12] Despite these provisions, the Constitutional Court held that no rights of a legislator were violated when the Speaker reassigned him, in response to his party's request, to a different standing committee because he intended not to vote according to the party line.

The Court reasoned that parties are allowed such leverage to implement their legislative programmes. To be sure, allowing each lawmaker the freedom to vote according to their own best judgment might be better for democratic intra-party decision-making process and for preventing the rise of oligarchies. The Court stated, however, that the principle of free mandate is not necessarily inconsistent with the parties' role

---

[10] National Assembly Act (hereafter 'NAA'), art 33(1) (Law No 16325, 16 April 2019). Lawmakers belonging to smaller parties with less than 20 seats may form a negotiation group with lawmakers from other parties.

[11] Article 46(2) reads: 'Members of the National Assembly shall give preference to national interests and shall perform their duties in accordance with their conscience.'

[12] 'As representatives of the entire nation, members of the National Assembly shall vote in accordance with their conscience without being bound by the will of their party.' NAA, art 114-2.

in articulating a unified position within the legislature. This entailed accepting the ability of a party to enforce its position among its members through various forms of pressure. The Court pointed out that, while a party could not strip nonconforming members of their seats in the National Assembly, it was free to discipline them and even expel them from the party. It thus rejected the nonconforming lawmaker's argument that his involuntary reassignment to a different standing committee constituted a violation of his constitutional right to vote in accordance with his own conscience.[13] The Constitutional Court maintained this stance in a later decision, in which it stated that the principle of free mandate is not absolute and must be balanced against the National Assembly's ability to perform its legislative function.[14] It characterised the reassignment of a lawmaker to a new standing committee as an exercise of the National Assembly's internal autonomous powers.

A political party's ability to enforce its position among its member lawmakers is further enhanced by a provision in the election law which states that proportional representatives shall lose their legislative seats if they renounce their party membership. That the said provision is intended to strengthen party discipline can be discerned from the fact that proportional representatives do not lose their seats if their party membership changes involuntarily – due to expulsion from the party, the party's merger with another party or its voluntary disbandment.[15] This is justified by the argument that, since proportional representatives are elected according to 'closed party lists', they owe their seats to their parties more than do their fellow lawmakers who are elected from local districts. Some commentators argue that this provision is unconstitutional on grounds that an Assembly member is a constitutionally mandated 'state organ', whereas a political party is merely a civil association (albeit a constitutionally protected one) which cannot be allowed to dispose of its elected members' legislative seats. Critics also point out that lawmakers from local districts are no less reliant on their parties in terms of support and organisation during elections; the said provision thus invidiously turns proportional representatives into 'second-class' lawmakers. While this rule has not been adjudicated in the Constitutional Court, it is worth noting a previous decision which ruled that, 'in the absence of legislation requiring otherwise', the mere fact that a proportional representative left a party should not result in

---

[13] Const Ct 2002 Hun-Ra 1 (30 October 2003).
[14] Const Ct 2019 Hun-Ra 1 (27 May 2020).
[15] Public Official Elections Act, art 192(4) (Law No 18791, 12 January 2021).

the forfeiture of that person's seat in the National Assembly.[16] Political parties apparently read this as an invitation to fill that absence by legislating the above rule.

C. Subsidies for Political Parties and Public Financing of Elections

Another factor that tends to encourage a disconnect between political parties and the electorate is state support for political parties and the system of public financing of elections. The Constitution explicitly authorises the provision of operational funds to political parties from the public coffers (art 8(3)). The justification is that parties would not be self-sustaining if left entirely to citizen support, even though, as essentially private associations, they should ideally be maintained by membership dues and voluntary contributions. Another justification is that state support for parties will help prevent the rise of plutocracy by protecting parties from undue influence by a few wealthy donors and thereby level the playing field among various parties. At the same time, the constitution also mandates that in principle all costs related to elections be borne by the state. It specifically provides that such costs cannot be imposed on political parties or candidates (art 116(2)). The justification is that this will ensure equal opportunity among candidates and parties with varying degrees of financial resources. It is also argued that bearing the cost of election will unduly restrict citizens' right to hold public office.[17]

Accordingly, the law has made it extremely difficult to make private donations to political parties, thereby making them essentially dependent on state support. According to the Political Funds Act, no foreigner, corporation or organisation is allowed to make political contributions.[18] A previous law was held unconstitutional, which had prohibited labour organisations from making political donations.[19] In response, the law was first revised in 2000 to remove the discriminatory treatment of labour organisations. Then, the law was revised again in 2004 to prohibit all organisations and corporations. In 2010, the Court upheld a similar

---

[16] Const Ct 92 Hun-Ma 153 (28 April 1994).
[17] Const Ct 2016 Hun-Ma 5224 (consolidated) (26 July 2018).
[18] Political Funds Act, art 31 (Law No 7191, 12 March 2004).
[19] Const Ct 95 Hun-Ma 154 (25 November 1999). The list of organisations banned from making political contributions also included public enterprises, news organisations, educational institutions, religious organisations, and corporations with over three years' continuous loss.

prohibition banning the use of corporate or organisation funds to make political donations.[20]

Individuals can only make contributions using their own name, and up to a very strict limit.[21] All contributions must be made to 'sponsor organisations' which may be set up by individual politicians running for, or holding, public office.[22] In 2006, the law was amended to eliminate sponsor organisations for political parties, in reaction to a revelation that parties had received illegal contributions from corporations by the 'truckload'. The Constitutional Court, however, held in 2015 that the total ban on sponsor organisations for political parties was an excessive response to the demand for transparency in political funding.[23] The law was revised again in 2017 to allow political parties to receive contributions.

Political parties are thus reliant on subsidies from the national treasury, which are also regulated by the Political Funds Act. The state is obligated to make appropriations each year for a certain amount (total number of voters multiplied by a 'subsidy unit price') to be allocated among political parties.[24] Half of the appropriated amount is distributed equally to all parties that formed a negotiating group within the National Assembly. Five per cent of the appropriated amount is then allocated to other parties that have more than five seats, and 2 per cent to parties with less than five seats. Half of the remainder is then distributed to the parties according to the ratio of their seats in the National Assembly. Any residual amount is allocated according to the ratio of votes obtained in the general election.[25] In addition, parties are also entitled to special subsidies from the national treasury for fielding female or disabled candidates in elections for public office.[26]

On top of these subsidies, the parties and candidates are reimbursed for any costs expended in relation to elections. Public financing of elections is premised on the idea that no one should be forced to spend one's own money in order to be elected as a public servant – since elections are public functions, they should be funded publicly. According to the

---

[20] Const Ct 2008 Hun-Ba 89 (28 December 2010).

[21] Total of KRW 20 million per year and KRW 5 million for the same party or candidate. Political Funds Act, art 11 (Law No 8880, 29 February 2008).

[22] Individuals may make an indirect contribution called a 'deposit' to national and regional election commissions, which will be distributed to the political parties.

[23] Const Ct 2013 Hun-Ba 168 (23 December 2015).

[24] Political Funds Act, art 25(1).

[25] Political Funds Act, art 27.

[26] Political Funds Act, arts 26 and 26-2.

Public Official Elections Act, in principle, any expense incurred for an election campaign will be reimbursed. This includes money spent for the campaign by the party and even the candidate's spouse, parents, and children. However, the law also provides a fairly extensive list of expenditures that are not recognised as 'election expenses'.[27] Also, for each type of election, the law specifies an upper limit for election expenses beyond which there is no reimbursement.[28] For critics, however, the system of public financing of elections and state subsidies for political parties results in double compensation. This is because the party subsidies disbursed every year already include funds to be used toward election campaigns and the parties are also reimbursed for having made expenditures during campaigns. After each election, there are reports of abuse whereby parties and candidates ended up enriching themselves by availing themselves of this system. Some even point out that using citizens' tax money to subsidise parties whose views and policies they do not necessarily support raises constitutional issues of freedom of expression.

More important for the health of the party system, excessive public support risks exacerbating the disconnect between political parties and the citizens. The Constitutional Court has also acknowledged that subsidisation of political parties may make them overly dependent on the state and less reliant on citizens' voluntary support.[29]

III. ORGANISATION OF THE NATIONAL ASSEMBLY

To be elected to the National Assembly, one must be at least 18 years of age.[30] Since the constitution contains no age requirement regarding candidacy for the National Assembly, this is a legislative issue. Previously, the minimum age was 25 but the law was changed recently to allow for better representation of youth in the political process. As there is no term limit, the lawmakers may be re-elected.

Once elected, Assembly members are considered representatives of the entire people, rather than a particular district. This is because the constitution provides that public officials are 'servants of the entire people' (art 7(1)) who should 'give preference to national interest' rather than regional or local interests (art 46(2)). Lawmakers are entitled to

---

[27] Public Official Elections Act, arts 120 and 122-2(2) (Law No 18790, 18 January 2022).
[28] Public Official Elections Act, art 121.
[29] 2013 Hun-Ba 168 (23 December 2015).
[30] Public Official Elections Act, art 16(2).

legislative immunity which enables them to engage in debate and legislative activities without fear of retaliation (art 45). They may not be arrested without the National Assembly's consent, unless they are caught in the act of committing a crime (art 44).

The constitution provides that the National Assembly shall be presided over by a Speaker and two Deputy Speakers (art 48). They are elected by the members of the Assembly through a secret ballot and serve for two years. By convention, the position of the Speaker is filled by a member of the party with the most legislative seats, and the two Deputy Speakers are divided between the two largest parties represented in the National Assembly. As the head of the entire National Assembly, the Speaker is expected to be neutral and not pursue partisan agenda. By law, maintenance of party membership is not allowed during the Speaker's term of office.[31] Yet, it is widely accepted that the Speaker will be a party politician. The law thus permits the reacquisition of party membership 90 days before general election if the Speaker is seeking re-election as a party candidate. It also provides that party membership is automatically regained at the end of the Speaker's two-year term.

The legislative work of the National Assembly is mostly done through committees composed of a small number of lawmakers. At present, there are 17 standing committees.[32] While one lawmaker is legally permitted to be a member of two or more standing committees, the Speaker is not allowed to join a standing committee.[33] Who is assigned to which standing committee is often a very sensitive issue. As seen, strong party discipline means that a party's leadership exerts considerable influence over committee assignments. The National Assembly is also authorised to create special committees on an ad hoc basis.

Legally, political parties are civil associations, which means that they are not part of the official organisation of the National Assembly. Lawmakers belonging to the same party form 'negotiation groups' which are officially recognised by law. The National Assembly Act provides that a party with 20 or more seats may form a negotiating group. In addition, 20 lawmakers who do not belong to any negotiating group may form a separate negotiating group of their own.[34] Thus, the assignment to standing committees is done through the negotiation group, particularly the floor leader of each party who becomes the head of that party's negotiation group.

[31] NAA, art 20-2 (Law No 6657, 7 March 2002).
[32] NAA, art 37(1).
[33] NAA, art 39.
[34] NAA, art 33(1).

IV. THE LEGISLATIVE PROCESS

The constitution distinguishes between regular and extraordinary sessions of the National Assembly. Regular sessions must be convened each year, the duration of which must not be longer than 100 days. Extraordinary sessions may be convened for maximum 30 days, upon the request of the president or one-fourth of the entire lawmakers (art 47). By statute, however, the distinction between regular and extraordinary sessions have become less meaningful. The National Assembly Act provides for a basic schedule whereby extraordinary sessions are to be held on a regular basis.[35]

Legislative bills may be proposed by members of the National Assembly or the Government (art 52). The National Assembly Act provides that bills may be introduced by 'ten or more members of the National Assembly or a committee of the National Assembly'.[36] A proposed bill is then referred to the relevant standing committee for review and vote, after which it is sent to the Legislation and Judiciary Committee for examination of its wording and coherence with other laws. The bill is passed upon deliberation and vote at the plenary session of the National Assembly. The bill becomes law after signing and promulgation by the president within 15 days of its passage. The president may veto the bill by returning it to the National Assembly with a request for reconsideration. In response, the National Assembly may override the veto by a two-thirds majority at a vote attended by at least half of its membership. Then, the bill becomes law without the president's promulgation.

If legislative bills and other agenda are not voted on or otherwise acted upon at the end of one session, they are passed onto the next session. Yet, continuity is only maintained between sessions of the same legislative period. In other words, bills not passed by the end of the lawmakers' term will not be carried over. They must be reintroduced after the election and the formation of a new National Assembly with a different membership.

---

[35] Extraordinary sessions are convened every February, April, June, and August, and the regular session commences on 1 September of each year. The regular session lasts for 100 days and extraordinary sessions for 30 days. NAA, arts 4 and 5. The precise duration of a session, however, is decided at the start of each session by a resolution of the lawmakers (art 7).

[36] NAA, arts 51 and 79. Previously, the consent of 20 lawmakers was needed to introduce a bill. This reduction has led to an explosion of bills introduced by Assembly members.

A. 'Backward' National Assembly and Legislative 'Railroading'

According to article 49 of the constitution, the default rule for legislation is a simple majority vote: a bill may be passed by a majority as long as more than half of all Assembly members are present. This standard decision-making rule, however, has long been blamed for the 'backwardness' of Korea's parliamentarian process. Since parties could ram through legislation if they controlled a simple majority in the National Assembly, they had no incentive to compromise with minority parties. The only thing that mattered was the power of numbers, which in turn led minority parties to put all their efforts into preventing bills they opposed from being brought to the floor for a vote. They would thus resort to physical force such as blocking entry into the main hall of the National Assembly building (even boarding up the doorways with wooden slabs and nails), occupying the Speaker's seat so that the plenary session cannot commence, or snatching away the Speaker's gavel so that the passage of a bill cannot be announced. Lawmakers engaging in scuffles and brawls in the hallowed halls of the National Assembly were not an uncommon sight.[37]

For its part, majority parties would do their best to avoid such confrontations by abruptly calling their member lawmakers to a vote and passing a bill with lightning speed, often dispensing entirely with any discussion or deliberation. They might do so, for example, by suddenly changing the venue for the vote to a different location, while privately informing only their own members of the change. Such tactics of legislative 'railroading' or 'run-away theft' enactments (*nalch'igi* in Korean[38]) were routinely decried by the minority parties who were left out of the voting process. They claimed that all laws enacted through such undemocratic procedure were invalid. They also argued that such deviant practice violated the minority lawmakers' right to participate in legislative processes.

The Constitutional Court partly agreed with the minority lawmakers. In several cases, it held that *nalch'igi* enactments violated the lawmakers' right to deliberate and vote on legislative bills. The Court, however, held each time that such violations were not sufficient grounds for invalidating laws that had been railroaded through the National Assembly.[39] Some

---

[37] J Keating, 'The World's Most Unruly Parliaments', *Foreign Policy* (September 2009).

[38] The term refers to 'purse snatching', ie, a thief's tactic of yanking a purse from victims' shoulder and running away with it.

[39] Const Ct 96 Hun-Ra 2 (16 July 1997); Const Ct 99 Hun-Ra 1 (24 February 2000); Const Ct 2009 Hun-Ra 8 (consolidated) (29 October 2009).

justices stated that the pronouncement of the passage of a bill should be respected as an act belonging to the National Assembly's autonomous decision-making powers, which should not be second-guessed unless there was a clear violation of the constitutional principle of majority rule (art 49) and the requirement that legislative sessions be open to the public (art 50). Others reasoned that the legislature's (specifically the Speaker's) act of pronouncing the passage of a bill is not an 'executive measure' that may become the subject of adjudication seeking invalidation or cancellation.

B. 'Advancing' the National Assembly by Restraining the Majority

In response to the criticism of the legislature's 'backwardness', the National Assembly Act was amended in 2012. The bill, labelled 'Law for the National Assembly's Advancement', introduced several major changes designed to put an end to the abuse of majority rule and the constant fracas within the legislature. The first change related to the power of the Speaker to bring a bill to the floor for a full vote. Previously, the Speaker had discretion to designate a deadline by which a bill should be deliberated by the relevant committees, after which it would automatically be sent to the plenary session for a vote by all members of the National Assembly. Since the Speaker is chosen among the majority party lawmakers, this meant that the majority party could force a vote on a bill, effectively skipping committee deliberations. Under the amended National Assembly Act, the Speaker may set a deadline for deliberation only when there is a natural catastrophe or a national emergency like war or armed conflict.[40] The aim was to severely limit the Speaker's power to bring a bill to the floor (and force a vote) by assigning a maximum time for deliberation.

The second change was the introduction of a 'fast-track' legislative process. When three-fifths of all members of the National Assembly agree, a bill may be placed on an expedited schedule – maximum 180 days for deliberation at the relevant standing committee and 90 days at the Legislation and Judiciary Committee. After 270 days, the bill is automatically brought to the plenary session and must be voted on within 60 days.[41] In other words, with the consent of a supermajority

---

[40] NAA, art 85(1).
[41] NAA, art 85-2. The same process may also be initiated with the consent of three-fifths of members of the relevant standing committee.

of 60 per cent of lawmakers, the fast-track process may be initiated, whereby a vote must be held on a bill within a maximum of 330 days even if the committees have not completed their deliberations and, more importantly, even if the minority parties are still holding out. The final vote is taken according to simple majority rule. It is therefore still possible to push through a bill in exceptional cases where three-fifths of the lawmakers agree on the need to expedite its enactment.

These amendments were effective to the extent that they resulted in a significant reduction of bills brought to the floor at the Speaker's discretion as well as the incidence of wrestling matches among lawmakers. As expected, however, parties that commanded a simple majority (less than three-fifths) were unhappy with the new system. For example, in 2016, the majority party wished to enact the North Korean Human Rights Act and urged the Speaker to set a deadline for its deliberation so that it might be brought to the plenary session. When the Speaker refused on grounds that there was no natural disaster or national emergency, the party filed a lawsuit at the Constitutional Court, arguing that the new provision limiting the Speaker's discretion was unconstitutional.[42] The Court rejected the argument by pointing out that limitation of the Speaker's discretion to bring a bill to the floor does not infringe upon lawmakers' constitutional right to deliberate and vote on legislative bills. These rights are activated only when a bill has been properly presented to the National Assembly, such that they could not be violated when there is no bill to vote on. The Court also stated that the majority rule mentioned in article 49 of the constitution is just a baseline from which the National Assembly may depart; as such, the requirement of three-fifths majority for initiating the fast-track process was not unconstitutional.

A third change in the National Assembly Act was the introduction of a form of filibuster or 'unlimited debate' on the floor of the National Assembly.[43] The goal was to provide a more civilised way for the minority to block the passage of bills. Rather than resorting to physical force, they are now expected to use debate as the means for holding up the legislative process. Under the new system, however, individual lawmakers cannot initiate unlimited debates. A request must be submitted to the Speaker with the signature of at least one-third of all members of the National Assembly. Also, when engaging in unlimited debate, lawmakers' speech

---

[42] Const Ct 2015 Hun-Ra 1 (26 May 2016).

[43] In a way this was a return to the original rule adopted in 1948 which had banned putting limits on the time for lawmakers' speech on the floor, unless there was a resolution by the National Assembly.

must be related to the item on the agenda.[44] Unlimited debate will
continue until there are no more lawmakers to take the floor or when
three-fifths of the National Assembly call for the termination of unlimited debate.[45] Also, expiration of the session's duration, decided upon by
the lawmakers at its beginning, brings the filibuster to an end.

The object of filibuster is not limited to legislative bills. The law
merely states that any item on the plenary session's agenda may be
debated endlessly. According to most commentators, however, when the
agenda is whether to consent to the appointment of officials, unlimited
debate is not permitted because, by custom, such votes are taken without debate. Personnel issues, in other words, are considered beyond the
scope of filibuster. Invoking that custom, the Speaker in 2013 ignored the
minority party's request for unlimited debate even though the request
had more than one-third of the lawmakers' signatures.

Another uncertainty was whether unlimited debate may be allowed at
the beginning of a session when the agenda is to decide on the duration of
that session. The Constitutional Court has held that this is not permitted
because unlimited debate presumes a session with its duration already
fixed.[46] Otherwise, the above-mentioned rule that unlimited debates
shall be terminated at the end of the session would be without meaning.
The Court reasoned that endlessly debating how long the session will be
would make it impossible even to begin the legislative process. Logically,
filibuster would be meaningless if there was no legislative process within
which the minority could oppose the majority.

A common theme throughout these three changes is the requirement
of three-fifths majority. While this is well within the bounds of the constitution, there is continuing criticism that it is blocking the passage of bills
and allowing a minority of 100 lawmakers to hold the entire legislative
process hostage. Defenders argue that reduction of scuffles within the
National Assembly is evidence of the new system's efficacy. It is worth
noting, however, that this approach to make the parliamentary system
more 'advanced' is premised on the assumption that three-fifths majority
would be a difficult threshold to pass in real life. In 2020, that assumption was proven wrong, when the government party obtained more than

[44] This is a general requirement that applies to all types of speech made by lawmakers.
NAA, art 102. This distinguishes the Korean system of filibuster from that of other countries (eg, United States) where legislators may read from materials unrelated to the issue at
hand, such as the Bible or even the phone book.
[45] NAA, art 106-2(6).
[46] Const Ct 2019 Hun-Ra 6 (27 May 2020).

180 seats in the National Assembly. This enabled it to initiate the fast-track process and to dispense with negotiating with the opposition, as well as terminating the minority's filibuster at will. Under such a situation, it is not surprising that the minority is once again resorting to physical force to stop what it calls the tyranny of the majority.

V. OVERSIGHT FUNCTIONS OF THE NATIONAL ASSEMBLY

In addition to legislation, the National Assembly performs various functions to ensure that the government is run according to law. As representatives of the people, its members are mandated with the mission to guard against abuse of state power, especially by the executive branch.

A. Powers Concerning Personnel Appointments

For certain constitutional organs, the legislature shares the appointment power with the executive and judicial branches. Three of the nine justices of the Constitutional Court (art 111(3)) and three of the nine members of the National Election Commission (art 114(2)) are selected by the National Assembly. Aside from these instances, the more common way for the National Assembly to exercise democratic oversight regarding personnel appointments is through its power to give consent to high-ranking public officials nominated by the president. The National Assembly's consent is a constitutional requirement for appointing the prime minister, the chairperson of the Board of Audit and Inspection, the president of the Constitutional Court, and justices of the Supreme Court (including the chief justice). In the case of the prime minister's appointment, if the National Assembly withholds its consent, this means that the president will be unable to form a cabinet because, technically, the prime minister must recommend the cabinet ministers to the president. In 1998, however, when the National Assembly's vote on whether to give consent to the nominee for prime minister (Kim Jong-pil) was cancelled, the newly elected President Kim Dae-jung asked the outgoing Prime Minister Koh Gun to recommend cabinet ministers and, after receiving Koh's resignation, proceeded to appoint Kim Jong-pil as 'acting' prime minister. The opposition Assembly members then initiated a competence dispute claiming that the president had violated the National Assembly's right of consent. The Constitutional Court dismissed the claim on grounds that the opposition lawmakers lacked standing because the right of consent that was allegedly violated belongs to the National Assembly, not to its members.[47] As a result, Kim Jong-pil served as an 'acting' prime minister for five months, at which time the National Assembly finally gave its consent. Commentators have criticised the Court for allowing such an unconstitutional condition to persist even though an 'acting' prime minister clearly has no legal basis.

The National Assembly's right of consent is typically exercised through personnel (confirmation) hearings. In cases where the National Assembly's right of appointment or right of consent is provided for in the constitution, the hearing is held by the Special Committee for Personnel Hearings.[48] By contrast, for those public officials who are required by the National Assembly Act to undergo confirmation hearings, the hearing is held by the standing committee that has jurisdiction over the organisation.[49] For example, the hearing for appointing the Minister of Foreign Affairs is held at the Foreign Affairs and Unification Committee. For appointing the prosecutor general, the hearing is held at the Legislation and Judiciary Committee. The range of public officials who require a confirmation hearing has steadily expanded through amendments to the National Assembly Act. Yet, unlike constitutionally mandated personnel hearings, the results of these statutorily mandated hearings are not binding. Even when the relevant standing committee concludes that the candidate is not suitable for the nominated position, the president is free to ignore it. The Constitutional Court confirmed this by holding that whether to abide by the findings of a hearings committee is ultimately a political issue to be decided by the president and not a legal issue.[50] Indeed, many presidents have appointed ministers and other high-ranking officials even when the relevant committees either opposed the appointment or failed even to hold a hearing.[51] Not surprisingly, this has given rise to criticism that statutorily mandated personnel hearings are useless and a waste of time. Since hearings based on the National Assembly Act have no basis in the constitution, critics even charge that it infringes on the president's constitutional powers of appointment and is a violation of separation of powers.

[47] Const Ct 98 Hun-Ra 1 (14 July 1998).
[48] NAA, art 46-3.
[49] NAA, act 65-2.
[50] Const Ct 2004 Hun-Na 1 (14 May 2004).
[51] Moon Jae-in holds the record for such appointments. During his presidency, 33 ministers and other high-ranking officials were appointed without or against the recommendation of the hearings committee.

B. Recommendation of Dismissal and Impeachment Powers

Another way for the National Assembly to act as a watchdog of the executive branch is by recommending to the president the dismissal of the prime minister or state councillor (ie, cabinet ministers) (art 63). This can be done when at least one-third of all members of the National Assembly makes a motion and then more than half of them agree. Since there is no limit to the grounds for the dismissal recommendations, legislators may hold ministers accountable for purely political reasons. The recommendation, however, is not legally binding upon the president.[52] As such, this power is seldom exercised.

A relatively more efficacious means to hold high-ranking officials accountable is through the impeachment procedure. This is more powerful because the result of the impeachment proceeding is legally binding. The constitution authorises the National Assembly to initiate impeachment proceedings against the president, government ministers, and other high-ranking officials.[53] The grounds for impeachment according to the constitution must be a violation of the constitution or statutes enacted by the National Assembly. Officials cannot be impeached for mere political misconduct or poor job performance or violations of administrative regulations or municipal ordinances. Even violations of the constitution and statutes, according to the Constitutional Court, must be 'grave enough' to merit removal from office.[54]

Proposing a motion for impeachment requires at least one-third of all Assembly members. The resolution to impeach then becomes final with the consent of a majority of all sitting lawmakers. To impeach the president, however, the constitution stipulates a higher threshold: one-half to make a motion and two-thirds to pass the resolution (art 65(2)). When the resolution to impeach is passed, it is filed at the Constitutional Court which adjudicates on the charges made by the National Assembly. During the adjudication, the chair of the National Assembly's Legislation and

---

[52] Const Ct 2004 Hun-Na 1 (14 May 2004). The Court suggested that the legislature's demand for dismissal of ministers could not be binding under the Korean constitution, since the president does not have a corresponding power to dissolve the legislature and call a general election.

[53] The scope of officials who can be impeached is specified in art 65(1): 'the President, the Prime Minister, members of the State Council, heads of Administrative Ministries, Justices of the Constitutional Court, judges, members of the National Election Commission, the Chairperson and members of the Board of Audit and Inspection, and other public officials designated by statutes'.

[54] For more on the standard of 'sufficient gravity', see ch 8.

Judiciary Committee acts as the primary prosecutor. Until the conclusion of the Court's adjudication, the impeached public official is suspended from office. If the Court determines that grave violations of the constitution or statutes have taken place, the official is dismissed from office. By statute, once the impeachment resolution is passed, the impeached official is not allowed to resign from office so as to evade the Court's official determination of wrongdoing.[55] The constitution specifically states that the dismissed official may still be subject to civil or criminal lawsuits (art 65(4)). For example, criminal charges were made against the former President Park Geun-hye even after she was dismissed from office through impeachment.

C. Inspection and Investigation of State Affairs

According to the constitution, the National Assembly may 'inspect state affairs' or 'investigate a specific aspect of state affairs' (art 61). Whereas the latter power is common to many countries' legislatures, the former is a rather unusual feature of the Korean constitution. The difference is that 'inspection of state affairs' is a general review of the affairs of all the other branches of the government, whereas 'investigation of a specific aspect of state affairs' is limited to a particular issue that requires the legislators' scrutiny. More importantly, whereas investigating a specific issue requires a motion by at least one-quarter of all Assembly members, the general inspection of state affairs needs no motion or vote and takes place according to a preset schedule every year.

By law, the general inspection of state affairs is to be conducted each year prior to the commencement of that year's regular session (1 September), for a period not exceeding 30 days. The exact schedule may be changed by a decision at the plenary session.[56] In practice, the inspection of state affairs has taken place during each year's regular session. Indeed, it is regarded as one of the regular session's most important agenda.

Government agencies which must submit to the National Assembly's inspection include: (i) all state agencies established under the Government Organisation Act; (ii) major municipal and provincial governments on

---

[55] NAA, art 134(2). What remains uncertain is whether the president, who has no superior, may resign after being impeached by the National Assembly.

[56] Inspection and Investigation of State Affairs Act, art 2(1) (Law No 15619, 17 April 2018).

matters delegated or funded by the central government; (iii) publicly funded institutions specified in the Act on the Management of Public Institutions, the Bank of Korea, the National Federation of Agricultural Cooperatives, and the National Federation of Fisheries Cooperatives.[57] These agencies and institutions are inspected by the specific standing committee that has jurisdiction over them.

To facilitate the inspection and investigation, the National Assembly is constitutionally empowered to demand necessary documents, summon witnesses, or hear testimonies or opinions (art 61(1)). Also, the committees in charge may form subcommittees and inspection teams. The committees may even subpoena unwilling witnesses and hold them in contempt of the National Assembly if they refuse to comply. Witnesses who perjure themselves or appraisers who offer false appraisal at the National Assembly are subject to punishment more severe than under ordinary criminal law.[58]

Whereas the investigation of specific issues is rarely used, the general inspection of state affairs can be an effective tool in the hands of the National Assembly to check the powers of the executive. Supporters claim that it is particularly useful for the minority parties to expose government wrongdoings and mismanagement, because no vote is needed to conduct the general inspection. Critics argue, however, that the whole process is unproductive because lawmakers are more interested in using the inspection as a media event to score political points with their constituents, rather than genuinely trying to find solutions to rectify problems. It is also unproductive because, during the National Assembly's general inspection, the entire government apparatus tends to come to a standstill as public officials, including cabinet ministers, are either busy responding to the lawmakers' demand for documents or on-call at the National Assembly for days waiting for their turn to testify and respond to questions. Some claim redundancy because, according to the Constitution, inspection of the books is the role of a separate constitutional agency, namely, the Board of Audit and Inspection.

D. Approval of National Budget and Expenditure

The National Assembly is empowered to review and approve the national budget bill for the coming year and the settlement of accounts for the

---

[57] Inspection and Investigation of State Affairs Act, art 7. In addition, other agencies may also be included if the plenary session deems it necessary.

[58] Act on Testimony, Appraisal etc before the National Assembly, arts 6 and 14 (Law No 15621, 17 April 2018).

previous year. Each year's regular session is usually dominated by the performance of this task, along with the annual inspection of state affairs.

It is the Government's responsibility to formulate the national budget bill and submit it to the National Assembly at least 90 days prior to the beginning of the next fiscal year (1 January).[59] The National Assembly then has until 'thirty days before the beginning of the fiscal year' (2 December) to adopt the budget (art 54(2)). The Government is entitled to provide an explanation of the budget bill at the plenary session in the form of a speech by the president or the prime minister and clarification by the Minister of Economy and Finance. Upon receiving the Government's budget bill, the relevant standing committees engage in a preliminary review of the respective parts of the bill, after which the entire budget bill is referred to the Special Committee on Budget and Accounts for comprehensive review and interpellation. Once the Special Committee approves it, the budget bill is sent to the plenary session for deliberation and vote. When it is passed by a simple majority at a plenary vote attended by at least half the lawmakers, the budget goes into effect. A budget approved by the National Assembly is not subject to the president's veto.

During its review of the budget bill, the National Assembly may reduce the Government's spending items, but it is not allowed to increase the spending for any item on the budget bill or create new items, without the Government's consent (art 57). To make changes to the budget bill, at least 50 lawmakers must agree to make a motion for amendment.[60] Also, the National Assembly cannot alter continuing expenditure items (for projects requiring disbursement over a period exceeding one fiscal year) which had been approved in previous years.

Due to the National Assembly's chronic failure to meet the 2 December deadline, a new rule was added in 2014 whereby the Special Committee is required to complete its review by 30 November; if it fails to do so, the bill is automatically referred to the plenary session the following day.[61] Also, the rule on filibuster stipulates that, in case of the budget bill, unlimited debate shall be terminated at midnight of 1 December.[62] Despite

---

[59] By statute, the Government must submit the budget bill no later than 120 days before the beginning of the fiscal year. National Finance Act, art 33 (Law No 11821, 28 May 2013). This rule, however, has rarely been observed.

[60] NAA, art 95(1). This is a higher threshold than ordinary motions for amendment which require the consent of 30 lawmakers.

[61] NAA, art 85-3(2). Exceptions may be made if the Speaker and the heads of negotiating groups reach an agreement.

[62] NAA, art 106-2(10).

these amendments, however, there have been fewer years when lawmakers met the December 2 deadline. The constitution actually provides for such eventualities. When the budget bill has not been passed by the beginning of a new fiscal year, the Government is authorised to disburse funds in line with the previous year's budget, for the limited purposes of maintaining the operation of government agencies, performing statutory duties, and sustaining pre-approved multi-year projects (art 54(3)).

During its regular session, the National Assembly also reviews and approves the Government's settlement of accounts for the previous year. The role is to make sure that the revenues and expenditures were duly implemented according to the budget. The constitution, however, does not contain an explicit provision for this power. It is indirectly mentioned in an article which provides that the Board of Audit and Inspection has the duty to report the results of its review of the national settlement of accounts (prepared by the Government) to the National Assembly (art 99). The same procedure as used for approving the national budget bill is followed. Upon reviewing the Board of Audit and Inspection's report, if the National Assembly finds illegal or improper execution of the budget, it may demand indemnification or disciplinary measures of the offending agency.[63]

As seen, the National Assembly conducts the annual inspection of state affairs, approves the national budget bill, and reviews the previous year's settlement of accounts during the 100-day regular session at the end of the year. This necessarily means that the lawmakers are pressed for time, which in turn makes it difficult for them to perform these solemn tasks thoroughly. The fact that members of the Special Committee on Budget and Accounts serve for only one year also means that they are not able to accumulate the expertise and experience needed for the proper performance of these tasks.

VI. CONCLUSION

Despite efforts to improve the quality of the legislative process, the National Assembly still suffers from low public esteem. Lawmakers are widely seen as merely following decisions made by their party leadership, while lacking the requisite expertise to engage in meaningful deliberation of bills or to inspect state affairs. This may be due to several factors.

[63] NAA, art 84(2).

The institutional structure mandated by the constitution and the legal system tends to place the legislature in a weaker position relative to the executive branch. Strong party discipline and the hierarchical culture of parties make it hard for individual lawmakers to develop a specialty or acquire sufficient experience in one field. This is not to say that the National Assembly is a passive institution. Lately, more legislative bills are being introduced by Assembly members than by the Government. Indeed, lawmakers tend to be quite assertive in exercising their powers and privileges. Especially, when the opposition party is in control of the National Assembly, the lawmakers are not hesitant to block policies and bills proposed by the president. Since an opposition-controlled National Assembly is a rather frequent phenomenon in Korea due to the mismatch of election cycles, one might conclude that the legislature has been successful in preventing the dominance of the executive. Even so, this has come at the price of government gridlocks and legislative stalemates, in which lawmakers often engage in physical blockage and shouting matches, rather than reasoned deliberation and principled arguments. Given Korea's constitutional history, this may be better than allowing executive dominance. To be a truly advanced democracy, however, Korea deserves a more professional legislature that can command the respect of the people.

FURTHER READING

Adesnik AD and Kim S, 'South Korea: The Puzzle of Two Transitions' in Kathryn Stoner and Michael McFaul (eds), *Transitions to Democracy* (Johns Hopkins University Press 2013).

Diamond L and Kim B-K (eds), *Consolidating Democracy in South Korea* (Lynne Rienner 2000).

Mobrand E, 'The Politics of Regulating Elections in South Korea: The Persistence of Restrictive Campaign Laws' (2015) 88 *Pacific Affairs* 791.

Mosler H, 'Judicialization of Politics and the Korean Constitutional Court: The Party Chapter Abolition Case' (2014) 47 *Verfassung in Recht und Übersee* 293.

Rhee W-Y, 'The Electoral Process and the Judicial Review of Elections in the Republic of Korea' in Po Jen Yap (ed), *Judicial Review of Elections in Asia* (Routledge 2016).

6

Courts in the Age of Democracy

Structure of the Judiciary – Appeals System – Constitutionality Review
by Ordinary Courts – Limits of Judicial Power – Judicial Independence
and Judicial Hierarchy – Judicial Reform and Democracy

HAPTER V OF the constitution is designated 'the Courts' and
its first article provides that 'judicial power' is vested in 'courts
composed of judges' and that 'courts' shall comprise a Supreme
Court as the highest court and various levels of courts (art 101).
The constitution also devotes a separate chapter (chapter VI) to the
Constitutional Court. What the constitution does not specify is the
precise relationship between the Supreme Court and the Constitutional
Court. Both institutions insist that neither is above the other, but this
'equality' can also be a source of tension. Some commentators claim
that the power of the Constitutional Court is not 'judicial power' but
a separate 'fourth' state power, because it is not part of the ordinary
court hierarchy. The Constitutional Court, however, understands itself
as exercising judicial power. This chapter will examine the role and
structure of the ordinary courts, ie, the Supreme Court and other lower
courts. The next chapter will discuss the Constitutional Court's powers
and organisation.

I. ORGANISATION OF THE JUDICIARY

The constitution only mentions the Supreme Court as the highest
court of the land, leaving the specifics of the judiciary's structure and
organisation to legislation. The Court Organisation Act is the organic
law for the judiciary. The basic structure is a three-tier system, with
the Supreme Court as the court of final appeal and a variety of lower
courts under it.

A. The Supreme Court

The Supreme Court is composed of 14 justices, including the chief justice.[1] This number is not specified in the constitution, which means that the number may be changed via legislative amendment. The chief justice is appointed by the president with the National Assembly's consent whereas other justices are appointed by the president on recommendation of the chief justice and with the National Assembly's consent (art 104(1) & (2)). The chief justice appoints one of the 13 associate justices as the Minister of National Court Administration (NCA), the body in charge of the operation of all ordinary courts throughout the country. Since this administrative position is a full-time job, this justice does not participate in the Supreme Court's adjudicative process. The number of justices who adjudicate cases is thus 12 associate justices, plus the chief justice. They constitute the 'collegiate panel' (full bench) of the Supreme Court, which hears cases and make decisions by majority vote. At least two-thirds of all justices must be present to constitute a full bench, which is presided over by the chief justice.

The constitution also authorises the establishment of 'divisions' (petty benches) within the Supreme Court (art 102(1)). By law, a division must consist of at least three justices. There are currently three divisions, each with four associate justices. Most cases are in fact decided by these divisions, provided there is no disagreement among the member justices. If a division's member justices cannot reach a unanimous decision, the case is referred to the full bench. For certain cases, adjudication by the full bench is required by law. They include cases involving the constitutionality or legality of administrative orders or regulations, and those requiring the change of the Court's own precedents on the interpretation and application of the constitution, statutes, orders, or regulations.[2]

The constitution states that judges who are not justices may be appointed to the Supreme Court (art 102(2)). Typically chosen from those with 10 or more years of experience, these judges serve as judicial researchers to assist the Supreme Court justices in their adjudicative work.[3] Each associate justice is assigned three judicial researchers. In addition, there are around 60 judicial researchers not assigned to any

---

[1] Court Organisation Act (hereafter 'COA'), art 4(2) (Law No 17689, 22 December 2020).

[2] COA, art 7(1).

[3] COA, art 24. The law also allows non-judges to be appointed judicial researchers.

particular justice, who provide assistance in terms of processing and preparing the cases to be reviewed by the Court. Having served as a Supreme Court judicial researcher is generally considered a plus in advancing a judge's career within the judiciary.

The Council of Supreme Court Justices is an official organ of the Supreme Court, whose primary function is to make decisions on administrative matters of the judiciary, such as the appointment of regular judges, the adoption and amendment of the Court's internal rules, and matters relating to the judiciary's budget. The NCA, which oversees the daily operation of the entire judiciary, is also an organ of the Supreme Court. Aside from the minister, NCA also has nearly 20 senior and junior judges appointed to various administrative positions.[4] Like the judges appointed to the Supreme Court as judicial researchers, those who serve at the NCA are usually regarded as the best and the brightest and are likely to rise to leadership positions within the judiciary.

Another organ established under the Supreme Court is the Judicial Research and Training Institute (JRTI), which oversees judges' training. Nearly 30 judges are appointed as professors at the JRTI. Prior to the change in the legal education and licensing system, introduced in 2009, everyone who passed the National Judicial Examination was required to attend the JRTI for two years before being licensed to practise law. Even those who became a prosecutor or a practising attorney had to attend the JRTI. Under the new system, however, anyone who passes the new National Bar Examination can practise law immediately. No longer an integral part of the licensing process, JRTI's mission is now limited to providing continuing education for judges. The last cohort of lawyers licensed under the older system graduated from JRTI in 2020.

Other bodies affiliated with the Supreme Court include the Judges Personnel Committee, which is a standing consultative body for deliberating on appointment, reappointment, and retirement of judges, and an ad hoc search committee convened by the chief justice whenever there is a vacancy on the Supreme Court, whose mandate is to recommend at least three candidates for each vacant seat.[5] Also, since 2007, a Sentencing Commission has been created under the Supreme Court to establish sentencing guidelines.

---

[4] This number was reduced from over 30, after accusations that the NCA abused its authority. See below.
[5] COA, arts 25-2 and 41-2.

B. Lower Courts

Aside from the Supreme Court, the Court Organisation Act provides that there shall be six other types of court.[6] Two of them have general jurisdiction over civil and criminal cases and four are courts with specialised jurisdictions.

As the court of first instance, District Courts are established in 18 different locations, each with numerous branch courts and local courts throughout the nation. High Courts, located in six major metropolitan regions, hear appeals from the District Courts. In principle, cases at the High Court are decided by three-judge panels, whereas at the District Court, cases may be heard by either a single-judge division or a three-judge panel.[7] For certain cases, typically those assigned to a single judge due to smaller litigation value and lighter sentences, the three-judge panel within the District Courts sits as the appellate division. Appeals from High Courts and the appellate division within District Courts are heard by the Supreme Court.

In addition to these courts of general jurisdiction, the Court Organisation Act provides for four types of courts with specialised jurisdiction. The Patent Court, established in 1998 in the city of Taejŏn, is at the same level as High Courts, and hears appeals from District Courts for cases involving patent and other intellectual property disputes. For cases involving family matters or juveniles, the Family Courts located in eight major cities are the courts of first instance. For cases involving administrative law issues such as tax, land appropriation, and labour-related matters, the Administrative Court, established in 1998 in Seoul, acts as the court of first instance. The latest addition to the courts with specialised jurisdiction is the Bankruptcy Court, established in 2017 in Seoul, which hears cases on debtor and corporate rehabilitation and bankruptcy issues. In areas where there is no Family Court, Administrative Court, or Bankruptcy Court, the District Court continues to have jurisdiction over such cases.

C. Military Courts

Military courts are special courts in the sense that they are an exception to the general principle governing the judiciary. They are subject to different rules regarding qualification of judges, the manner of their

---

[6] COA, art 3(1).
[7] COA, art 7(3).

recruitment, and the system of appeals. Their legal basis is not the Court Organisation Act, but the Military Court Act. They constitute an exception to the constitutional right to be tried by 'judges qualified under the constitution and statutes' (art 27). This is because, according to the Military Court Act, cases are decided by military judicial officers which includes not only military judges but also 'adjudicators' who are selected from high-ranking officers with 'knowledge of law' and 'good character and sufficient learning to be a military judicial officer'.[8] In other words, adjudicators need not be licensed as lawyers.

Military courts also are an exception because, in certain instances, their decisions are not appealable. Even though appeals from military court are generally heard by the Supreme Court (art 110(2)), under extraordinary martial law, crimes by soldiers and military employees, crimes of military espionage, and certain other crimes may be tried without the possibility of appeal (art 110(4)). When the sentence prescribed is capital punishment, however, the case may be appealed. Given that military courts are specifically provided for in the constitution, the Constitutional Court has held that they are not unconstitutional despite these exceptions to the general principle regarding the judiciary.[9]

II. POWERS OF THE JUDICIARY

The most important power of the courts is the power of adjudication. The Court Organisation Act declares that the courts shall adjudicate 'all legal disputes and litigations', except as otherwise prescribed by the constitution.[10] The judiciary is thus entrusted with the power to decide civil, criminal, administrative, family, patent, and bankruptcy cases. As for constitutional issues, the Supreme Court decides on the constitutionality of all laws other than statutes enacted by the National Assembly. When statutes' constitutionality is in question, ordinary courts refer the issue to the Constitutional Court.

A. Supreme Court as the Court of Last Resort

The Supreme Court is the court of final instance for cases on appeal from High Courts and other appellate level courts, including appellate

---

[8] Military Court Act, art 24 (Law No 17367, 9 June 2020).
[9] Const Ct 93 Hun-Ba 25 (31 October 1996).
[10] COA, art 2(1).

military courts. Whereas lower-level courts deal with both questions of law and fact, the Supreme Court only addresses questions of law. If it finds that a lower court misinterpreted the law, it remands the case to be re-adjudicated according to the correct interpretation.

The Court, however, is currently faced with seemingly inconsistent demands. On the one hand, it is expected to be the ultimate defender of individual rights by making sure that every single case that it reviews is decided correctly. For every litigant who appeals to the Supreme Court, that is what 'justice' means. On the other hand, it is also expected to be the articulator of a judicial vision for the entire society, by interpreting the law in a way that meets the challenges of a changing society and by ensuring consistency of legal interpretation throughout the nation's courts. The reality is that the Court simply does not have the resources and time to meet both demands. With no discretion to select which cases to hear, it is inundated each year with cases on appeal from lower courts. In 2020, the number of cases the Supreme Court decided on the merits was 38,809 (out of 46,231 cases filed).[11] In order to dispose of such a high caseload, the Court must resort to reviewing cases via the four-justice divisions, and rarely decides by the full bench. Since 1987, a system of 'discontinuance of trial' has been in use, which allows the Court to summarily dismiss appeals unless the lower court's judgment shows serious misapplication of the constitution, other laws, or the Court's own precedents. Yet, this makes it difficult for it to act as a deliberative body for formulating national judicial policy. Critics charge that, even at the level of individual cases, it is failing to provide justice because, with so many cases to decide, it is humanly impossible to give proper attention to each case.

Since the early 2000s, numerous proposals have been put forward to address this problem. One proposal is to give discretion to the Court to choose only those cases with national consequence, similar to the US Supreme Court's writ of certiorari. Another is to establish a separate tribunal (either within or without the Supreme Court) dedicated to hearing ordinary appeals from the lower courts, thereby freeing the 13 Supreme Court justices to concentrate on cases with national significance and to ensure consistency throughout the court system. The former idea has been met with much resistance from the general public. For many citizens, a three-tier court system means having the right to be heard by the Supreme Court as a matter of course. Having to obtain permission to

---

[11] 2021 *Sabŏp Yŏn'gam* [*Judicial Yearbook 2021*] (Pŏpwŏnhaengjŏngch'ŏ 2021), 674.

appeal to the Supreme Court sounds like an infringement of the constitutionally guaranteed right to a fair trial. In fact, the Constitutional Court has held that the right to appeal to the Supreme Court is not a constitutionally guaranteed right.[12] Nevertheless, due to the criticism that the judiciary is trying to limit access to justice, discussion of late has focused on creating a separate tribunal of final appeal to review most cases, with the purpose of turning the Supreme Court into what is called in the Korean context, a 'policy court'. As of this writing, however, no concrete decision has been made.

For a small category of cases, the Supreme Court acts as the court of first and last instance. According to the Public Official Elections Act, disputes regarding elections for selecting the president and members of the National Assembly must be litigated at the Supreme Court. These include litigations disputing the validity of the election itself, as well as litigations challenging the result of an otherwise valid election.[13] The Supreme Court also hears cases disputing the validity of a national referendum, which may be filed by any voter who obtains the signature of at least one hundred thousand voters.[14] Another case in which the Supreme Court has original jurisdiction is when a judge objects to disciplinary actions taken by the Judicial Disciplinary Committee, set up under the Supreme Court.[15] Decisions on these cases cannot be appealed.

B. Constitutionality Review

All courts, including military courts, have the power to request the Constitutional Court's adjudication on the constitutionality of statutes enacted by the National Assembly. According to the constitution, such a request may be made when the constitutionality of a statute 'is at issue in a trial' (art 107(1)).[16] This means that (a) there must be a concrete case pending at a court, (b) the statute whose constitutionality is in question must be applied in the said case, and (c) the court will adjudicate the case differently depending on whether the said statute is constitutional or not.[17] In other words, request for constitutionality review may not be

---

[12] Const Ct 90 Hun-Ba 25 (26 June 1992).
[13] Public Official Elections Act, arts 222 and 223.
[14] Referendum Act, art 92.
[15] Discipline of Judges Act, art 27 (Law No 15250, 19 December 2017).
[16] A more literal translation might be 'is a precondition to the adjudication'.
[17] Const Ct 92 Hun-Ka 8 (24 December 1992).

made in the abstract without any concrete case, or before the statute is duly enacted and takes effect.

The request for constitutionality review may be made at the court's own discretion or on motion by a party to the case.[18] The request must be founded on a 'reasonable doubt' regarding the constitutionality of the statute. This requires more than simple scepticism according to the judge's own personal views.[19] The court's decision on whether to make a request to the Constitutional Court may not be appealed.[20] In case, however, the court rejects a party's motion and refuses to make a request to the Constitutional Court, the party has the option to go directly to the Constitutional Court and file a constitutional complaint requesting review of the statute to be applied in the case.[21] When a court wishes to request the Constitutional Court's review, the request must be made through the Supreme Court.[22] As this is merely an administrative procedure, the Supreme Court may not screen or block the lower court's request.

Regarding legal norms other than statutes passed by the National Assembly, questions of their constitutionality and/or legality is determined by the Supreme Court (art 107(2)). When a court must apply, for example, a presidential order, an administrative regulation or other government measures to adjudicate a case, and when there is doubt as to their consistency with the constitution or with any statute enacted by the National Assembly, the power of review ultimately lies with the Supreme Court. The constitution uses the same language 'is at issue in a trial' to ensure that the constitutionality and/or legality of a specific law must be in doubt in a concrete case. No power of abstract review is granted.

By authorising the Supreme Court to determine the constitutionality of orders, regulations, and measures, the Constitution effectively divides the power of constitutionality review between two institutions. The Constitutional Court is responsible for reviewing the constitutionality of statutes, while the Supreme Court reviews the constitutionality of other 'lower' norms within the legal hierarchy. As will be seen, this division of labour is the source of some confusion and tension, especially when the two courts have different views on what is required by the Constitution.

---

[18] Constitutional Court Act (hereafter 'CCA'), art 41(1).
[19] Const Ct 93 Hun-Ka 2 (23 December 1993).
[20] CCA, art 41(4).
[21] CCA, art 68(2).
[22] CCA, art 41(5).

C. Limits of Judicial Power

The judiciary's power of adjudication is essentially passive in the sense that it cannot be exercised unless there is a concrete legal dispute initiated by a party with the requisite standing and the issue is ripe for judicial resolution and is not moot. In certain instances, the Constitution specifically precludes the exercise of the courts' judicial powers. When the National Assembly reviews the qualifications of its members, takes disciplinary actions against its members, or expels its members, such decisions cannot be challenged in the courts (art 64(4)). The Constitutional Court's exclusive jurisdiction over the five types of cases specified in the constitution may also be regarded as an exception to the judicial power of regular courts (art 111).

Some types of disputes are considered beyond the competence of judges. Commonly discussed under the rubric of 'act of state' (*t'ongch'i haengwi*), the issue is whether certain action or decision taken by the state is so political that it should be exempt from the courts' review.[23] Although the Supreme Court has mentioned the concept of act of state in a few cases, the trend seems to be toward restricting the scope of issues deemed too political to be reviewed by the judiciary.[24]

Three cases involved the justiciability of the president's decision to declare extraordinary martial law. The first one was with regard to the martial law declared in 1964 in response to demonstrations staged by thousands of university students protesting the Park Chung-hee government's secret negotiations with Japan to normalise diplomatic relations.[25] The second one involved the declaration of martial law by the then-acting-President Choi Kyu-ha, following Park's assassination in 1979.[26] Both decisions concluded that the judiciary has no power to review the president's declarations of extraordinary martial law, unless they were void *ab initio* due to obvious procedural flaws. The 1964 decision stressed that assessing the propriety of the president's discretionary power to declare martial law required political judgment best exercised by the National Assembly. The 1979 decision stated that engaging in such assessment was beyond the essential limits inherent in the concept of judicial power.

---

[23] The Korean term is a translation of the German *Regierungsakt* or the French *acte de gouvernement*, and is an analogue of the political question doctrine in the United States.

[24] For discussion of similar issues with regard to the Constitutional Court, see chs 4 and 8.

[25] Sup Ct 64 Ch'o 3 (21 July 1964).

[26] Sup Ct 79 Ch'o 70 (7 December 1979).

The third decision was rendered in 1997, after Korea's transition to democracy, in relation to the government's decision in 1980 to place the entire country under martial law in response to the protests in the southwestern city of Kwangju.[27] In this case, the Supreme Court held that the coup d'état by which the former presidents Chun Doo-hwan and Roh Tae-woo and their subordinates assumed control of the government constituted, *inter alia*, crimes of insurrection and mutiny. Regarding the concept of 'act of state', the Court first reiterated its previous stance that the judiciary has no power to review the propriety of a declaration of martial law, barring some egregious violations of the law. Yet, it also reserved for itself the power to review the criminality of such a declaration if it was done for the purpose of subverting the nation's constitutional order.[28] The Court then found that the declaration of martial law by the military junta was indeed a means for subverting the nation's constitutional order.

This approach of simultaneously acknowledging the category of 'act of state' lying outside the scope of judicial power and asserting the right to review such acts in case of egregious illegality was presaged in an earlier decision of the Supreme Court. In 1985, the Court decided on the continuing validity of a repressive emergency decree issued by the president under the previous *Yushin* Constitution. In a concurring opinion, Justice Yi Hoe-ch'ang admitted that, given the judiciary's focus on legality, its review of an act of state requiring highly political judgment made by the president may fail to give due consideration to whether the decision served greater legitimate political objectives. He also suggested that courts should exercise restraint on such matters in the interest of preserving the judiciary's own neutrality and independence. Nevertheless, he asserted that when citizens' basic rights are involved, an act of state should be subject to review and that this lies squarely within the concept of judicial power.[29]

In a 2004 case involving the government's actions toward North Korea, the Supreme Court adopted a similar approach. Repeating almost verbatim Justice Yi's reasoning in the 1985 case, it acknowledged that certain decisions require highly political consideration and should not be reviewed by the judiciary, and yet concluded that in the instant

---

[27] Sup Ct 96 Do 3376 (17 April 1997).

[28] According to art 87 of the Criminal Code, the crime of insurrection is defined, in part, as engaging in 'collective violence for the purpose of subverting the nation's constitutional order'. More detailed definition of the phrase 'subverting the nation's constitutional order' is given in art 91.

[29] Sup Ct 74 To 3501 (29 January 1985) (Yi Hoe-ch'ang, J, concurring). M S-H Kim, *Constitutional Transition and the Travail of Judges* (Cambridge University Press 2019) 274.

case the defendants' actions did not constitute such an act of state.[30] The Court stated that the decision to hold a summit meeting between North and South Koreas requires political judgment of the highest order, which may not be amenable to review by the courts whose narrow focus on legality may result in neglecting broader political purposiveness and legitimateness. Regarding, however, the acts of presidential advisers who sent US$450 million to North Korea for the purpose of securing the summit meeting without going through the proper legal channels, the Court declared that these were subject to judicial review. It thus held that providing such funds in return for obtaining the right to conduct business in the North, without notifying the Minister of Economy and Finance or obtaining the approval of the Minister of Unification, as required by law, was a violation of the principle of rule of law which could not be justified in the name of 'act of state'.[31]

III. JUDICIAL INDEPENDENCE

Judicial independence is a corollary of the principle of separation of powers. It requires that judicial power be exercised by a body different from the legislative and executive branches. This means that, at the institutional level, the judiciary should have the autonomy and power to define its own domain and to defend itself. It also means that the process of adjudication in the courtroom should be free from outside pressure or political influence, to ensure that each dispute is settled only according to the dictates of the law. To secure these goals, judges must also be provided with the security and assurance needed to make decisions without fear of attack or retaliation.

A. Institutional Independence of the Courts

To maintain the judiciary as an independent branch of the government, it must be given autonomy in terms of rule-making authority,

---

[30] Sup Ct 2003 Do 7878 (26 March 2004).

[31] The illegal transfer of funds to North Korea took place in 2000 under the presidency of Kim Dae-jung in preparation for his meeting with the North Korean leader Kim Jong-Il. A special prosecutor was appointed in 2003, after Kim left office, to investigate the charges. Although the former president was not charged, all defendants (including his chief adviser, the head of the National Intelligence Agency, the head of the Korea Development Bank, and the CEO of Hyundai-Asan) were found guilty of violating the Foreign Exchange Transactions Act, the South-North Exchange and Cooperation Act, and the Act on the Aggravated Punishment of Specific Economic Crimes.

financial resources, and personnel decisions. The constitution provides that the Supreme Court has the power to enact regulations regarding adjudicative processes and the judiciary's internal administration (art 108). This rule-making authority, however, must be exercised within the limits of statutes enacted by the National Assembly. Since the judiciary does not have the power to propose any legislative bills, it is dependent on the good will of the National Assembly and the Government for laws establishing the various courts and their jurisdictions. The courts thus have no power to propose or amend laws affecting their own status or jurisdiction. The Court Organisation Act, however, allows the chief justice of the Supreme Court to make suggestions in writing to the National Assembly regarding the enactment or amendment of bills pertaining to the courts' organisation, personnel, and adjudicative processes.[32]

The judicial budget is part of the national budget, which is drawn up by the executive and approved by the legislature. This means that the courts' autonomy in terms of financial resources may be limited. The Court Organisation Act only provides that the judiciary's independence and autonomy must be respected when formulating the courts' budget.[33] According to the National Finance Act, the government has the duty to respect the opinion of heads of independent state bodies, and to consult with them in advance when adjustment to their budget is needed. The State Council is required to hear the views of heads of the independent state bodies, when reducing the amount of their expenditure budget.[34] In practice, judges who staff the NCA are often seen lobbying members of the National Assembly, trying to persuade them not to cut the judicial budget. The subordinate status of the judiciary vis-à-vis the legislature was graphically on display during National Assembly's deliberation of the judiciary's budget for 2021, when a lawmaker in the Legislation and Judiciary Committee essentially demanded that the Minister of the NCA must 'beg for his life' if he did not wish to see the elimination of a budget item for the digital database of court decisions.[35]

---

[32] COA, art 9(3).
[33] COA, art 82(2).
[34] National Finance Act, art 40.
[35] Ch'oe H-r, 'Pak Pŏm-gye, Taebŏpkwan e "Uiwŏnnim Sallyŏjuseyo" Haebora' [Pak Pŏm-gye to Supreme Court Justice, says, "Please save me, Mr MP"], *Dong-A Ilbo* (6 November 2020).

B. Independence of Adjudicative Process

The constitution provides: 'Judges shall rule independently according to their conscience and in conformity with the constitution and legislative acts' (art 103). Judges must be free from external pressure or influence in adjudicating cases. Neither the executive nor the legislative branch is allowed to interfere in court proceedings. The law specifically excludes cases currently pending at courts from the scope of the National Assembly's otherwise expansive power to inspect and investigate state matters.[36] To ensure the independence and fairness of adjudication, judges are barred from assuming any legislative or executive positions or participating in any political movement.[37] The ban on interference in the adjudicative process also applies to those coming from within the judiciary. Higher courts may not interfere with cases being adjudicated by lower courts. Neither the chief judge of a court nor the presiding judge of a panel may interfere with the individual judge's adjudication. As will be seen, however, complaints about interference from the judiciary's leadership, particularly the National Court Administration, are sometimes heard.

Of special interest is the phrase 'independently according to their conscience'. This expression was absent from the constitution's text until the adoption of the 1962 Constitution of the Third Republic. It is unclear why the phrase was inserted, but apparently it was copied from Japan's post-war constitution.[38] The meaning of 'conscience' is the source of some controversy because it may be interpreted as permitting judges to rely on their personal political, moral, and religious convictions when deciding cases. Commentators use such labels as 'subjective conscience' to refer to the individual judge's personal beliefs and 'objective conscience' to refer to something like values and standards inherent in the law or professional norms that come with the practice of being a judge. Critics claim, however, that such a clear-cut distinction cannot be made between one's personal and professional beliefs.[39]

---

[36] Inspection and Investigation of State Affairs Act, art 8.

[37] COA, art 49. The same provision also prohibits judges from engaging in any activity for financial profit or becoming an officer of a corporation regardless of monetary compensation.

[38] The Constitution of Japan, art 76(3).

[39] Yang K, *Hŏnpŏp Kangŭi* [*Constitutional Law Lectures*] (10th edn, Pŏpmunsa 2021) 1323. For a similar discussion in the Japanese context, see Y Hasebe, 'Judges' Conscience and Constitutional Reasoning' (2020) 27 *Academia Sinica Law Journal* 1.

146   *Courts in the Age of Democracy*

In this connection, a small controversy arose in 2017 when a relatively young judge posted a statement on the court's internal social media that each judge should be free to rely on his/her individual worldview and philosophy in deciding cases and that it was time to acknowledge the diversity of political viewpoints among judges. Referring to article 103 of the constitution, he even asserted that the Supreme Court's precedents merely contain 'other people's interpretations' which should be reviewed according to the individual judge's conscience. In response, other judges warned that respecting diversity among judges and deciding cases based on political reasoning are two different things, and that confusing the two will only undermine judicial independence.[40] Whatever 'conscience' may mean, most commentators agree that it cannot be a licence for idiosyncratic arbitrary decision-making that cannot be supported by the text and structure of the laws.

One specific context in which the judges' conscience may become an issue is the scope of their sentencing powers. While the Sentencing Commission under the Supreme Court establishes sentencing guidelines, they are not legally binding. If the actual sentence is outside the guidelines' range, the court is required to provide its reasons.[41] Sometimes, the legislature may restrict the scope of judges' sentencing powers via statutes. The Constitutional Court, however, has held that extreme restrictions on judges' sentencing powers may be unconstitutional. For example, regarding a statute that prescribed heavier punishments for certain economic crimes, not allowing the judge to suspend the sentence unless there were specifically prescribed reasons for mitigation was held to be an excessive restraint on the judge's power to choose and determine the sentence.[42] In a similar vein, a provision in the Military Criminal Code, which prescribed only the death sentence for the crime of murdering one's superior officer, was held unconstitutional.[43]

---

[40] Kim S-m, 'Hyŏnjik P'ansa, "Chaep'an i kot Chŏngch'i" Kŭl ... 'Sabŏp Chŏngch'ihwa Nollan [Current Judge's Statement "Adjudication is Politics" Sparks Debate on Politicisation of Judiciary]' *JoongAng Ilbo* (1 September 2017).
[41] COA, art 81-7.
[42] Const Ct 2006 Hun-Ka 5 (27 April 2006).
[43] Const Ct 2006 Hun-Ka 13 (29 November 2007). The main ground for unconstitutionality was that the prescribed punishment was disproportionately heavy compared to the crime itself.

C. Independence of Judges

A crucial foundation of judicial independence is the court's autonomy in the appointment and recruitment of judges, as well as the guarantee of their term of office during which they cannot be dismissed arbitrarily.

The constitution provides that the qualifications for becoming a judge shall be specified by the National Assembly's legislative enactment (art 101(3)). According to the Court Organisation Act, to be appointed to the Supreme Court, one must be at least 45 years of age and 20 years or more must have passed since being licensed to practise law.[44] The Attorney-at-Law Act provides that to be licensed as a lawyer, one must have either passed the National Judicial Examination and graduated from the JRTI or passed the new National Bar Examination.[45] With the introduction of the new examination system in 2012, the older licensing system was gradually phased out until it was last administered in 2017. Thus, currently, passing the National Bar Exam is the only way to be qualified as attorney-at-law.

For judges other than Supreme Court justices, there is no age requirement but at least 10 years must have passed since being licensed as a lawyer.[46] This is a major change from the older system under which judges used to be recruited from fresh graduates of the JRTI. The change was instituted with the transition to a new system of legal education. With the goal of training lawyers with diverse background and experience, three-year post-graduate level law schools were established in 2009 and only those who attended such law schools are now eligible to take the new National Bar Exam. Previously, legal education was provided at the undergraduate level, but one did not have to be a graduate of a law department or be a law major to be eligible to take the National Judicial Exam. The new system thus more closely integrated the legal education system with the examination system for licensing new lawyers. This was accompanied by a change in the method of recruiting and promoting judges. Under the old system, new judges were recruited from each year's graduating class of the JRTI, while many of their classmates became public prosecutors or practising attorneys. The transition to the new system was an opportunity for the judiciary to change the courtroom

---

[44] COA, art 42(1).
[45] Attorney-at-Law Act, art 4 (Law No 17828, 5 January 2021).
[46] COA, art 42(2).

dynamic between the bench and the bar. By recruiting more experienced lawyers, judges could be more senior in age and have better knowledge of the law compared to the litigants (public prosecutors and attorneys). Another rationale for the new hiring system for judges was to bring more diversity into the judiciary and to break from the hierarchical bureau-cratised system in which judges were basically promoted according to seniority, like other public officials.

The requirement of 10 or more years of experience, however, will be implemented in phases. A minimum of five years of experience will be required until the end of 2024, and seven years until 2028.[47] Even with this phased introduction, the judiciary is concerned that there will not be enough experienced lawyers applying for judgeship. The NCA has pointed out that the total number of judges has been steadily declining since the transition to the new recruitment system and that many seats on the bench throughout the nation remain vacant. Much will depend on the specific method of recruiting experienced lawyers as judges, as well as on making judgeship an attractive career path, in terms of both benefits and prestige.

According to the constitution, the power of appointing regular judges currently lies with the chief justice. Appointments are made with the consent of the Council of Supreme Court Justices (art 104(3)). Neither the executive nor the legislative branch has any role in appointing judges. This may be seen as a deliberate choice to avoid the system under the *Yushin* Constitution, which gave the president the power to appoint all judges.

By law, the chief justice also has the power to assign judges to various posts within the court system.[48] Judges are typically rotated throughout the nation's courts after serving two to three years at a given post. In the past, the usual practice was that a judge who served at a court in the Seoul metropolitan area would next be assigned to a court away from the nation's capital, and vice-versa. According to the Constitutional Court, a judge may challenge assignment to a given post via constitutional complaint but must first go through adjudication at the Administrative Court.[49] Beginning 2021, judges have the option to request serving for

---

[47] This represented a delay of three years compared to the original schedule adopted in 2013.

[48] COA, art 44.

[49] Const Ct 92 Hun-Ma 247 (23 December 1993). Regarding the chief justice's refusal to hire a person as a judge, the Constitutional Court has held that it may not be challenged via constitutional complaint because such challenge must be made via Administrative Court

longer periods at one post (up to five years in Seoul and seven to 10 years outside Seoul). This is intended to enhance judges' professional expertise and to reduce delays in adjudication caused by frequent rotation.

The chief justice has the ultimate power of evaluating judges' performance and professionalism.[50] Such evaluations are then used to decide renewal of appointments and assignments of posts. In other words, judges' promotion depends on these evaluations. Although the Court Organisation Act recognises only three categories of judges (chief justice, Supreme Court justices, and regular judges), the reality is that there are numerous unofficial ranks within the judiciary. The fact that powers concerning personnel matters are concentrated in the hands of the chief justice may be problematic for individual judges' independence. They may have to compromise their opinion and decide according to the views of the chief justice if they wish to be promoted to the next rank. Given that the chief justice is appointed by the president, a further possibility is that judges may be influenced indirectly by the views and wishes of the president.

The fact that judges are appointed for a fixed term of office as well as being subject to mandatory retirement age may also be detrimental to judicial independence. The chief justice is appointed for a single six-year term; other justices of the Supreme Court are appointed for a renewable six-year term; regular judges are appointed for a renewable term of 10 years (art 105). Retirement age for Supreme Court justices is 70, whereas regular judges must retire at 65.[51] Despite the possibility of reappointment, in practice all justices have served only one term. This means that the Supreme Court's 'turnover rate' is fairly high, allowing the president to appoint many new justices during the president's five-year term. In some cases, one president may be able to replace all 14 justices, thereby changing the entire makeup of the Supreme Court. Aside from the issue of continuity of the highest court's jurisprudence, the fact that the executive power may reshape the Court in its own image can be problematic for judicial independence.

For regular judges, their appointment may be renewed at the end of their 10-year term. According to the law, appointments will not be renewed if (a) a physical or mental impairment makes it impossible to

---

and because constitutional complaints may not be filed to contest a court's decision. Const Ct 2001 Hun-Ma 245 (20 December 2001).

[50] COA, art 44-2. Each year the chief judge of each court evaluates the performance of judges assigned to that court and submits the evaluation to the chief justice.

[51] COA, art 45(4).

150 Courts in the Age of Democracy

discharge the normal duties of a judge; (b) a demonstrably unsatisfactory performance record makes it impossible to discharge the normal duties of a judge; or (c) there is a demonstrable difficulty in maintaining one's dignity as a judge.[52] While these grounds have become more specific than in the past, the ultimate decision on whether to renew a judge's appointment lies with the chief justice. Non-renewals are rare, but critics charge that they are mostly used to punish judges who publicly express critical views about the judiciary and its leadership.

According to the constitution, the only way that judges may be dismissed during their term of office is via impeachment or a sentence of at least imprisonment without prison labour (art 106(1)).[53] The same article also disallows disadvantageous treatment of judges except through disciplinary action.[54] By contrast, the constitution states that judges may be relieved from office in case of serious mental or physical impairment which prevents them from discharging their official duties (art 106(2)). This decision is also made by the chief justice, except when relieving a Supreme Court justice from office, which is done by the president at the chief justice's recommendation.[55]

IV. POLITICS OF JUDICIAL REFORM

Calls for making the judiciary less bureaucratic and more democratic have been intensifying in recent years. Many observers note that, unlike the days of authoritarian governments, the primary threat to judicial independence is now from within the judiciary due to its hierarchical structure and concentration of power.[56] The problem, for many critics, is the fact that the judiciary's leadership has been unresponsive to demands for reform coming from the junior judges and civic groups, which in turn is undermining the citizens' trust in the courts' decisions. They point to the widespread perception that judges are an elite group, out of touch

---

[52] COA, art 45-2(2).

[53] According to the Criminal Code, punishments heavier than imprisonment without prison labour are the death penalty and imprisonment with prison labour. Criminal Code, art 41 (Law No 17571, 8 December 2020).

[54] Judges may be subject to three types of disciplinary actions: suspension, salary reduction, and reprimand. Discipline of Judges Act, art 3.

[55] COA, art 47.

[56] J Kim, 'Courts in the Republic of Korea: Featuring a Built-in Authoritarian Legacy of Centralization and Bureaucratization' in J-r Yeh and W-C Chang (eds), *Asian Courts in Context* (Cambridge University Press 2015).

with ordinary people's lives, as well as the popular complaint that only the well-connected and wealthy are able to obtain justice. The cynical phrase 'without money, guilty; with money, not guilty' is often cited as a reflection of the citizens' diminishing trust in the judiciary. Also, the fact that many judges including Supreme Court justices leave office at the end of their term to become practising attorneys who then represent clients before their former colleagues, and who actually win many cases, has undermined the people's faith in the integrity of the judicial process.[57]

A. Citizen Participation in the Judiciary

One approach to judicial reform advocated for many years by civic groups has been allowing ordinary citizens' participation in the adjudicative process. The argument is that this will enhance the democratic legitimacy of court decisions and reduce the gap between the commoners' sense of justice and the decisions rendered by the elite judges.

The Act on Citizen Participation in Criminal Trials was finally enacted in 2007, introducing for the first time in Korean history a limited form of jury trial.[58] Under the new system, the defendant has the right to request a jury trial if the charge is for a crime that carries a sentence of at least one year of imprisonment, which are tried by a three-judge panel. The Constitutional Court has held that the right to a jury trial is not a constitutionally guaranteed right and that it is not a violation of equality principle to have lesser crimes tried by single judges.[59]

The number of jurors depends on the gravity of the crime: nine for crimes punishable by death penalty or life imprisonment and seven for all other crimes. If the defendant admits to the material facts of the alleged crime, the case may proceed with five jurors.[60] The jury's responsibility includes determination of guilt or innocence, as well as making recommmendation on sentencing.[61] The jury's participation in sentencing may be problematic because at this stage previous crimes may be considered, whereas at the stage of determining guilt, evidence of previous crimes can be highly prejudicial.

---

[57] Kim (n 56) 133.
[58] This largely coincided with the changes in the legal education and licensing system mentioned above.
[59] Const Ct 2014 Han-Ba 447 (30 July 2015).
[60] Act on Citizen Participation in Criminal Trials (hereafter 'Citizen Participation Act'), art 13(1) (Law No 14839, 26 July 2017).
[61] Citizen Participation Act, art 12.

The Korean system of jury trial reserves a significant role for the judges. In certain situations, the court may reject the defendant's request for a jury trial: if certain jurors are unable to perform their duties or if co-defendants do not wish to be tried by a jury, or if the victim of sexual crimes wishes to avoid a jury trial.[62] Before deliberating, the jury receives instruction from the presiding judge, which includes a summary of the alleged facts and applicable laws, essential points of the arguments by the defence, and admissibility of evidence. The jury may seek to hear the judge's opinion before reaching its decision. Indeed, it is required to hear the judge's opinion if it cannot reach a unanimous guilty verdict. The jury then decides by majority vote. If the verdict is guilty, then the jury discusses the proper sentence with the judge and makes its recommendation. Beyond such high degree of judge-jury interaction, which may undermine the autonomy of the jury, the judges have ultimate control of the trial in the sense that the jury's verdict and sentencing recommendation are not legally binding.[63] The judge is free to disregard them so long as the judge explains why a different decision has been reached.[64]

Whether such a system will enhance the democratic legitimacy of the judicial process and promote the people's trust in court decisions remains to be seen.[65] For its part, the Supreme Court has tried to promote greater respect for jury trials by holding that a unanimous not-guilty verdict by the jury in which the judges concurred may not be reversed by the appeals court which only interrogated witnesses for the victims and decided without a jury.[66] Yet, the fact is that jury trials remain seriously under-utilised. More importantly, despite numerous proposals to increase its use, there is a fundamental limitation because the constitution protects the right to be tried by qualified judges (art 27(1)). Expansion of jury trials may risk infringing upon this basic right.

B. Problems of Hierarchy and Abuse of Judicial Administrative Power

Allegations that the judiciary's leadership exerts various forms of undue pressure on judges have been made for many years. In 2009, it was

---

[62] Citizen Participation Act, art 9.

[63] Citizen Participation Act, art 46(5).

[64] Citizen Participation Act, art 48(4).

[65] For an optimistic view and discussion on possible ways for improvement, see S Han, 'Jury Trials in South Korea: The Situation, Achievements, and Suggestions for Improvements' (2020) 10 *Yonsei Law Journal* 29.

[66] Sup Ct 2009 Do 14065 (25 March 2010).

reported that one of the Supreme Court justices, during his tenure as the chief judge of the Seoul Central District Court, had sent emails to judges in charge of cases against alleged violators of the Act on Assembly and Demonstration, urging them to conclude them 'swiftly' and 'in accordance with current laws'.[67] The Public Officials Ethics Committee under the Supreme Court concluded that the justice's actions were improper interference in the adjudicative process and recommended that a serious warning be issued by the chief justice. Many inside and outside the judiciary were disappointed that no disciplinary actions were taken against the justice and that he was allowed to serve out his term despite numerous calls for resignation.[68]

Less than 10 years later, in 2017, similar news of internal pressure and even surveillance emerged which engulfed the judiciary in a crisis of unprecedented proportions. It was alleged that the National Court Administration had compiled a 'blacklist' of judges thought to be critical of the judiciary's leadership and pressured a 'study group' of progressive judges to reduce the size of its meeting. The Supreme Court investigated the allegations and concluded that, although the NCA may have used its powers improperly, there was no blacklist or any attempt to systematically disadvantage specific judges. Upon the retirement of Chief Justice Yang Seung-tae in September 2017, a judge with a more progressive reputation was appointed to succeed him by then-President Moon Jae-in. In response to continuing demands from the judges and the public, the new Chief Justice Kim Myŏng-su agreed to a re-investigate the matter. The second investigative commission announced that while there was no 'blacklist', the NCA had compiled reports of certain judges' activities and political orientation, as well as analyses of lower courts' adjudication of certain cases in which the former President Park had shown interest. Critics charged that the very fact the NCA compiled such documents is an abuse of its powers and a violation of judges' independence. The Supreme Court then formed a third investigative commission, which concluded in May 2018 that the NCA had indeed engaged in 'surveillance' of judges critical of the judiciary's leadership, but that no blacklist designed to systematically harm their careers was ever compiled. The new Chief Justice Kim made a public apology to the nation promising to ensure that such abuse of the Court's administrative powers is never repeated

---

[67] At the time, the constitutionality of the applicable provision, which prohibited nighttime demonstrations, was being litigated at the Constitutional Court.

[68] Kim (n 56) 128–29.

and assured active cooperation with any criminal investigation by the public prosecutors.

Meanwhile, a group of law professors in February 2018 filed a criminal complaint against the former Chief Justice Yang and the former Vice Minister of NCA. Then, in June 2018, over 2,000 practising attorneys signed a declaration condemning the Supreme Court for violating judges' independence and demanded a thorough investigation and punishment of responsible parties. An informal conference of 'representatives' the nation's judges was also convened, which similarly demanded an immediate investigation.

Eventually, President Moon in September 2018 joined the call for a full investigation of abuses of the Supreme Court's administrative powers, which resulted in a prolonged process in which over a hundred judges were summoned and interrogated by the prosecutors as potential criminals. Allegations were made that the NCA under the former Chief Justice Yang had tried to 'bargain' with the former President Park. It was reported that Supreme Court promised to decide certain cases in the government's favour in return for the president's support for the Court's plan to create a separate court of final appeal, which would alleviate the Supreme Court's caseload. On 24 January 2019, in a humiliating development for the judiciary, former Chief Justice Yang was arrested on charges of manipulating court rulings and abusing his authority to influence the promotion of judges.[69] Eventually, 14 judges were indicted, including Yang and two other former Supreme Court justices. The cases are still ongoing as of this writing and it will likely take years before the entire legal proceedings are concluded. Already, however, the crisis has been devastating for the people's trust in the courts. Most judges regard it as a colossal disgrace for the judiciary, and many think that charges are groundless or overblown. In defence of the accused judges, some point out that the cases that were allegedly used to 'bargain' with the president had already been decided before any attempt was made to argue for the need of a separate appellate review court. Other judges, however, think that the criminal investigation is a welcome first step toward transforming the judiciary toward a more transparent and democratic institution. A few have even called for the impeachment of the senior judges responsible for causing the judicial crisis.

<hr>

[69] Choe S-H, 'Ex-Chief Justice of South Korea Is Arrested on Case-Rigging Charges' *The New York Times* (23 January 2019).

C. Reforming the Judiciary: Democratisation or Politicisation?

This crisis of the judiciary has spurred a few changes in the law regarding court organisation and the status of judges. One reform intended to make the judiciary less hierarchical was the elimination in 2020 of the rank of 'High Court presiding judge'. Previously, attaining that rank had been regarded as a necessary step before being promoted to the position of the chief judge of a district court or a family court. Also, change was made to the composition of the three-judge panels, used in both district and high courts. These used to be a hierarchical body composed of a senior presiding judge and two junior judges, but now a panel can be composed of three judges of the same seniority. The aim is to change the dynamic within the panel by making it less hierarchical to enhance the level of deliberation among the judges.

   Another effort to make the entire court system more democratic and to lessen the concentration of powers in the office of the chief justice was the introduction of a recommendation system for selecting chief judges. Beginning 2022, the chief judges of 13 district courts are chosen from a list of candidates recommended by judges currently serving at those courts. Also, the National Conference of Judges' Representatives was given official status in 2018 via the adoption of a Supreme Court regulation specifying its rules and method of choosing the representatives. Its primary mandate is to make suggestions regarding matters of judicial administration and judges' independence.[70]

   While these reforms were undertaken in the name of democratisation, they raise the issue of politicisation of the judiciary. According to critics, the so-called reforms only resulted in the takeover of the judiciary's leadership by more politically oriented judges. The charge is that judges with progressive political views have been promoted by Chief Justice Kim to form a new inner circle within the judiciary. Kim has been criticised for being as biased as his predecessor, while overtly courting politicians' favour. In 2020, when a senior judge implicated in the abuse of judicial administrative power under the former Chief Justice Yang submitted his resignation, Kim refused to accept it. He reportedly told the senior judge that he could not accept the resignation because the National Assembly was preparing to impeach the senior judge. Since impeachment can be directed only against currently serving judges, the

---

[70] Regulation on National Conference of Judges' Representatives, art 6(1) (Supreme Court Regulation No 2839, 4 April 2019).

National Assembly would not be able to impeach him if Kim allowed him to resign. The chief justice was apparently more interested in cooperating with the politicians than in protecting a member of the judiciary. Critics charged that judicial independence was being abandoned by the head of the judiciary.

Ironically, democratisation of the judiciary, led by politically oriented judges who used to advocate the independence of individual judges against interference from the judicial leadership, may be exposing the judiciary to external political influence. For these judges, judging is essentially a political act and it may be acceptable to use their position to pursue political goals. Similarly, they may not be so concerned about using to the courts as a base for advancing explicitly political interests and policies. After Chief Justice Kim took office, at least two judges left the court to join the then-ruling party of President Moon and became career politicians as members of the National Assembly. Other judges left to become senior officials at the Office of the President, where they defended and promoted the Moon administration's policy goals. Such explicitly partisan behaviour on the part of former members of the judiciary may call into question the fairness and impartiality of decisions they issued before their resignation. It may even undermine the public's trust in the courts as an independent and unbiased institution.

To address such concerns, the law was amended in 2020 to prohibit a former judge from assuming any position at the Office of the President unless two years have passed since retiring from the judiciary. Also, judges may not be seconded to, or hold any concurrent position at, the Office of the President.[71] The revised law also provides that no person may be hired as a judge unless three years have passed since that person's resignation from the Office of the President. Similar restrictions apply to former members of political parties and former advisers to presidential candidates.[72] For former candidates for elected offices, five years must have elapsed before such persons can be hired as a judge. As regards judges resigning from the court to become candidates for elected offices, bills have been proposed to require the passage of certain minimum time after resignation, but so far they have all been defeated, on grounds that such a restriction will infringe upon the constitutionally guaranteed right to run for elected office.

---

[71] COA, art 50-2.
[72] COA, art 43.

V. CONCLUSION

Under a system which grants so much power to the chief justice, potential is always there for abuse. Proper reform may require changing the constitution. Even without constitutional revision, however, the power of appointing judges and evaluating their performance can be assigned by statute to a committee comprising members of not only the bench but also the bar and perhaps even the civil society. There is broad agreement across the political spectrum for making the courts more transparent and less hierarchical. There are even calls for making it more accountable to 'the people'. Yet, it should be clear that judicial reform must be carried out to advance the rule of law. In an age in which popular sovereignty has become the ultimate source of legitimacy, the task of reforming the courts will require a delicate balancing act of heeding the calls for democracy while avoiding excessive politicisation of the judiciary.

FURTHER READING

Chisholm N, 'The Faces of Judicial Independence: Democratic versus Bureaucratic Accountability in Judicial Selection, Training, and Promotion in South Korea and Taiwan' (2014) 62 *American Journal of Comparative Law* 893.

Choi D and Rokumoto K (eds), *Judicial System Transformation in the Globalizing World: Korea and Japan* (Seoul National University Press 2007).

Hans V, 'Reflections on the Korean Jury Trial' (2014) 14 *Journal of Korean Law* 81.

Rhee W-Y, 'Judicial Appointment in the Republic of Korea from Democracy Perspectives' (2010) 9 *Journal of Korean Law* 53.

7

Constitutional Court: Guardian of the Constitution?

Appointment of Justices – Procedural Rules for Adjudication – Constitutionality Review of Legislation and Tensions with the Supreme Court – Constitutional Complaints and Exceptions – Impeachment Proceedings – Dissolving Political Parties – Competence Disputes

THE ESTABLISHMENT OF the Constitutional Court of Korea was a result of the historic transition to democracy in 1987. The 1960 Constitution of the short-lived Second Republic had provided for a constitutional court, but this was never realised due to Park Chung-hee's coup the following year. Constitutional adjudication was thus virtually unknown in Korea until the current constitution was adopted.[1] There are five types of cases adjudicated by the Constitutional Court: (i) review of a statute's constitutionality; (ii) impeachment of public officials; (iii) dissolution of political parties; (iv) competence disputes among different government agencies; and (v) constitutional complaints filed by individual citizens (art 111(1)). Some of these are more political than others, but it is quite evident that all of them call for judgment that goes beyond the narrow judicial application of settled legal norms. Yet, the Korean system of constitutional adjudication is relatively more 'judicial' in that all justices of the Court must be qualified as judges. This creates interesting dynamics because the Court often insists that its decisions are not based on political considerations, whereas some of the cases seem to require a high level of political judgment. This chapter will examine the organisation and jurisdiction of the current Constitutional Court, with a view to explaining its role and limitations in maintaining the integrity of Korea's constitutional order.

---

[1] For rare exceptions during the Third Republic, see M S-H Kim, *Constitutional Transition and the Travail of Judges: The Courts of South Korea* (Cambridge University Press 2019) 43–44, 58–60, 75–89.

I. FROM UNCERTAIN BEGINNINGS
TO JUDICIALISATION OF POLITICS

The Constitutional Court officially started receiving cases in 1988 after the National Assembly enacted the Constitutional Court Act. However, during its early years, its caseload was very low. Most citizens were unfamiliar with the Court's functions. Many were sceptical about its ability to provide meaningful solutions to constitutional problems and its long-term viability. Even the National Assembly which enacted its organic law apparently thought that the Court would not meet very often. The original Constitutional Court Act provided that only six of the nine justices were to be full-time members.[2] With relatively few cases to decide, the Court had to cultivate its business and reputation. One member of the first cohort of justices recalled that his colleagues took deliberate care to discuss the merits of a case even if it could be dismissed on procedural grounds.[3] They wished to signal to the people that their claims would be carefully considered by the new Court.

Before long, citizens began to make active use of the Court, and its caseload swelled. Particularly, the constitutional complaint became a popular channel for individuals with grievances against the government to express their discontent and hopefully obtain redress. The Court soon earned an 'activist' reputation. Its early popularity may also have resulted from association with Korea's transition from authoritarian rule to democracy. Unlike the Supreme Court, it was not burdened with a chequered past and could position itself as a key agent in democratic consolidation. A few of its earlier decisions are noteworthy in this regard. Through the case of the Kukje Corporation which had been forced into bankruptcy during the Chun Doo-hwan administration (1980–1988), the Court issued a constitutional reprimand against past governments' high-handed economic and political practices.[4] The Court also held that the notorious National Security Law was unconstitutional unless it was given a narrow interpretation as specified by the Court itself.[5] While it stopped short of striking it down entirely, the Court warned against abusing the

---

[2] Constitutional Court Act (hereafter 'CCA'), art 13 (Law No 4017, 5 August 1988). This provision was deleted in 1991.
[3] Yi S-y, 'Hŏnpŏp Chaep'an 10 Nyŏn ŭi Hoego wa Chŏnmang [A Retrospective on Ten Years of Constitutional Adjudication]' (1999) 27(3) *Kongpŏp Yŏn'gu* 107.
[4] Const Ct 89 Hun-Ma 31 (29 July 1993). For an analysis of this case, see JM West, '*Kukje* and Beyond: Constitutionalism and the Market' (1998) 3 *Segye Hŏnpŏp Yŏn'gu* 321.
[5] Const Ct 89 Hun-Ka 113 (2 April 1990).

law to undermine the rule of law and citizens' basic rights. Several decisions related to the prosecutions of former presidents Chun Doo-hwan and Roh Tae-woo (1988–1993) for 'crimes destructive of constitutional order' further contributed to the Court's image as a champion of transitional justice.[6]

Such a positive reputation currently coexists with increasing criticism from commentators and politicians that the Court is 'judicialising politics' by encroaching on areas best left to the public and their representatives.[7] The year 2004 may be the symbolic turning point when scepticism began to be expressed about the democratic propriety of 'nine unelected judges' deciding momentous constitutional issues. That year saw the much-noted presidential impeachment case against Roh Moo-hyun (2003–2008).[8] Confronted with the spectacle of a judicial body adjudicating a political clash between the president and the legislature, many citizens began asking why this Court should resolve such highly political issues. That year, the Court also invoked the controversial notion of a 'customary constitution' to invalidate a law passed with bipartisan support to relocate the nation's administrative capital.[9] This decision sparked a series of criticisms not only because the idea of a customary constitution had previously been unheard of, but because the Constitutional Court seemed to authorise itself to create new constitutional norms from any longstanding fact, further encroaching on the prerogative of the sovereign people as agents of constituent power.[10]

Rising concerns about the democratic legitimacy of the Constitutional Court and 'judicialisation of politics' may have led to elected national representatives 'politicising the court'. In 2006 the Court was embroiled in a political controversy (described below) over the appointment of its chief justice, the president of the Court. For months, the National Assembly, whose consent is required for appointing the Court's president, engaged in a political war of attrition over whether the candidate was even eligible.[11] Having become aware of the Constitutional Court's

---

[6] For these cases, see ch 9.

[7] J Kim and J Park, 'Causes and Conditions for Sustainable Judicialization of Politics in Korea' in B Dressel (ed), *The Judicialization of Politics in Asia* (Routledge 2012).

[8] Const Ct 2004 Hun-Na 1 (14 May 2004).

[9] Const Ct 2004 Hun-Ma 554 (consolidated) (21 October 2004).

[10] C Hahm and SH Kim, 'Constitutionalism on Trial in South Korea' (2005) 16 *Journal of Democracy* 28.

[11] For a discussion of this controversy, see C Hahm, 'Beyond "Law vs. Politics" in Constitutional Adjudication: Lessons from South Korea' (2012) 10 *International Journal of Constitutional Law* 6, 9–13.

tremendous influence over political issues, lawmakers on both sides of the aisle wished to ensure that someone with like-minded political views would lead the Court. With such expansive powers, the Court could act as the 'guardian of the Constitution', but this also meant that it could be a powerful tool for the government's partisan agenda. Although the Court has not since seen such overt politicisation, the National Assembly now scrutinises each new nominee for the Court from more partisan and ideological standpoints.

II. ORGANISATION OF THE COURT

The Constitutional Court comprises nine justices who must be qualified to sit on regular courts (art 111(2)). While the president has formal appointment power, for three seats, the president must appoint whomever the National Assembly nominates and, for another three, whomever the Supreme Court's chief justice designates (art 111(3)).

To be appointed to the Court, one must be over 40 years of age, and at least 15 years must have passed since being licensed as an attorney.[12] In practice, most justices are former judges, with a few former prosecutors. In the Court's early years, some had illustrious careers as practising attorneys before their court appointment. Recently, however, even the few who were practising when appointed were retirees from the judiciary or prosecutor's office, leading to criticism that the Court is composed of elite jurists and lacks diversity. The academia has persistently criticised the licensing requirement, which typically disqualifies law professors, regardless of their expertise and reputation. In time, this may change since the new legal education and licensing system adopted in 2009 has led to higher bar passage rates so that law school graduates who become professors will be more likely to be licensed attorneys.

The justices are aided by professional researchers who sort out the issues and write draft opinions. Initially, researchers were judges on loan from the judiciary. The Court later created an independent cohort of researchers who are licensed to practice law. The Court also appoints law professors for a two-year term as consultants on foreign constitutional law. In addition, it hosts the Constitutional Adjudication Research Institute, founded in 2011, where academic researchers investigate long-term constitutional issues likely to arise in the future.

---

[12] CCA, art 5(1).

A. Term of Office

The justices serve renewable six-year terms (art 112(1)), but single terms have become well-established, with only a few justices reappointed during the Court's early years. What remains unclear is the term for the president of the Court because the constitution provides only that the president shall be appointed 'from among the justices' (art 111(4)). Suppose the candidate had already been a Court justice. Does this person start a new six-year term upon appointment as president or serve only the time remaining in the original appointment as a justice? Interestingly, this was not an issue until 2006, 18 years after the Court had opened. Until then, no president of the Court had been a sitting justice, and no one read 'from among the justices' literally to mean that one must first become a justice of the Court to be eligible for court president. In 2006, however, President Roh Moo-hyun chose Chŏn Hyo-suk, a justice who had been on the Court for three years, to become its president. Chŏn was asked to first resign from the Court to ensure that she would start a new six-year term. This set off a political row in the National Assembly, with opposition lawmakers claiming that a new six-year term would deviously extend a sitting justice's term. They argued that, since Chŏn had resigned from the Court, her nomination violated the 'from among the justices' clause. Ultimately, Roh withdrew Chŏn's nomination at her request, ending the political controversy. In recent years, a convention may be taking shape, as subsequent presidents of the Court have served only the remaining years of their original term.

By statute, the justices must retire at age 70.[13] When the Constitutional Court was first created, the retirement age was 65, and only the president of the Court retired at 70. This was changed in 2014 to allow more experienced individuals to serve and to achieve parity with Supreme Court justices.[14] The combination of relatively short single terms and retirement at 70 leads to a rather quick turnover and, occasionally, an opportunity for the Republic's president to appoint an entirely new bench, which may undermine the Court's independence. The Constitution bars the justices from joining a political party or participating in political activities (art 112(2)). They may be dismissed only upon impeachment or imprisonment (art 112(3)).

---

[13] CCA, art 7(2).
[14] In 2011, the retirement age for Supreme Court justices was raised to 70.

B. Equal Share for the Three Branches?

By allocating the appointment of the justices to the three branches of the government, the constitution seems to give them an equal share in the Court's composition. In practice, however, the president has a far greater influence on their appointment. Since the Supreme Court's chief justice is also a presidential appointee, the three seats designated by the chief justice will most likely reflect the president's wishes. Of the three seats filled by the National Assembly, one is assigned to the government party, the second to the opposition party, while the third is a compromise choice. Since the government party's candidate is likely to meet the president's approval, the president's influence actually extends over the appointment of at least seven justices.

C. Confirmation Hearings at the National Assembly

The constitution requires that all nine justices be qualified to serve as judges. Yet, the Korean system also invites more political debate over appointments by requiring candidates to undergo public confirmation hearings at the National Assembly. The 2006 deadlock over the nomination of Chŏn for the Court's president is but one example of the politicians' interest in the appointment process.

Originally, not all justices underwent National Assembly scrutiny. The constitution requires only that the Court's president be appointed with the Assembly's consent (art 111(4)). By statute, the three justices nominated by the National Assembly must undergo a hearing before a special committee of the Assembly. As for the remaining six justices, no hearing was required until 2005. This was considered a serious design defect given that all 14 justices of the Supreme Court are constitutionally required to undergo legislative scrutiny.[15] It was argued that justices for the court that reviews the constitutionality of statutes enacted by the National Assembly should also be scrutinised by the legislature. In 2005, the National Assembly amended the Constitutional Court Act to remedy this defect. Now all candidates for the Court must undergo confirmation hearings.[16]

---

[15] J Kim, 'Some Problems with the Korean Constitutional Adjudication System' (2001) 1(2) *Journal of Korean Law* 17, 24–25.

[16] CCA, art 6(2) (Law No 7622, 29 July 2005); National Assembly Act, art 65-2 (Law No 8685, 14 December 2007).

A few differences remain. For the Court's president and the justices nominated by the National Assembly, the Special Personnel Hearings Committee conducts the hearing. For justices chosen by the Republic's president or the chief justice, hearings take place in the Legislation and Judiciary Committee. More importantly, even under the changed rules, a vote by the full session of the National Assembly is not required for the justices scrutinised by the Legislation and Judiciary Committee. Further, if the confirmation hearing before the Legislation and Judiciary Committee is not completed within 30 days, the president may proceed with the appointment.[17] In sum, even though candidates chosen by the president and the chief justice must now undergo hearings at the National Assembly, the lawmakers' consent is not an absolute requirement. Critics charge that this undercuts the whole point of subjecting candidates to scrutiny by the people's representatives.

Despite these differences, the fact that all candidates for the Constitutional Court must now stand before politicians for questioning means that the appointment process may become politicised. Having contributed to the consolidation of Korea's democracy, the Court itself has now become the object of demands for more democratic oversight. Compared to its putative European models, it may claim better democratic credentials on account of the legislature's scrutiny, but it is also more likely be exposed to political controversy.

III. PROCEDURAL RULES FOR ADJUDICATION

Final decisions of the Constitutional Court are rendered by the full nine-justice bench,[18] and at least seven justices are required to begin deliberations.[19] The constitution requires a supermajority for most types of cases. Six or more justices must concur to conclude that a statute is unconstitutional, an impeached official be dismissed, a political party be dissolved, or a constitutional complaint be upheld (art 113(1)). A simple majority is sufficient only for competence disputes. By statute, the same supermajority is required for overruling the Court's precedent or revising its interpretation of the constitution or statutes.[20]

---

[17] Law on Personnel Hearings, arts 3 and 9 (Law No 7627, 29 July 2005).
[18] CCA, art 22.
[19] CCA, art 23(1).
[20] CCA, art 23(2).

Oral arguments are integral to cases on impeachment, dissolution of political parties, and competence disputes. For reviewing a statute's constitutionality and adjudicating constitutional complaints, oral arguments are not required, although they may be held if the full bench deems them necessary.[21] Generally, oral arguments and pronouncement of the Court's decisions are open to the public unless the Court is concerned about national security, public peace and order, or good public morals.

All justices who participated in a decision must publicly indicate their opinions,[22] and each justice's position must be individually identifiable. Until 2005, justices were required to indicate their opinions only for cases that decided the constitutionality of statutes, competence disputes, and constitutional complaints. This caused a controversy in 2004, when the Court decided the impeachment case against then-president Roh Moo-hyun. Citing the law then in force, the Court did not reveal the justices' votes, even while acknowledging internal disagreement. This provoked criticism that justices should take responsibility for their views rather than hide behind anonymity. In response, the National Assembly revised the Constitutional Court Act to require that justices indicate their views on all decisions issued by the Court.

The Court is legally required to announce its final decision within 180 days of a case's filing, unless vacancies on the Court make it impossible for seven justices to adjudicate the case.[23] In reality, however, the Court's adjudication frequently exceeds this time limit. The Court has read the time limit as a 'directive' and concluded that failure to comply with the requirement is not a violation of citizens' constitutional right to a speedy trial (art 27(3)).[24]

The parties must have legal representation in all Constitutional Court proceedings, so a private individual may not file a case or participate in proceedings unless properly represented by an attorney.[25] Self-representation is allowed only if the party is a licensed attorney. This rule, however, has practical relevance only for constitutional complaints because, as will be seen, other adjudications do not involve private individuals.

---

[21] CCA, art 30.
[22] CCA, art 36(3).
[23] CCA, art 38.
[24] Const Ct 2007 Hun-Ma 732 (30 July 2009).
[25] CCA, art 25(3).

IV. REVIEW OF STATUTES' CONSTITUTIONALITY

The Constitutional Court has exclusive jurisdiction over the constitutionality of statutes enacted by the National Assembly. If a statute's constitutionality is disputed in a case pending at an ordinary court and the case's outcome depends on whether the statute is constitutional, the ordinary court must request and follow the Constitutional Court's determination. The 'court' which can make a request refers to the adjudicator in charge of a case, which could be a single judge or a panel of judges, at all levels of the judicial hierarchy.

A. Initiation of the Review Process: A Two-Track System

An ordinary court adjudicating a case may request a constitutionality review *sua sponte* or on motion by a party to the case. The adjudicating court is free to deny the party's motion to request the Constitutional Court's review, and that denial is not appealable. But the party may then directly request the Court's review by filing an 'article 68(2) constitutional complaint'.[26] This means that even though the formal process of 'constitutionality review of statutes' is triggered by ordinary courts, citizens may also trigger a review. Citizens, however, must be a party to a case, and must first make a motion to the adjudicating court for a constitutionality review, which is then denied, before filing the article 68(2) constitutional complaint.

Whoever triggers the review process, the requirements for making the request are the same and the Court adjudicates them in the same manner. However, when a court initiates the process, the case is suspended until the Constitutional Court's determination,[27] whereas, when the party triggers the review, the ordinary court may proceed to a final judgment on the assumption that the statute is constitutional. In the latter scenario, if the statute is declared unconstitutional after final judgment, the party's only recourse is to seek a retrial. The difference stems from the system's higher regard for the ordinary court's professional assessment of constitutionality and the need for minimising abuse of the review system by discontented private individuals.[28]

---

[26] CCA, art 68(2).
[27] CCA, art 42(1).
[28] Cheon K-S, *Hanguk Hŏnpŏpnon* [*Korean Constitutional Law*] (Chiphyŏnje, 2016) 867.

Allowing parties to file a constitutional complaint to trigger the Court's review of a statute's constitutionality is an innovation unique to the Korean system. This means that in Korea there are two types of constitutional complaints. One, just mentioned, is for requesting a review of a statute's constitutionality. The other, explained below, is the 'article 68(1) constitutional complaint' which is for redressing public authorities' violation of individuals' constitutional rights.

B. Review of Statutes Only

The Court's review is only for concrete cases where a statute's constitutionality will determine the case's outcome. Thus, abstract or *a priori* review is not part of the Korean system. The Court may review 'legislative acts' which means statutes passed by the National Assembly. Articles of the constitution are not reviewable by the Court. According to the Constitutional Court, all articles of the Korean constitution are of equal status, so one article cannot be reviewed in light of another.[29] While it may seem obvious that a constitutional provision cannot be ruled unconstitutional, the issue was actually litigated at the Court. The claim involved article 29(2), which precludes members of the military and police who sustain damages during combat duties or drills from filing a tort claim against the state, if they are entitled to statutory compensation. This essentially carves out an exception to article 29(1), which guarantees all citizens the right to file a tort claim against the state for damages sustained from public officials' unlawful acts. The exception has been part of constitutional text since the 1972 *Yushin* Constitution. The year before, an almost identical provision in the State Tort Claims Act was held unconstitutional by the Supreme Court, which then had the power of judicial review.[30] That law had been enacted in 1967 due to government concerns that increased state tort claims by service members injured in the Vietnam War might deplete the National Treasury. The Supreme Court's decision reportedly provoked the wrath of President Park Chung-hee, who responded by inserting the same language in the *Yushin* Constitution to preclude any claims of unconstitutionality and then restoring the problematic article to the State Tort Claims Act. Even after the demise of the *Yushin* Constitution, the subsequent

---

[29] Const Ct 95 Hun-Ba 3 (28 Dec 1995); Const Ct 2000 Hun-Ba 38 (22 February 2001).
[30] Sup Ct 70 Da 1010 (22 June 1971).

constitutions of 1980 and 1987 retained the same provision. When injured service members challenged the constitutionality of the statutory and constitutional provisions, the Constitutional Court concluded that the statute was not unconstitutional because the constitution allowed it and a constitutional provision cannot be subject to the Court's review because it is part of the constitution.

C. Division of Labour with the Supreme Court

The Constitutional Court reviews the constitutionality of only statutes legislated by the National Assembly. The constitutionality of other legal norms issued by various state agencies is not within the Court's jurisdiction. When the constitutionality of, say, presidential orders, administrative regulations, and government measures is at issue in a concrete case, the Supreme Court has the final say (art 107(2)). This division of labour between the two courts is apparently intended to allow the Constitutional Court to focus on ensuring the constitutional integrity of the highest legal norms – statutes enacted by the national legislature – while leaving the constitutionality of other types of laws to the Supreme Court. Yet, this arrangement can sometimes cause problems.

To begin with, inconsistency between the two courts' interpretations of the constitution is always possible. Although the two courts review different types of norms in the legal hierarchy, laws are often integrally related. Many administrative regulations are issued under authorisation from a statute enacted by the National Assembly. The Supreme Court might find that a regulation is constitutional in one case, while the Constitutional Court, in a different case, finds unconstitutional the statute that authorised the regulation. Moreover, even if the Supreme Court finds a regulation unconstitutional, it can only withhold the regulation's application to the case at hand, as its decisions are binding only on the parties (*inter partes*). A Constitutional Court determination would be needed to void the regulation for all persons (*erga omnes*). Yet, the two courts' division of labour seems to preclude this pronouncement because the Constitutional Court can only review statutes passed by the National Assembly.

As a partial remedy to this problem, the Constitutional Court has held that it has jurisdiction to review orders and regulations that directly infringe upon an individual's constitutional rights without waiting for their implementation in a specific case. It held, for example, that the complainant's rights were violated by a Supreme Court regulation that delegated to the Minister of National Court Administration unlimited discretion to decide whether to hold examinations for selecting judicial scriveners.[31]

D. Binding Effect of Unconstitutionality Judgments

When the Constitutional Court finds a statute unconstitutional, the judgment is binding on the entire judiciary, other state agencies, and local governments. In principle, a statute held unconstitutional loses effect from the day the decision is announced.[32] However, statutes or statutory provisions relating to criminal punishment lose effect retroactively. A person convicted under a statute later held unconstitutional may request a retrial.

E. Modified Judgments: Tension with the Supreme Court

Sometimes, the Constitutional Court issues a judgment of 'limited unconstitutionality,' which means that the challenged statute or provision is unconstitutional if given a certain interpretation. This takes the form of a declaration that the law 'is unconstitutional insofar as it is interpreted to mean ...'. The Court issues such judgments when the law's text is amenable to a range of interpretations, some of which are unconstitutional. At other times, the Court issues a judgment of 'limited constitutionality' by declaring that the challenged law 'is not unconstitutional insofar as it is interpreted to mean ...'. In such decisions, the Court stipulates the constitutionally acceptable interpretation from a range of possible readings.

The Court issues these modified judgments to surgically remove constitutionally problematic interpretations while respecting the statute's text as enacted by the legislature. These judgments do not bring about any textual change, but from then on, the statute must be interpreted according to the Court's instructions.

An example of a limited unconstitutionality judgment is the Court's decision on the Act on Registration of Periodic Publications, where it held that article 7(1)(ix) of the law is unconstitutional if interpreted to

---

[31] Const Ct 89 Hun-Ma 178 (15 October 1990).
[32] CCA, art 47(1).

mean that, to be registered, a newspaper publisher must own the printing facilities.[33] It reasoned that, since printing facilities can be leased or rented, requiring ownership would result in an undue restriction on freedom of the press. An example of a limited constitutionality judgment is the Court's decision on the National Security Law, where it stated that article 7(5) 'is not unconstitutional insofar as it is interpreted narrowly to mandate punishment for the enumerated activities only in cases when there is a clear danger of substantive harm to the integrity and security of the state or the free democratic basic order'.[34] In this case, the Court held that the crime of 'praising and encouraging' the activities of the North Korean regime is punishable only if they entail a clear threat to national security.

As justification for issuing these modified judgments, the Court cites the need for maintaining coherence and uniformity throughout the legal system, respecting the legislature's choices, and maintaining legal stability. The principle is that a judicial body should, to the extent possible, choose an interpretation congruent with the constitution while respecting and preserving the legislation's textual integrity. This 'presumption of constitutionality' was articulated by the US Supreme Court and taken up by the German Federal Constitutional Court as the principle that statutes must be interpreted in conformity with the constitution. Modified judgments are said to be modelled on the German Court's practice of issuing 'variants' of decisions (*Entscheidungsvarianten*).[35]

Unfortunately, the Korean Supreme Court has not recognised modified judgments of limited constitutionality and limited unconstitutionality. The rationale is that just as the Constitutional Court has exclusive interpretive authority over the constitution, the ordinary courts have exclusive interpretive authority over statutes (and other inferior laws). The Supreme Court points out that modified judgments have no basis in the law, as the Constitutional Court's mandate is limited to deciding 'whether a statute is in violation of the Constitution', not whether a particular statutory interpretation violates the constitution.[36] It also argues that the Constitutional Court's review power is meant to restrain legislative activities, not judicial interpretations. On this view,

---

[33] Const Ct 90 Hun-Ka 23 (26 June 1992).

[34] Const Ct 90 Hun-Ka 11 (25 June 1990).

[35] For the German practice, see W Heun, *The Constitution of Germany: A Contextual Analysis* (Hart Publishing 2011) 177–78.

[36] CCA, art 41(1). On this view, the German model is inapposite because there the varieties of decisions are provided for by law.

these modified judgments merely express the Constitutional Court's opinion on how the challenged statute should be interpreted and do not bind the ordinary courts. Even if the Constitutional Court's interpretation of the statute accords with the constitution, that interpretation is not the constitution which must be followed by ordinary courts. There is no reason to treat the Constitutional Court's interpretation as superior to the Supreme Court's interpretation of the same statute.

As can be expected, this causes confusion and harm to individual citizens. For example, after obtaining a Constitutional Court judgment of limited unconstitutionality regarding a statutory provision that prescribed a penalty or imposed a tax, the litigant might seek a retrial of the original case, which found the person guilty or obligated to pay the tax. The ordinary courts, however, would refuse to recognise the binding force of the Constitutional Court's decision and dismiss the case. This leaves the person without practical redress, despite the Constitutional Court's decision that the statutory provision, as ordinary courts interpret it, is unconstitutional.

Another type of modified judgment is when the Court agrees that a law is unconstitutional but refrains from striking it down immediately because removing the problematic law would leave the legal system without any norm to regulate similar situations. Instead, the Court issues a judgment of 'not in conformity with the constitution' in which it specifies a deadline by which the legislature must cure the constitutional infirmity. The Supreme Court has respected this form of modified judgment as having the same binding effect as judgments of simple unconstitutionality.

V. ADJUDICATION OF CONSTITUTIONAL COMPLAINTS

The Korean system has two types of constitutional complaints. An 'article 68(2) complaint' (discussed above) permits the party in a concrete case before an ordinary court to request the Court's review of a statute's constitutionality. A second procedure, the 'article 68(1) complaint', redresses the violation of a person's constitutional rights. This is intended to provide relief when all other avenues for rectifying the violation of rights have proven ineffectual. The complainant must show an infringement of a specific basic right directly resulting from a public authority's act or omission. If the Constitutional Court affirms the complaint, it can nullify the act that caused the violation or declare unconstitutional the omission that caused it. The Court is not reviewing the constitutionality of a statute but pronouncing a direct violation of specific constitutional rights by state power.

This constitutional complaint is filed to contest the improper 'exercise or non-exercise of public power'.[37] The term 'public power' includes legislative, executive, and judicial powers. Thus, in principle, anyone whose constitutional rights have been violated by an act or omission by the legislative, executive, or judicial branch may file a constitutional complaint. In practice, however, there are significant restrictions on the scope of state acts and omissions that may be challenged via constitutional complaints.

A. Complaints against Judicial Decisions not Allowed

Most importantly, the law explicitly excludes 'adjudications by courts',[38] precluding individuals from filing constitutional complaints to claim that a court decision violated their constitutional rights. The justification is that, if constitutional complaints against court judgments are allowed, the Constitutional Court will become another appeals court, above the Supreme Court. This exemption came about due to the judiciary's strenuous lobbying during the drafting of the Constitutional Court Act. While ready to accept a separate specialised court for constitutional matters, the ordinary courts were not willing to be reviewed by it. This is another feature of the Korean system of constitutional complaints that is different from the German system, its putative model.

This is the background to the Korean 'innovation', mentioned above, of using the constitutional complaint to challenge the constitutionality of statutes in concrete cases (art 68(2) complaint). This innovation effectively provides a limited means to contest the disposition of an ordinary court (ie, a decision not to request the Constitutional Court's review) by enabling the parties to trigger the Court's review directly. While the parties may not contest the ordinary court's final judgment via a constitutional complaint, they can challenge the court's 'intermediate' decision refusing to request a constitutional review. Since ordinary courts' final judgments are exempt from constitutional complaints, challenging the exercise of judicial power via this route is nearly impossible.

---

[37] CCA, art 68(1).
[38] CCA, art 68(1).

Critics point out that the likelihood of the judiciary violating constitutional rights is not necessarily any smaller than executive or legislative violations. Some have challenged the constitutionality of article 68(1) of the Constitutional Court Act, which exempts judicial decisions from constitutional complaints. The Court's response was that it is not unconstitutional given that the National Assembly has broad discretion over how to structure the constitutional complaint system.[39]

The Court, however, has carved out an exception: when an ordinary court applies a law previously held unconstitutional by the Constitutional Court, that judgment can be contested via constitutional complaints. It reasoned that the integrity and coherence of the constitutional order could not be maintained if ordinary courts continued to apply a statute that was declared unconstitutional. In a few cases, it employed this reasoning and cancelled a judgment of the Supreme Court.[40] It thus held that article 68(1) of the Constitutional Court Act is unconstitutional insofar as it is interpreted to mean that constitutional complaints are disallowed against judicial decisions that apply laws previously held unconstitutional by the Court. Since this was a 'limited unconstitutionality' decision, however, the Supreme Court refuses to recognise it as binding.

B. Complaints against Legislation and Executive Acts

Legislation can, in theory, be challenged via constitutional complaints. Most legislation, however, do not violate the rights of individuals until implemented and applied to specific cases. If the application of certain legislation in a specific case produces harm to a party, the proper route for relief is to seek a review of the legislation's constitutionality. This means that a constitutional complaint against legislation is extremely rare. The Constitution Court has nonetheless acknowledge the possibility that rights could be violated by legislation before any process of execution by government agency or application by the judiciary.[41] Administrative agencies' rules and regulations are also difficult to challenge via constitutional complaint because, in principle, these administrative norms are

[39] Const Ct 96 Hun-Ma 172 (24 December 1997).
[40] Const Ct 96 Hun-Ma 172 (24 December 1997); Const Ct 2014 Hun-Ma 760 (30 December 2022).
[41] Const Ct 91 Hun-Ma 192 (12 November 1992) (when the mere enactment of a law restricts freedom, imposes duty, or deprives legal status).

only valid internally and not binding on the general public, making it difficult to establish that they directly infringe anyone's rights. Yet, the Court has held that sometimes even an administrative regulation may, in tandem with the statute that authorised its adoption, bind the public and be a proper target of a constitutional complaint if rights violation occurred.[42]

Acts of the executive branch are the most common target of constitutional complaints because more people are at the receiving end of administrative agencies' dispositions and measures. Yet, there is an important limit which stems from the exclusion of judicial decisions mentioned above. In most cases, there is an administrative appeals procedure within the executive branch for contesting administrative dispositions. If relief is not forthcoming, the aggrieved person may file suit in the Administrative Court. If that court denies the claim, no constitutional complaint is permitted because challenging court judgments is not permitted by law. As a result, challenging administrative dispositions through a constitutional complaint, when they can be contested via administrative appeals, is all but impossible.

By law, state inaction or the 'non-exercise of public power' may become the target of constitutional complaints. Omissions by a public authority may be unconstitutional if they result in violating individuals' constitutional rights. Yet, the complainant must show that the public authority did not take any action despite a legal duty to act. In sum, the scope of state actions or inactions that may be challenged by a constitutional complaint is rather narrow.

C. Direct, Personal, and Present Violations

The complainant must show a violation of a specific constitutionally protected right, not merely that an act or omission of public power violated general constitutional principles, such as separation of powers or popular sovereignty. Moreover, the contested act or omission must directly cause the violation of a right belonging to the complainant personally. The violation must also be ongoing when the complaint is filed with the Court. If the infringement has ended and there is no present harm, then the proper route for relief is via state tort claims as provided in article 29 of the constitution.

---

[42] Const Ct 99 Hun-Ma 455 (20 July 2000) (allowing complaints against administrative guideline regulating operating hours of dance clubs).

The Constitutional Court has relaxed these requirements in certain situations. A revision to the criminal law may be challenged via a constitutional complaint prior to any prosecution or conviction under the revised law. The Court reasoned that the revision had effected a change in the rights and duties of individuals and that the 'directness' requirement does not mean that a person must actually be prosecuted under the revised law.[43] Similarly, the requirement that the rights violation be 'present' can be eased if it is fairly certain that the complainant will eventually be sanctioned by the law.[44] The Court has also permitted constitutional complaints against violations that were no longer 'present', if it is highly likely that the same violation will be repeated or resolving the case is of such importance to the preservation of the constitutional order that clarification is necessary.[45]

D. Principle of Subsidiarity

The constitutional complaint is designed to be an individual's last resort for a rights violation. The principle of subsidiarity requires complainants to exhaust all other avenues for relief before filing a complaint, and the Court will dismiss the complaint if another avenue is available under other statutes. The Court has eased this requirement where other avenues for relief were not exhausted through no fault of the complainant or where there was little possibility of obtaining relief through other avenues.[46]

As seen, however, subsidiarity can effectively exempt certain acts of the executive branch from constitutional complaints. The principle requires that the administrative appeals process be exhausted, which includes appealing to the Administrative Court. Yet, the Administrative Court's judgment may not be contested through a constitutional complaint because judicial decisions are exempt from the Constitutional Court's review. The Court has recognised an exception if an administrative disposition was the subject matter of a judicial decision that was cancelled for having applied a statute previously declared unconstitutional by the Court.[47] In that case, a constitutional complaint against the original administrative disposition is allowed.

---

[43] Const Ct 94 Hun-Ma 213 (29 February 1996).
[44] Const Ct 98 Hun-Ma 168 (15 October 1998).
[45] Const Ct 91 Hun-Ma 111 (28 January 1992).
[46] Const Ct 91 Hun-Ma 80 (28 December 1995).
[47] Const Ct 96 Hun-Ma 172 (consolidated) (24 December 1997).

VI. IMPEACHMENT PROCEEDINGS

The Constitutional Court has jurisdiction over impeachment cases. When the National Assembly passes a motion to impeach a public official, the case must be adjudicated by the Court. Unlike other countries where impeachment takes place within the legislature (ie, initiated and prosecuted by the lower house and decided by the upper house), with minimum judicial input, the Korean system takes a more 'judicial approach'. The constitution limits the grounds for impeachment to violations of 'the Constitution and legislative acts' (art 65(1)).

A. 'In the Performance of Official Duties'

According to the constitution, public officials subject to impeachment include 'the President, the Prime Minister, members of the State Council, heads of Administrative Ministries, Justices of the Constitutional Court, judges, members of the National Election Commission, the Chairperson and members of the Board of Audit and Inspection' (art 65(1)). This list is not exhaustive, as the same provision states that 'other public officials designated by legislative act' may be impeached. Public prosecutors and the head of the National Police Agency are examples of public officials who may be impeached according to statutes.[48] To date, the Court has adjudicated four impeachment cases – two against the president, one against a judge, and another against a cabinet minister.

Impeachable offences are limited to those committed in the performance of official duties. The Court has ruled that wrongdoings, however serious, are not impeachable if they occurred prior to the commencement of the official's term of office. It thus declined to consider the National Assembly's charge that Roh Moo-hyun had engaged in corruption before becoming president.

B. Legal Offence of Sufficient Gravity

Given that the constitution specifically states that officials may be impeached when they have 'violated the Constitution or legislative enactments', the Constitutional Court has emphasised that impeachment

---

[48] Prosecutors' Office Act, art 37 (Law No 9815, 2 November 2009); Police Act, art 11(6) (Law No 10745, 30 May 2011).

proceedings require legal decisions, and no political consideration should be involved in the decision.[49] Mere mismanagement of state affairs or pursuing misguided policies cannot be bases for impeachment. Further, the Court has stated that despite the wording of this clause, not all infractions of the constitution or statutes are impeachable offences. Only those violations that are 'grave enough' from the constitutional standpoint deserve the extreme and unappealable judgment of dismissal from office.[50] This is particularly so in the case of presidential impeachments because the Court must respect the president's democratic mandate, which comes from the people through a direct nationwide election. The president's legal offence must be sufficiently grave to merit the Court's nullification of the people's electoral choice.

The Court announced what appears to be a 'balancing test' to determine when an offence is grave enough to merit dismissal. In the 2004 presidential impeachment case against Roh Moo-hyun, the Court stated that the decision must be based on a comparison of the offence's harm to the constitutional order with the national loss likely to arise from dismissing a democratically elected president. This was repeated almost verbatim in 2017 when the Court decided the impeachment of Park Geun-hye: the benefit from the president's dismissal should overwhelmingly outweigh the societal cost occasioned by such an extraordinary measure.[51]

In the 2004 decision, the Court also stated that, since impeachment is a means to protect the constitutional order, dismissal would be justified when necessary to safeguard the constitution and repair the damaged constitutional order. The Court explained that 'constitutional order' refers to the 'free democratic basic order' of the constitution, which has two components – the principle of the rule of law and the principle of democracy. It further specified that elements of 'rule of law' include the protection of basic human rights, separation of powers, and judicial independence, whereas 'democracy' consists of parliamentary representation, a multi-party system, and electoral institutions.

The Court has stated that, considering that the president's democratic legitimacy comes directly from the people, dismissal would be warranted when the president, by committing the alleged wrongdoings, has betrayed the people's trust. According to the Court, examples of

---

[49] Const Ct 2004 Hun-Na 1 (14 May 2004).

[50] On whether the Court really adhered to this position, see Y Lee, 'Law, Politics, and Impeachment: The Impeachment of Roh Moo-hyun from a Comparative Constitutional Perspective' (2005) 53 *American Journal of Comparative Law* 403.

[51] Const Ct 2016 Hun-Na 1 (10 March 2017).

betrayal of trust might include abuse of power to engage in bribery and other forms of corruption, acts that clearly harm the national interest, encroaching upon the powers of the legislature and other state agencies, using state power to persecute citizens, and actively seeking to manipulate election results. If the president is found to have engaged in any such acts, the Court reasoned that it is difficult to expect that the president would protect the free democratic basic order or faithfully execute the duties of that office.

Having laid out these standards, the Court in 2004 found that Roh Moo-hyun had violated the constitution and laws on three counts: failing to remain neutral in relation to a general election; defying the National Election Commission's ruling admonishing him to maintain neutrality; and promising to hold a confidence referendum contrary to the constitution's requirements. In the end, however, it held that these were not a grave enough threat to the constitutional order and reinstated him to the presidency.[52]

By contrast, in 2017, the Court concluded that Park Geun-hye had betrayed the people's trust by, *inter alia*, abusing her powers to enrich a personal friend; allowing this friend to influence state affairs; coercing corporations to donate funds to establish foundations for the friend's benefit; and attempting to deny and cover up these acts when questioned by the legislature and media. It indicated that Park's apologies to the nation were insincere, and she failed to follow through with her promise to cooperate with the prosecutor's investigation. Declaring that 'no clear will to uphold the Constitution can be discerned' on the president's part, the Court concluded that her violations of the constitution and laws were a betrayal of the people's trust, which must be deemed a grave legal violation that cannot be tolerated if the constitution is to be safeguarded.[53]

C. Effect of the Court's Decision

If the Constitutional Court finds that the impeached official has committed a sufficiently grave constitutional offence, the only sanction it can prescribe is removal from office (art 65(4)). When the impeached official is no longer in office, the Court must dismiss the case. In a case where

---

[52] Const Ct 2004 Hun-Na 1 (14 May 2004).

[53] For critical analysis, see C Hahm, 'Constitutional Court of Korea: Guardian of the Constitution or Mouthpiece of the Government?' in A HY Chen and A Harding (eds), *Constitutional Courts in Asia: A Comparative Perspective* (Cambridge University Press 2018) 158–63.

the National Assembly's motion for impeachment was filed just before the expiration of a judge's term of office, the Court dismissed the case because by the time oral arguments were heard the impeached judge had already retired. In effect, the case was moot because, even if the charges could be substantiated, the judge could not be dismissed.[54]

Upon removal from office by the Constitutional Court, the official may face criminal prosecution or civil lawsuits, but ordinary courts would decide these. The dismissed official is statutorily barred from becoming a public official for five years.[55]

VII. DISSOLUTION OF UNCONSTITUTIONAL POLITICAL PARTIES

The Constitutional Court makes the final decision, upon the government's request, on whether to disband a political party. The constitution provides political parties special protection as the primary means for formulating the people's political will. The same constitutional article provides a process for forcefully dissolving political parties if their goals and activities are inconsistent with the constitution's fundamental principles (art 8(4)). While the state may abuse this process to oppress dissidents, it is intended to provide a measure of protection for political parties by requiring Constitutional Court approval rather than merely an order from the president or other administrative measures. The process was first introduced via the 1960 constitutional revision and has been a part of Korea's constitutional order ever since.

According to the constitution, only the executive branch may initiate the process. Private citizens may not request that the Constitutional Court adjudicate the constitutionality of a political party. To date, the Court has adjudicated only one case on a political party's constitutionality – the Unified Progressive Party (UPP) case.[56]

A. Grounds for Dissolution

The standard for dissolving a political party is when its 'goals or activities are contrary to the democratic basic order' (art 8(4)). The Constitutional

---

[54] Const Ct 2021 Hun-Na 1 (28 October 2021).
[55] CCA, art 54(2).
[56] Const Ct 2013 Hun-Da 1 (19 December 2014). For more on this case, see ch 3.

Court has characterised this as an instantiation of 'militant democracy' (*streitbare Demokratie*), which seeks to protect democracy from forces intent on destroying it.[57] In the UPP case, the Court interpreted 'democratic basic order' as a political order 'premised on a pluralistic worldview which presumes that all political viewpoints have relative truth-value and degrees of reasonableness' and which rejects all forms of violent and arbitrary rule, operates on the principles of democratic decision-making and freedom and equality, and respects the majority while being solicitous of the minority.[58]

It concluded that a party following the ideology of the North Korean regime as absolute truth is inconsistent with the pluralism and value relativism that underly South Korea's constitutional democracy. The Court pointed out that the concrete meaning of 'democratic basic order' must be understood in light of the specific circumstances of Korea's constitutional order and geopolitical situation. Abstract theorising about democracy will not do; the security threat faced by the South Korean state must be considered. It concluded that the UPP's goals and activities were geared toward rejecting not only democracy's basic principles, such as parliamentary procedures, rule of law, and the electoral system, but the Republic of Korea's very existence.

Given that dissolving a political party seriously restricts citizens' political rights, it must be a last resort. In the UPP case, the Court stated that dissolution must satisfy the principle of proportionality. Disbanding a party is allowed only when the benefit from dissolution (ie, preservation of the values of the democratic basic order, such as popular sovereignty, fundamental rights, multi-party system, and separation of powers) is greater than the cost of restricting the freedom of political parties and there are no other less intrusive means.

B. Effects of the Court's Decision

Dissolution of a political party is effective upon announcement of the Constitutional Court's ruling.[59] Any property held by the dissolved party shall be escheated to the National Treasury.[60] Establishing a new

---

[57] Const Ct 99 Hun-Ma 135 (23 December 1999).
[58] Const Ct 2013 Hun-Da 1 (19 December 2014).
[59] CCA, art 59.
[60] Political Parties Act, art 48(2) (Law No 15750, 14 August 2018).

political party with the same platform as the dissolved party or creating another party with the same name is prohibited by law.[61] However, the constitution and statutes are unclear on whether lawmakers, who are members of the dissolved party, retain their seats in the legislature. In the UPP case, the Court offered its clarification, ruling that party members shall be stripped of their National Assembly seats. Otherwise, the Court reasoned, the goal of protecting the democratic basic order would not be fully realised because former party members could pursue the same unconstitutional political goals and activities in the National Assembly.[62]

VIII. ADJUDICATION OF COMPETENCE DISPUTES

Competence disputes are a constitutional adjudication designed to settle jurisdictional disagreements among public authorities. The disagreement is typically over whether a certain state agency or local government has a specific power (or 'competence') under the constitution or statutes and whether another state agency or local government has improperly encroached upon this competence. By adjudicating such disputes, the Constitutional Court clarifies the jurisdictional boundaries of public authorities and maintains the proper relationship among them.

The constitution specifies three types of competence disputes: (i) between state agencies; (ii) between a state agency and local government; and (iii) between local governments (art 111(1) item 4). According to statute, 'state agencies' include the National Assembly, the Government, the courts, and the National Election Commission. 'Local governments' include various types of cities, provinces, and counties (*gu*).[63]

Any of these entities may request the Constitutional Court's adjudication when one of its constitutionally or statutorily granted competences has been infringed by another public authority's act or omission, or when there is an imminent danger of infringement.[64] If the Court finds that an infringement has occurred, it may cancel or nullify the infringing act. If the infringement occurred due to an omission,

---

[61] Political Parties Act, arts 40 and 41(2).

[62] For a critical view of this decision, see J Kim, 'Dissolution of the Unified Progressive Party Case in Korea: A Critical Review with Reference to the European Court of Human Rights Case Law' (2017) 10 *Journal of East Asia and International Law* 139.

[63] CCA, art 62(1).

[64] CCA, art 61(2).

despite a legal duty to act, the Court may order the infringing party to take the required action.[65]

The Constitutional Court initially read the statutory enumeration of state agencies and local governments as exhaustive and ruled that other entities not listed in the law were not eligible to initiate a competence dispute. In particular, public offices constituting a subpart of state agencies, such as individual members of the National Assembly, were deemed ineligible to file a competence dispute. It thus held that a dispute between the Speaker of the National Assembly and other Assembly members was an internal dispute within a 'state agency' and not the subject matter of a competence dispute.[66] The Court later changed its position to recognise the eligibility of unlisted public offices if they were created by the constitution and granted an independent competence that could be exercised autonomously. According to this view, National Assembly members may file a competence dispute against the Speaker on the grounds that the latter's disposition has infringed their rights as independent state agencies. For example, in a few cases, the Court upheld the claims of opposition lawmakers who argued that their rights to deliberate and vote on legislative bills were infringed upon by the Speaker's announcement that the bills had passed. Opposition members filed these disputes after discovering that the ruling party had surreptitiously and hastily passed bills at irregular sessions (eg, in the middle of the night or at a location other than the main hall of the National Assembly building). The Court agreed that these tactics violated the rights of the opposition lawmakers as independent state agencies – a legislative 'railroading'.[67]

Although National Assembly members are now considered a 'state agency', they still may not act on behalf of the entire National Assembly in a competence dispute with the president. When the government in 2005 entered into an international agreement without National Assembly consent, several opposition lawmakers filed a competence dispute claiming that the Assembly's right to consent had been violated. The Court ruled that, although the National Assembly has the standing to contest the government's action, individual lawmakers cannot act as a 'third party litigant' on behalf of the entire Assembly.[68]

---

[65] CCA, art 66(2).

[66] Const Ct 90 Hun-Ra 11 (29 April 1995).

[67] Const Ct 96 Hun-Ra 2 (16 July 1997); Const Ct 99 Hun-Ra 1 (24 February 2000); Const Ct 2009 Hun-Ra 8 (consolidated) (29 October 2009). The Court, however, did not declare invalid the laws adopted through these tactics. For more on these decisions and on the 2012 revision to the National Assembly Act designed to prevent legislative railroading, see ch 5.

[68] Const Ct 2005 Hun-Ra 8 (26 July 2007).

Regarding a local government's eligibility to file competence disputes, the Constitutional Court has distinguished between competencies relating to self-government and those delegated by a state agency. A local government cannot claim infringement of a power delegated by the central government. The power to approve a project for urban planning, for example, is a competence belonging to the Minister of Construction and Transportation, though delegated to city mayors and county heads. Thus, a city or county government may not file a competence dispute claiming that another public authority has violated this power.[69]

Disputes between subparts ('organs') of local governments (eg, between the governor and legislature of the same province) are not the subject matter of competence disputes. They are instead heard by the Supreme Court as 'agency suits' regulated under the Administrative Litigation Act.[70]

IX. CONCLUSION

The Constitutional Court has no discretion in choosing which cases to decide. Its caseload has steadily grown over the years, and since 2017, the Court has received around 2,700 cases every year. Of these, constitutional complaints seeking redress for rights violation (art 68(1) complaints) account for roughly 75 per cent and constitutionality review of statutes initiated by parties (art 68(2) complaints) for roughly 22 per cent. The number of constitutionality reviews sought by the adjudicating courts has ranged from 20 to 40 each year, while competence disputes almost always have remained in the single digits. So, about three-quarters of the cases are filed by private citizens claiming that state power has violated their rights. About two-thirds of these are dismissed for lack of standing and other procedural defects. They are typically disposed of at a preliminary review by a panel of three justices.[71]

Nevertheless, the Court has become an extremely busy institution due to its popular reputation as one of the more trustworthy government institutions. This perception was aided by some of its earlier decisions regarded as facilitating Korea's democratic transition. There

---

[69] Const Ct 98 Hun-Ra 4 (22 July 1999).
[70] The Supreme Court has original jurisdiction over such disputes. Local Autonomy Act, art 107(3) (Law No 16057, 24 December 2018).
[71] CCA, art 72.

is no question that the Court has contributed to turning the constitution from mere parchment into a living norm. At the same time, its ongoing rivalry with the Supreme Court has revealed that the Constitutional Court is also an 'interested' institution. Its more recent rulings on politically charged issues, such as impeachment and dissolution of a political party, as well as the justices' confirmation hearings, have made clear that the Court is not immune from the larger society's increasing polarisation and that it can be swayed by political pressure and public opinion. How it deals with these challenges will determine whether it will be regarded as the constitution's guardian or just another political actor pursuing self-interest.

FURTHER READING

Chon J, 'The Effect of Constitutional Adjudication on the Judicial Branch: The Relationship between the Constitutional Court and the Ordinary Court' in J-R Yeh (ed), *The Functional Transformation of Courts: Taiwan and Korea in Comparison* (V&R Academic 2015).

Hahm C, 'Beyond "Law vs. Politics" in Constitutional Adjudication: Lessons from South Korea' (2012) 10 *International Journal of Constitutional Law* 6.

Hahm C, 'Constitutional Court of Korea: Guardian of the Constitution or Mouthpiece of the Government?' in A HY Chen and A Harding (eds), *Constitutional Courts in Asia: A Comparative Perspective* (Cambridge University Press 2018).

Hahm C and Kim SH, 'Constitutionalism on Trial in South Korea' (2005) 16 *Journal of Democracy* 28.

Hong JS, 'Signaling the Turn: The Supermajority Requirement and Judicial Power on the Constitutional Court of Korea' (2019) 67 *American Journal of Comparative Law* 177.

Kim J, 'Dissolution of the Unified Progressive Party Case in Korea: A Critical Review with Reference to the European Court of Human Rights Case Law' (2017) 10 *Journal of East Asia and International Law* 139.

Kim S, 'From Remonstrance to Impeachment: A Curious Case of "Confucian Constitutionalism" in South Korea' (2019) 44 *Law & Social Inquiry* 586.

Lee K-K, 'The Past and Future of Constitutional Adjudication in Korea' in L Mayali and J Yoo (eds), *Current Issues in Korean Law* (The Robbins Collection 2014).

Lee Y, 'Law, Politics, and Impeachment: The Impeachment of Roh Moo-Hyun from a Comparative Constitutional Perspective' (2005) 53 *American Journal of Comparative Law* 403.

Rhee W-Y, 'Decision of the Korean Constitutional Court of Nonconformity of Statute with the Constitution and the Subsequent National Assembly Legislative Process in Korea's Constitutional Democracy' (2021) 20 *Journal of Korean Law* 1.

Yang K, 'In the Name of Constitutional Law: Reflections on Recent Korean Constitutional Adjudication with Special Reference to President Park' (2019) 49 *Hong Kong Law Journal* 979.

8

Expansion of Constitutional Rights

Traditional Aversion to Rights Claims – Anti-Communism and Bifurcation of Rights Discourse – Dignity and Worth as Human Beings – Proportionality Principle – Essential Core of Basic Rights – Diversity and Rights Protection – International Human Rights Norms in Korean Context

IMMEDIATELY FOLLOWING ITS General Provisions chapter, the Korean constitution features a comprehensive catalogue of basic rights – the 'Rights and Duties of Citizens'. Having a bill of rights, of course, is different from actual enjoyment of those rights. For most of Korea's modern history, authoritarian rulers focused on economic development while largely regarding the constitution's rights provisions as decorative. Various international human rights organisations regularly listed Korea among states with poor human rights records. Some human rights activists still reproach the country for prioritising efficiency over individual rights. For example, at the beginning of the 2020 Covid-19 pandemic, the government's zeal to trace and stem the virus' spread was faulted for insensitivity to citizens' privacy rights. Overall, however, the situation has improved dramatically since the democratic transition in 1987, and the Constitutional Court has often provided an important venue for contesting and correcting rights violations. Korea has come a long way since the late nineteenth century when a handful of intellectuals introduced the concept of individual rights to modernise the country. This chapter will start with a brief review of the history of rights discourse in Korea and then examine the Constitutional Court's invocation of the ideal of human dignity and the proportionality principle as a means for protecting basic rights. It will then note some recent developments which reflect the increasing diversity in contemporary Korean society, as well as the relevance of international human rights norms for the domestic rights discourse.

I. RIGHTS DURING DYNASTIC AND COLONIAL PERIODS

According to some scholars, Koreans had no conception of rights before the end of the nineteenth century. Having adopted Confucianism as state teaching during the dynastic period, Korea's political and ethical discourse emphasised a person's duty toward family and community. Claiming something for oneself was thus deemed selfish and unseemly. Individuals had entitlements specific to their status and rank, but these were never articulated as legally enforceable rights.[1] Even when the language of rights was introduced at the end of the nineteenth century, it is not clear that the dimension of individual claims was fully appreciated. Early attempts to translate the concept of rights using Confucian terms tended to highlight the concept's relation to 'objective' justice or the ruler's righteousness rather than its 'subjective' dimension of enforcing individuals' claims.[2] On this view, advocates of rights were intent not so much on underscoring the individual's inviolability as safeguarding the state against outside enemies. Emphasising 'people's rights' was considered a means to make the state more responsive to public demands, which would in turn better equip the state to resist foreign aggression.[3] This was a common feature of East Asian rights discourse during the late nineteenth and early twentieth centuries when intellectuals from China, Japan, and Korea were more concerned about Western imperialism, though to different degrees. The language of rights was a tool for buttressing national sovereignty.

Korea did not realise this goal because it became a colony of Japan in 1910. Not surprisingly, protection of Koreans' rights was not a priority for the colonial government. Although Koreans were formally subjects of the Japanese emperor, the colonial legal system ensured that their rights were inferior to those of Japanese in the main islands. The constitution of the Japanese Empire and other laws that specified individual rights were not enforced in Korea. Koreans enjoyed practically no political rights as they could not participate in parliamentary elections held in

---

[1] One scholar has called pre-modern Korea a society that offered 'remedies without rights'. W Shaw, 'Korea before Rights' in W Shaw (ed), *Human Rights in Korea* (Harvard Council on East Asian Studies 1991).

[2] Y-H Chung, 'Confucianism and Human Rights: The Reception of the Concept of People's Rights During the Enlightenment Period in Korea' (2000) 27 *Korean Social Science Journal* 1.

[3] V Chandra, 'Korean Human-Rights Consciousness in an Era of Transition: A Survey of Late-Nineteenth-Century Developments' in W Shaw (ed), *Human Rights in Korea* (Harvard Council on East Asian Studies 1991).

Japan proper. No representative assembly was established in Korea for its residents. Civic rights, including freedom of speech, assembly, and the press, were severely curtailed under codes such as the Newspaper Law, the Publication Law, and the Security Preservation Law.

Outside Korea, independence fighters created the Provisional Government of the Republic of Korea in Shanghai, which adopted the Provisional Charter of 1919. This document exhibited an embryonic understanding that a constitution's purpose was to guarantee individual rights. Yet, as a congregation of activists and intellectuals in exile, the provisional government could not meaningfully protect the rights of those residing in Korea. Even the skeletal rights provisions in the KPG constitution were dropped in later revisions, to be restored only in 1944 as preparations for state building began with Japan's impending defeat.

When liberation came in August 1945 after Japan's surrender to the Allied Powers, Korea was placed under the control of the United States and Soviet Union. American authorities in the southern part, which became the Republic of Korea, proclaimed that the occupation's purpose was, in part, to protect the Korean people's 'personal and religious rights' and promised that their 'property rights will be respected'.[4] The US military government in 1946 created a legislative body that gave Koreans a partial political voice, with half of the members elected indirectly.[5] In April 1948, the US commanding officer issued a 'Proclamation on the Rights of the Korean People' in preparation for the nation's first general election the following month. This was effectively the first bill of rights with the force of law in Korea, in contrast to the constitutions of the provisional government.

II. ANTI-COMMUNISM AND RIGHTS DISCOURSE

On 10 May 1948, Korean citizens exercised their right to vote and elected their political representatives. Universal franchise was practised for the first time in the nation's history. The 95.5 per cent turnout of eligible electors demonstrated the people's appreciation of the event's historic significance. This founding election established the National Assembly, which adopted the Founding Constitution that included an extensive bill of rights.

---

[4] Proclamation No 1 by General of the Army Douglas MacArthur (7 September 1945).
[5] C Hahm and SH Kim, *Making We the People: Democratic Constitutional Founding in Postwar Japan and South Korea* (Cambridge University Press 2015) 253–54.

A written constitution with a bill of rights, however, does not directly translate into implementation. The outbreak of the Korean War in 1950, less than two years after the Republic's founding, meant that the individual's right to survival and national security would be prioritised over all other rights. Even before the war, the new republic was racked with violence and lawlessness caused by communist insurgents. Under siege practically from the minute it was born, the Republic enacted the National Security Law in November 1948 to address these threats.

A. Anti-Communism as Official State Ideology

When the war ended in July 1953, the border between North and South Koreas remained essentially where it was when the war began. The Republic of Korea survived the war, aided by the United Nations' military intervention, but with approximately three million dead and the entire country in ruins, the state's foremost goal was preventing mass starvation. A liberal society, respecting civil and political rights, seemed a luxury to the ruling elite, whose immediate concerns were protecting the country from another communist invasion and reconstructing the economic infrastructure. Thus began a long period where fierce anti-communism and state-led economic development defined every aspect of South Korean society.

In this context, individual rights suffered from what may now seem a paranoic obsession with ferreting out North Korean infiltration or anyone sympathetic to that communist regime. President Syngman Rhee (1948–1960) regarded the North as a mortal enemy, and he promoted 'northward unification' as South Korea's mission. Following his resignation, the Chang Myŏn administration of the Second Republic (1960–1961) drafted the Anti-Communism Act, but decided to shelve it due to political opposition. The bill was promptly passed after Park Chung-hee came to power in 1961. Park's government cited, as justification for the military coup, the society-wide chaos stoked by leftist politicians and student groups in the wake of Rhee's resignation. It made 'anti-communism' the first principle of the South Korean state and called on the public to build a nation strong enough to prevail in the competition with the communist North.[6]

---

[6] The first item of the six 'Revolutionary Pledges' announced by the military leaders promised to redouble the government's dedication to anti-communism.

Elevation of anti-communism as state ideology entailed a significant restriction of political and civil rights. The study of Marxist and socialist philosophies was banned even for purely academic purposes. Anyone suspected of colluding or sympathising with North Korea was swiftly prosecuted and punished. Restriction of rights became more severe in 1972 with the adoption of the *Yushin* Constitution. The National Security Law and presidential emergency decrees were often invoked to curb any criticism of the government. Criticising the *Yushin* Constitution or calling for constitutional reform became a crime. Violations of emergency decrees were tried by military courts. Student demonstrations and assemblies were banned, as were boycotts of classes or exams. One emergency decree prohibited 'rumourmongering and spreading distorted facts', banned any criticism of the Republic of Korea or its constitution, and permitted warrantless searches and arrests of violators. The government justified the *Yushin* system as a 'Korean-style democracy', which demanded political stability under strong presidential leadership during the period of state-building.[7]

Under President Chun Doo-hwan, who came to power in a coup d'état after Park's death in 1979, the constitution was revised in 1980 to limit the president's power to issue emergency decrees, but the National Security Law continued to be used to suppress pro-North student activists and other opposition groups. Chun justified his coup as necessary for fortifying national security and safeguarding the state from possible North Korean aggression. While the government no longer touted the *Yushin* era notion of 'Korean-style democracy', it continued to promote 'indigenisation of democracy' as one of its missions, implying that 'Western-style' democracy was unsuitable for Korea.

B. Bifurcation of Rights Discourse

The authoritarian governments' promotion of anti-communist ideology, while understandable, has had an unfortunate effect on South Korean rights discourse. At the time, government critics could claim to be fighting for democracy and individual rights, and attorneys defending political dissidents were known as 'human rights' lawyers, creating an almost

---

[7] YJ Kim, 'Park Chung Hee's Governing Ideas: Impact on National Consciousness and Identity' in H-A Kim and CW Sorensen (eds), *Reassessing the Park Chung Hee Era, 1961–1979: Development, Political Thought, Democracy, and Cultural Influence* (University of Washington Press 2011) 100–03.

subversive connotation for that term. Since many dissidents were cast, rightly or wrongly, as North Korean sympathisers, favouring democracy and human rights has ironically become linked with a friendly stance toward the totalitarian regime in the North. Many student activists during the 1980s did study the thoughts of Kim Il-sung, the North's first president, and routinely invoked the North's argument that South Korea was run by 'comprador capitalists' serving Western imperial interests. Some activists took instructions from North Korean authorities. Since the democratic transition in 1987, these former student activists have been honoured for fighting the authoritarian governments and are now considered to have played an important role in bringing democracy to South Korea. For many leaders of the 'democracy movement' who later entered politics, their imprisonment for violating the National Security Law is a badge of honour. By contrast, critics of the North's human rights record or its belligerent attitude toward the South are often cast as being beholden to a 'Cold War mentality'. As a result, in the current political terrain, curiously enough, a 'pro-North' stance is associated with peace and democracy, while a hawkish view toward the North is associated with authoritarianism and the developmental state.

This resulted in an interesting 'division of labour' among Korean advocacy groups. Groups that criticise human rights abuses by North Korea are faulted for undermining the peace process and neglecting rights violations within South Korea, whereas those that focus on the rights of the disadvantaged and underprivileged in South Korea are often criticised for turning a blind eye to the plight of their northern brethren.[8] This politicised division of labour is unfortunate; not only do human rights protections suffer, but neither side seems to exhibit a robust commitment to the sanctity of the individual per se. Pro-North 'progressives' may favour peace and reconciliation, but their politics overridingly value the Korean ethnic nation or, more precisely, national unification via reconciliation of the two Koreas. Anti-North 'conservatives', by contrast, claim to value political and economic freedom, but their basic orientation may be more about safeguarding the state than the individual. Thus, Korean rights discourse has long been marked by the opposition between nationalists and statists, leaving little room for a truly liberal perspective that values the individual's rights and autonomy. This landscape may be changing due to the recent proliferation of groups demanding enhanced rights protection. With increasing calls for protecting the rights of the

---

[8] Y-h Kim, *Quest for Freedom: Struggling for a Democratic North Korea* (J Cha and P Ward trs, BookBaby 2018).

disabled, women, foreign workers, sexual minorities, and other traditionally marginalised individuals, the recent discursive terrain appears more focused on specific individuals in diverse circumstances.

III. HUMAN DIGNITY AND UNENUMERATED RIGHTS

The bill of rights chapter of the Korean constitution is bookended by a proclamation that every citizen is endowed with 'human dignity and worth' and the 'right to pursue happiness' (art 10) and a statement that the enumerated rights are not exhaustive (art 37(1)). These two provisions have served as basis for recognising rights with no textual basis. The Constitutional Court has particularly focused on the human dignity clause to expand constitutionally protected rights.

Interestingly, Korea's first constitution, adopted in 1948, had no provision on human dignity. The term 'dignity and worth as human beings' first entered the constitution with the 1962 revision. The 1980 revision added a clause guaranteeing everyone's 'right to pursue happiness' and declared it a state duty to guarantee the individual's 'inalienable fundamental human rights'. Despite this relatively late entry into constitutional text, courts and commentators universally regard 'human dignity and worth' as the highest principle of Korea's constitutional order. It is described as the constitution's most fundamental value, the goal at which all other rights provisions are directed, or the guiding principle for implementing other basic rights. Some scholars even claim that the human dignity provision is part of the core commitment of the sovereign people of Korea, which cannot be altered even through amendment.[9]

A. Human Dignity as a Source of Rights

Despite such acclamations, the concrete meaning of 'human dignity and worth' remains the subject of ongoing debate. For some commentators, the concept expresses the constitution's highest 'objective' principle; it should not be understood as the basis for any 'subjective' rights of individuals. Similarly, the 'right' to pursue happiness is merely an ethical desideratum that arises from human dignity rather than a concrete right.[10] Some Constitutional Court decisions likewise refer to the human

---

[9] Han S-W, *Hŏnpŏphak* [*Study of Constitutional Law*] (Pŏpmunsa 2016) 533.
[10] Huh Y, *Hanguk Hŏnpŏpnon* [*Korean Constitutional Law*] (Pakyŏngsa 2021) 351–59.

dignity and worth clause as 'the highest constitutional value'[11] and 'the ultimate goal and fundamental principle of all basic rights protection'.[12] In other decisions, however, the Court has provided a more concrete and expansive reading of the clause by using it as the basis for recognising concrete rights not enumerated in the constitution. The Court has held numerous laws and government actions unconstitutional for violating rights derived from the human dignity and worth clause. What remains unclear is the precise interpretive mechanism for deriving a specific justiciable right from the clause.

In several decisions, the Court appears to follow a two-step process. First, it derives a 'general right to personhood' (*ilbanjŏk inkyŏkkwŏn*) from the human dignity and worth clause and then uses this general right to develop more specific rights. The Court has, for example, taken this route to recognise a 'right of reply' for individuals whose dignity has been harmed by the mass media.[13] Based on the same reasoning, it has recognised the individual's 'right of self-determination regarding the use of personal information'.[14] More recent examples include parents' right to access information regarding the sex of their unborn child,[15] a sperm or ovum donor's right to decide how to dispose of the embryo,[16] and an individual's right not to be photographed without consent.[17]

In other cases, the process appears to be a one-step derivation. The Constitutional Court has declared that certain state actions directly violate a concrete 'right to personhood, which flows from human dignity and worth'. These cases invariably pertain to inhumane or degrading treatment of individuals within the criminal justice system. For example, the Court found that this right was violated when an inmate was forced to wear a prison uniform in a detention centre before an official guilty verdict,[18] to use unsanitary toilets in detention cells with almost no privacy,[19] or to endure excessive and humiliating bodily searches.[20] These decisions suggest that the Court regards such degrading treatments as a more direct affront to human dignity.

---

[11] Const Ct 2013 Hun-Ba 322 (consolidated) (31 May 2018).
[12] Const Ct 2000 Hun-Ma 327 (18 July 2002).
[13] Const Ct 89 Hun-Ma 165 (16 September 1991).
[14] Const Ct 2003 Hun-Ma 282 (consolidated) (21 July 2005).
[15] Const Ct 2004 Hun-Ma 1010 (consolidated) (31 July 2008).
[16] Const Ct 2005 Hun-Ma 346 (27 May 2010).
[17] Const Ct 2012 Hun-Ma 652 (27 March 2014).
[18] Const Ct 97 Hun-Ma 137 (consolidated) (27 May 1999).
[19] Const Ct 2000 Hun-Ma 546 (19 July 2001).
[20] Const Ct 2000 Hun-Ma 327 (18 July 2002).

B. Human Dignity as a Justiciable Right?

The Constitutional Court's eagerness to use article 10's human dignity clause to expand rights is evident from its frequent description of the clause as a provision on the 'individual's right to personhood'. In other words, rather than *deriving* an unenumerated right from the clause, the Court seems to read it as a provision on a concrete, enumerated right – the right to personhood. On this reading, article 10 is no longer a statement of the highest abstract value from which new rights can be inferred but rather an article protecting a concrete right that merely needs more specification for the given context.[21] According to this approach, article 37(1), which proclaims protection for unenumerated rights, need not be invoked when article 10 is at issue because 'human dignity and worth' is just another name for the concrete right to personhood. Some commentators have warned that this approach may create interpretive difficulties for the Court because, once human dignity is regarded as a concrete right, the Court will have to start distinguishing acceptable restraints on human dignity from unacceptable restraints. Also, if article 10 is read as just another rights provision, how will it serve as the guiding principle for implementing other constitutional rights? Nevertheless, the Court has adopted this approach in decisions that recognised the right to choose one's marriage partner[22] and the right to decide on matters regarding pregnancy and childbirth.[23] These rights were specific instances of the right of self-determination which is presumed in individual's concrete right to personhood guaranteed by article 10.

In a few cases, the Court has found a direct violation of article 10 without specifying the violation of any 'right'. It held that the state violated a prison inmate's human dignity and worth by forcing him to wear double steel manacles and a leather manacle for long periods, making it difficult to 'maintain even the minimum level of dignity as a human being'.[24] Similarly, a prisoner's human dignity and worth were violated when forced to share a prison cell so small that an inmate of average height had to sleep on his side to avoid touching other cellmates.[25]

---

[21] The German Basic Law, in addition to the proclamation on the inviolability of human dignity, includes a guarantee of the 'right to the free development of one's *Persönlichkeit*' (art 2(1)). Although the Korean constitution lacks such a provision, Korean jurists have read that right into the human dignity clause.

[22] Const Ct 95 Hun-Ka 6 (consolidated) (16 July 1997).

[23] Const Ct 2010 Hun-Ba 402 (23 August 2012).

[24] Const Ct 2001 Hun-Ma 163 (18 December 2003).

[25] Const Ct 2013 Hun-Ma 142 (29 December 2016).

The Court evidently viewed human dignity and worth not as a source for deriving new rights but as a concrete justiciable norm that individuals can invoke for protection. In the prison cell case, the Court even dispensed with first considering whether other specific rights were violated, which contradicted previous decisions where the Court's subsidiarity approach relied on the human dignity clause only when it could not find a violation of other specific enumerated rights.

C. Limiting Rights with Human Dignity

The Court's expansive reading of the human dignity clause does not always result in new rights or stronger protection of existing rights. Depending on the context, human dignity can be, and has been, cited to restrict rights. Several decisions have invoked the human dignity ideal to reject claims seeking to expand the scope of basic rights. As regards the criminalisation of prostitution, the Court acknowledged that it entails restricting the right to sexual self-determination, privacy rights, and freedom to choose one's profession. Nevertheless, it held that the sale of sex is fundamentally at odds with human dignity, which deserves protection even if such rights are restrained.[26] Similarly, the Court upheld the ban on selling cord blood,[27] despite the attendant restriction on the freedom of contract and right to property. It reasoned that treating this blood as an object of commercial transactions – a mere 'thing' detached from personhood – violates human dignity, and that such restrictions are permissible to protect human dignity.[28]

Both sides invoke human dignity on some issues, such as the death penalty's constitutionality. For abolitionists, capital punishment violates human dignity because the state treats the individual merely as a means to prevent crime. For the Constitutional Court, however, this penalty may be justified in exceptional circumstances where it is 'unavoidable and necessary to protect other lives or other public goods with a value comparable to that of the criminal's life'.[29] One justice posited that, when a person shows no regard for others' lives, taking that person's life might be justified to protect human dignity and uphold the value of human life.[30]

---

[26] Const Ct 2013 Hun-Ka 2 (31 March 2016).

[27] Cord blood, which remains in the placenta and the attached umbilical cord after childbirth, contains stem cells that can be utilised in medical research and life sciences.

[28] Const Ct 2016 Hun-Ba 38 (30 November 2017).

[29] Const Ct 95 Hun-Ba 1 (28 November 1996).

[30] Const Ct 2008 Hun-Ka 23 (25 February 2010) (Justice Song Du-hwan).

For critics, this flexibility shows that the human dignity concept lacks specificity and rigor, so it should not be used in legal discourse to support a particular viewpoint.[31] Nevertheless, the Constitutional Court seems intent on expanding its reliance on human dignity without necessarily clarifying the concept's precise meaning or reconciling its inconsistent use. This phenomenon is partially caused by the indiscriminate invocation of human dignity by countless litigants seeking redress for grievances. After making arguments based on specific constitutional rights, claimants tend to add that, if nothing else, the legislation or other state action violated their human dignity. In many cases, these invocations border on the frivolous, and the Court has tended to dismiss them summarily. Consequently, while the human dignity clause is mentioned in a plethora of cases, the Court's jurisprudence on this foundational concept remains underarticulated.[32]

IV. RESTRAINING BASIC RIGHTS

One implication of the Constitutional Court's death penalty decisions is that no right is absolute under the Korean constitution.[33] For example, even though the Court has characterised the right to life as a 'transcendental and natural-law right', suggesting that no textual basis is needed, the Court found that this right may be restrained according to the constitution's article 37(2) standard for limiting basic rights. This article restricts rights 'only when necessary for national security, the maintenance of law and order, or public welfare'. It is widely agreed that this provision enshrines the proportionality principle even though the word 'proportionality' is not in the text. The Constitutional Court has also suggested that proportionality is an inherent part of the rule of law.[34]

---

[31] SS Lee, 'Hŏnpŏp Chaep'anso Kyŏlchŏngmun ŭl t'onghaesŏ bon In'gan Chonŏm ŭi Ŭimi: Chonŏm Kaenyŏm ŭi Kwayong kwa Namyong [Meaning of Human Dignity as Seen Through the Constitutional Court's Decisions: Overuse and Abuse of Human Dignity Concept]' (2019) 8 *Sŏgang Pŏmnyul Nonch'ong* 111.

[32] C Hahm, 'Constitutional Discourse on Human Dignity in South Korea: A Critical Appraisal' in J C-S Hsu (ed), *Human Dignity in Asia: Dialogue between Law and Culture* (Cambridge University Press 2022) 64–66.

[33] This contrasts with German constitutional law, where the human dignity provision is understood to be both absolute and unamendable.

[34] Const Ct 92 Hun-Ka 17 (27 March 1997). The Court has also applied the proportionality principle in its decisions on presidential impeachment and dissolution of political parties. See ch 7.

A. Proportionality and Arbitrariness Tests

The proportionality test – commonly referred to as the 'prohibition of excessive restriction' – is generally understood as a four-part analysis: (i) the legitimacy of the purpose of the legislation or administrative act that restrains a right; (ii) the suitability of the means chosen by the legislation or administrative act to achieve the said purpose; (iii) a minimum degree of restraint on the right (least restrictive means); and (iv) preponderance of public interest served by restraint over the damage to right-holder's interest (balance of interests). If any part is not met, the restraint on the right is unconstitutional.

In theory, this is a uniform test, with no different 'levels of scrutiny'. In practice, however, the Constitutional Court has applied the test differently depending on the right being restrained, although the exact standard for differentiation is a subject of debate. Generally, the Court tends to review legislation less strictly when it deems that the legislature has broad discretion in setting the rules. In some cases, the Court appears to adopt a 'relaxed' proportionality standard, while in others, it seemingly applies a test resembling the 'rational basis test' used by United States courts.[35] For example, while the Court purported to apply the proportionality test to determine the proper scope for regulating commercial advertisements, it relaxed the 'least restrictiveness' step and advanced a different standard. Since commercial advertisements differ from political and civil speech, the Court only reviewed whether the restraint on speech was 'needed to attain the legislative purpose' rather than whether it was the least restrictive means.[36]

Similarly, the Court has generally taken a deferential approach to reviewing legislation restricting property rights. This approach is partly due to the constitution's specific directive that property rights' substance and limits be determined by legislation (art 23(1)) and that the exercise of property rights be consistent with public welfare (art 23(2)). The Court thus accords the legislature a wide range of discretion and tends to apply a more lenient standard in reviewing restrictions on property rights, especially where the right carries a greater 'social relevance or function' which can justify greater legislative intervention. For example, it applied a relaxed standard to review a law regulating the licence to operate marine passenger transportation services, as this has a greater

---

[35] YJ Shin, 'Proportionality in South Korea: Contextualizing the Cosmopolitan Rights Grammar' in PJ Yap (ed), *Proportionality in Asia* (Cambridge University Press 2020) 88–97.
[36] Const Ct 2003 Hun-Ka 3 (27 October 2005).

'public character' than the basic right to private property.[37] In another case, the Court seemingly dispensed altogether with the four-step analysis and applied a rational basis test to determine whether the legislature arbitrarily specified a short time limit (statute of limitations) for filing a tort claim.[38] It merely compared the public interest served by the time limit with the harm to the right-holder, concluding that there was no imbalance describable as legislative arbitrariness.

The right to equality is another area where the Court might apply a relatively less stringent standard in reviewing legislation. In most cases, it seeks to ensure only that the legislature did not arbitrarily treat persons differently. So, unequal treatment is generally acceptable if the Court can find a rational basis for it. However, the stricter proportionality test must be applied in two types of cases: (i) when the constitution specifically calls for equality; or (ii) when unequal treatment results in a serious restraint on related basic rights.[39] It thus applied the proportionality test to a national exam system for recruiting public servants, which automatically granted extra points to male applicants who had completed military service. The Court pointed out that the constitution explicitly calls for gender equality in the areas of labour and employment (art 32(4)), and that the exam system's unequal treatment seriously restrained women's basic constitutional right to hold public office (art 25).

B. Essential Core of Basic Rights

After declaring that restrictions on rights may be only for 'national security, maintenance of law and order, or public welfare', the constitution further provides that legitimate restrictions based on those grounds may not infringe on the 'essential content' (*bonjilchŏgin naeyong*) of the restricted right (art 37(2)). Another instance of German influence,[40] this clause has been part of the Korean constitution since the 1960 revision.[41] Perhaps this was included to provide stronger protection for basic rights, but its exact meaning and function are somewhat controversial.

[37] Const Ct 2015 Hun-Ma 552 (22 February 2018).
[38] Const Ct 2004 Hun-Ba 90 (26 May 2005).
[39] Const Ct 98 Hun-Ma 363 (23 December 1999).
[40] Article 19(2) of the German Basic Law provides: 'In no case may the essence of a basic right be affected.'
[41] It was deleted in the 1972 *Yushin* Constitution but restored in 1980.

The practical interpretive issue is whether this ban on infringing a right's essential content is in addition to requiring that the legislation pass the proportionality test. Thus, can a law be held unconstitutional for infringing a basic right's essential content, even after it was found that (i) the law's purpose was legitimate, (ii) the means chosen to achieve that purpose were suitable, (iii) there were no less restrictive means, and (iv) the public interest served by the restriction outweighed the damage to the right-holder? Sometimes, the Constitutional Court has separately analysed whether a right's essential content was infringed.[42] In death penalty cases, however, it has rejected arguments that capital punishment infringes the essential content of the right to life. The Court seemed to state that, under exceptional circumstances justified by the proportionality principle, taking a life does not necessarily infringe this right's essential content.[43] The implication is that a separate analysis regarding the right's essential content is unnecessary once the proportionality test is met. In fact, the Court has decided most cases by applying the four-step proportionality analysis without mentioning the ban on infringing essential content.

V. RIGHTS IN A DIVERSE SOCIETY

Until recently, Koreans proudly claimed to be one of the world's most homogeneous nations. There are indeed no official ethnic or linguistic minorities in Korea, and, while regional differences often fuel political animosity, every Korean is considered a member of the same nation. This sense of homogeneity tended to promote uniformity and conformity. In the area of basic rights, recognition of difference was not a priority. This has begun to change.

A. Multiculturalism as Official Identity

Since the 1990s, foreign workers have entered Korea under 'industrial trainee' programmes. In 2004, the government instituted the employment

---

[42] Const Ct 88 Hun-Ka 13 (22 December 1989).
[43] Const Ct 95 Hun-Ba 1 (28 November 1996); Const Ct 2008 Hun-Ka 23 (25 February 2010). The Court also relied on the fact that the constitution contains a provision presuming the constitutionality of capital punishment. Article 110(4) provides that, under extraordinary martial law, military trials may be concluded without the possibility of appeal, except when the defendant has been sentenced to death.

permit system, allowing Korean firms to employ these workers legally, and as of 2021, over 855,000 foreign workers are employed in Korea. More importantly, an increasing number of families consists of marriage between a Korean and a non-Korean immigrant. In 2019, 10 per cent of new marriages were between a Korean and a non-Korean immigrant or naturalised spouse. Since 2014, their children have exceeded 1 per cent of students enrolled in primary and secondary schools. 'Multicultural family' has become part of the legal vocabulary, and a state agency is now devoted to promoting their welfare. The government's official position is that Korea is a multicultural society.

There is growing acceptance of various non-conformist groups that had long been 'invisible' to the majority and the legal system. Advocacy organisations have dramatically increased, and minorities' willingness to bring claims to the Constitutional Court has enhanced their visibility.

B. Military Service, Conscientious Objection and Gender Equality

Military service in Korea has long been a sensitive issue. It is widely considered a burden that should be borne equally, and any suspicion of preferential treatment, especially for members of the society's leadership class, is likely to provoke a vocal outcry. The constitution provides that all citizens have the duty of national defence under conditions prescribed by legislation (art 39(1)). Against that background, arguing for a personal moral or religious exception has been very difficult.

The Constitutional Court has dealt with conscientious objections on four occasions. Each time at issue was the Military Service Act, which requires all male citizens to serve in the military and prescribes punishment (up to three years' imprisonment) for failing to fulfil this duty.[44] In the first three decisions, the Court held that the legislature's failure to provide an alternative service was constitutional.[45] Although the constitution protects freedom of conscience (art 19), this could not be a basis for refusing to fulfil military duties or demanding alternative service. The Court pointed to the Republic of Korea's unique security threat, the difficulty of ascertaining the genuineness of personal convictions, and the risk of exacerbating social dissensus by allowing exceptions for persons

---

[44] Military Service Act, arts 3 and 88 (Law No 19081, 12 December 2022).
[45] Const Ct 2002 Hun-Ka 1 (26 August 2004); Const Ct 2004 Hun-Ba 61 (28 October 2004); Const Ct 2008 Hun-Ka 22 (30 August 2011).

of unusual faith or conviction. It also made clear that the legislature has wide discretion in deciding how citizens specifically discharge this duty, while gently urging it to consider introducing an alternative service.

The Court changed its position in 2018, holding that the failure to offer alternative service for conscientious objectors did not conform with the constitution.[46] Applying the proportionality test, it found that, although the Military Service Act's goal (preparing manpower for national defence) was legitimate, it failed to employ the least restrictive means. It declared that the public interest served by criminalising conscientious objectors did not outweigh the harm to those individuals. The Court reasoned that allowing alternative service was far more socially beneficial than imprisoning objectors and would minimally affect combat readiness. It explained that the government could design an alternative service system that deterred abuse by individuals merely wishing to avoid military duty, and thus avoid criticisms of unfairness.

As a result of this decision, the legislature revised the law, and since 2020, conscientious objectors have worked in corrections facilities instead of undergoing combat training. The service period is 36 months, almost twice the length of regular military duty, which has attracted criticism from groups like the Jehovah's Witness. The legislature apparently thought that a longer service period was needed to prevent abuse and deflect criticism.

Gender equality is another issue related to military service. The Military Service Act requires only males to serve; females can serve voluntarily. The Constitutional Court has held that this does not violate the constitutional guarantee of equality. Applying the arbitrariness test, it reasoned that this dissimilar treatment is not unreasonable discrimination given the genders' physical differences.[47]

C. Regulating Homosexuality

Despite Korea's culturally conservative reputation, its society has recently shown remarkable tolerance, if not acceptance, of alternative gender and sexual identities.[48] This contrasts with politicians' persistent reluctance to advocate the rights of 'sexual minorities' or pass protective legislation. This is partly due to conservative evangelical Protestant opposition, which

---

[46] Const Ct 2011 Hun-Ba 379 (consolidated) (28 June 2018).

[47] Const Ct 2006 Hun-Ma 328 (25 November 2010).

[48] G Youn, 'Attitudinal Changes Toward Homosexuality During the Past Two Decades (1994–2014) in Korea' (2018) 65 *Journal of Homosexuality* 100.

has so far blocked any change toward legal recognition of the LGBT+ community.

Korean law does not recognise same-sex marriage. Municipal offices have routinely rejected same-sex couples' applications to register their marriage on the grounds that 'marriage' is legally defined as a union of man and woman. Lower courts have upheld this exclusion, explaining that including same-sex relationships within the meaning of 'marriage' is beyond acceptable interpretation.[49] This seems consistent with the Supreme Court's position that allowing married persons to change their gender on official identification documents is not permitted because that would effectively recognise same-sex marriage.[50] The Constitution apparently regards marriage as a heterosexual relationship. Article 36(1) states that marriage and family life must be 'entered into and sustained on the basis of ... equality of the two sexes'. The Constitutional Court has consistently defined marriage as a union between a man and a woman.[51] Legislative efforts to recognise a civil union have not gathered much support. Meanwhile, an appellate court has recently ruled that a same-sex partner should be recognised as a 'dependent' for the purposes of national health insurance, even if they are not legally married.[52] Similarly, some private employers have begun providing the same benefits as heterosexual couples.

There is one area where certain homosexual behaviour is criminalised. The Military Criminal Code has provided that 'sodomy and other indecent acts' between military service members shall be punishable by imprisonment of up to two years ('anal sex' replaced 'sodomy' in 2013, but otherwise the provision remains the same).[53] On three occasions, the Constitutional Court has upheld this punishment.[54] It reasoned that the punishment is limited to military members and the public interest in maintaining discipline and combat readiness overrides the right to sexual self-determination and secrecy of private life. As of this writing, other cases are pending at the Constitutional Court. Issues include whether heterosexual anal sex is also prohibited, whether the phrase 'other indecent acts' is too vague, and whether punishment is permissible when there is no coercion.

---

[49] Seoul Western Dist Ct 2014 Ho-pa 1842 (25 May 2016).
[50] Sup Ct 2009 Sŭ 117 (2 September 2011).
[51] Const Ct 2009 Hun-Ba 146 (24 November 2011).
[52] Seoul High Ct 2022 Nu 32797 (21 February 2023).
[53] Military Criminal Code, art 92-6 (Law No 11734, 5 April 2013).
[54] Const Ct 2001 Hun-Ba 70 (27 June 2002); Const Ct 2008 Hun-Ka 21 (31 March 2011); Const Ct 2012 Hun-Ba 258 (28 July 2016).

Meanwhile, the Supreme Court recently seemed to contradict the Constitutional Court's position.[55] Taking a progressive view, the Court overturned the convictions of two male servicemembers who engaged in consensual sex outside the military setting. The Court reasoned that the code does not apply in those circumstances and criminalisation violates servicemembers' constitutional rights to sexual autonomy, non-discrimination, human dignity, and the pursuit of happiness. The Court also noted that homosexual activity no longer arouses shame and revulsion among ordinary people or contravenes sound moral sensibilities regarding sex.

D. Debate Over the Comprehensive Anti-Discrimination Act

One indication that diversity and multiculturalism are, at least rhetorically, replacing ethnic homogeneity as Koreans' self-image might be the Seoul metropolitan government's Student Human Rights Ordinance (2012). Article 5 provides a right to non-discrimination and prohibits discrimination based on, *inter alia*, country of origin, ethnicity, disability, race, skin colour, sexual orientation, and gender identity. Although fiercely opposed by conservative groups, particularly evangelical Protestant churches, the ordinance passed as originally drafted.[56] Previously, the National Human Rights Commission Act (2001) defined a 'discriminatory act violating the right to equality' with a similarly extensive list of prohibited discrimination.[57] However, the Act did not provide substantive rights, and the National Human Rights Commission only has the power to issue advisory opinions (discussed below). Rights activists are thus calling for a national, comprehensive anti-discrimination statute specifying prohibited discriminatory acts and punishments for violations.

The National Human Rights Commission drafted a bill under instructions from President Roh Moo-hyun, whose campaign pledged an anti-discrimination law. The government introduced the first bill in 2007, but conservative Protestant groups and the business community strongly opposed it. Although legislators tried to compromise by removing several prohibited grounds of discrimination, the bill's

[55] Sup Ct 2019 Do 3027 (21 Apr 2022) (full bench).
[56] J Kim and SS Hong, 'Discovering Diversity: The Anti-Discrimination Legislation Movement in South Korea' in CL Arrington and P Goedde (eds), *Rights Claiming in South Korea* (Cambridge University Press 2021) 262.
[57] National Human Rights Commission of Korea Act, art 2 item 3 (Law No 17126, 24 March 2020).

promoters refused to accept the dilution.[58] Ever since, a few lawmakers have proposed different bills, but so far none have been passed, due in part to politicians' reluctance to take on controversial issues. Lack of social consensus is also often cited as the reason for not rushing to enact the law.

Primary opposition continues from conservative Protestant groups, which have recently become quite vocal. They argue that their right to religious freedom will be infringed by a law preventing them from teaching and acting on their beliefs, particularly regarding human sexuality. Although not as vocal, the education and business sectors have expressed concerns about any law banning differential treatment according to 'level of education'. Regarding one proposed bill, the Ministry of Education requested that this item be deleted from the list of prohibited reasons for unequal treatment. For the business community, a mandate to treat alike persons with different educational backgrounds infringes on private enterprises' right to autonomous management. The proposal to ban unequal treatment based on 'forms of employment' has likewise elicited criticism. Critics are particularly concerned that some bills place the burden of proof on the accused violators, requiring them to prove that they did not discriminate. Proposals for punitive damages are also criticised as unfair double punishment.[59]

Whatever anti-discrimination legislation is adopted, it must address these issues. Meanwhile, vocal opposition, particularly from the Protestant churches, has only enhanced the visibility of sexual minorities who have mobilised in response to the opposition. If nothing else, the debate over a comprehensive anti-discrimination law has placed diversity firmly on Korea's social and political agendas.

VI. INTERNATIONAL CONTEXT OF RIGHTS PROTECTION

The Republic of Korea is a state party to most international human rights instruments. While the formal ratification of these treaties does not necessarily indicate a state's commitment to protecting individual rights, Korea's accession to them was motivated at least partly by a desire to be seen as a respectable member of the international community. For

---

[58] Kim and Hong (n 56) 259–60.

[59] Han Y-n, Yi Y-g, and Kim S-h, '23gae Sayu ga Mwŏgillae … Wae Ch'abyŏlkŭmjipŏp e Nara ga Tŭlssŏgina [What Are the 23 Grounds? Why Is the Nation up in Arms over the Anti-Discrimination Act?]' *Chosun Ilbo* (3 July 2021).

example, Korea joined the International Convention on the Elimination of All Forms of Racial Discrimination (CERD) in 1978 during President Park Chung-hee's *Yushin* era when the government hoped to deflect international criticism of the human rights record during Park's 'Korean-style democracy'. Similarly, Korea acceded to the Convention on the Elimination of All Forms of Discrimination against Women (CEDAW) in 1984 under Chun Doo-hwan's presidency when 'creation of an advanced fatherland' (*sŏnjin joguk ch'angjo*) was the government's motto.

After its transition to democracy, Korea has further sought to become a responsible participant in international human rights discourse. In 1990, Korea ratified the International Covenant on Economic, Social, and Cultural Rights (ICESCR) and the International Covenant on Civil and Political Rights (ICCPR), as well as the ICCPR's Optional Protocol, which provides for individual communication to the UN Human Rights Committee. This was followed by the ratification of the Convention on the Rights of the Child (CRC) in 1991 and the Convention Against Torture and Other Cruel, Inhuman or Degrading Treatment or Punishment (CAT) in 1995. Since 2008, Korea has been a state party to the Convention on the Rights of Persons with Disabilities (CRPD).

A. Domestic Relevance of International Human Rights

Regarding implementation of these international human rights instruments, there is some debate over their status within the hierarchy of legal norms and their role in constitutional adjudication. According to Korea's constitutional text, international treaties 'shall have the same effect as the domestic laws of the Republic of Korea' (art 6(2)). The general understanding is that international legal instruments shall be accorded the same level of authority as the National Assembly's legislative enactments.[60] Therefore, international human rights treaties should theoretically have the same force as domestic statutes in Korean courts. While some commentators argue that international human rights norms should be accorded authority equal to the constitution or at least higher than statutes, the Constitutional Court has consistently interpreted 'same effect as the domestic laws' to mean the same force as statutes enacted by the National Assembly.

---

[60] This is particularly true of those treaties that the National Assembly ratified according to article 60(1) of the constitution.

Consequently, the Constitutional Court seldom relies directly on international human rights treaties when concluding that a law or government action violated an individual's rights. When an international human rights norm is mentioned, it is mostly to provide supplementary support for a conclusion that the Court has reached on independent grounds.[61] The debate sometimes revolves around whether a domestic statute that conflicts with an international human rights treaty violates the constitutional principle, embodied in article 6(1), of respecting international law. Individual claimants would argue that a domestic statute, which conflicts with an international instrument's specific human rights provision, necessarily results in an unconstitutional violation of the government's duty to abide by international law. The Court, however, has held that inconsistency between a domestic statute and an international human rights treaty does not *ipso facto* mean that the state is failing to uphold its duties under international law.[62] The Court has more often referred to international human rights treaties to support its conclusion that the limitation of rights under domestic law is consistent with international human rights standards. Some recent decisions suggest the Court's willingness to engage more deeply with international human rights norms, as it invoked not merely the textual provisions of international instruments but also various textual interpretations by treaty bodies and international courts. The Court, however, has yet to directly cite international human rights law when striking down a statute.[63]

B. National Human Rights Commission

International influence on Korean human rights practice may be more visible outside the courts. In 2001, the National Human Rights Commission was created in accordance with the Paris Principles adopted by the UN General Assembly in 1993 and the recommendation of the

[61] Y Won, 'The Role of International Human Rights Law in South Korean Constitutional Court Practice: An Empirical Study of Decisions from 1988 to 2015' (2018) 16 *International Journal of Constitutional Law* 596.

[62] Chon J, 'Hŏnpŏp Chaep'anso ŭi Kukche Inkwŏn Choyak Chŏkyong [Application of International Human Rights Treaties by the Constitutional Court]' (2019) 170-2 *Chŏsŭt'isŭ* [Justice] 507.

[63] Won Y, 'Hŏnpŏp Chaep'anso Wihŏn Kyŏlchŏng kwa Kukche Inkwŏnpŏp [Unconstitutionality Rulings by the Constitutional Court and International Human Rights Law]' (2020) 65(2) *Kukchepŏp Hakhoe Nonch'ong* 127.

World Conference on Human Rights in Vienna earlier that year. During Kim Dae-jung's 1997 presidential campaign, he pledged to establish a national human rights institution and make human rights the centre-piece of his administration. The pledge attracted popular support partly because, for many Koreans, including political elites, advancing human rights was deemed a crucial step toward attaining 'advanced nation' status (*sŏnjin'guk*).[64]

The commission's actual establishment revealed the difficulty, perhaps inherent in the Paris Principles, of creating a watchdog agency which has sufficient independence from the government but which can command the authority of a government agency. The original bill for the commission's organic law, drafted by the Ministry of Justice, envisioned a special 'legal person' with members appointed by the president at the suggestion of the justice minister. Its mandate would be limited to 'recommendations' regarding human rights violations committed by law enforcement agencies. This was criticised as undermining, if not negating, the project of creating an independent national human rights institution. Human rights activists argued that the commission should be given a 'quasi-constitutional' status with a broad mandate, with independent powers of investigation, and the means to enforce its decisions.

The commission was eventually established as a state agency but one that does not belong to the legislative, executive, or judicial branch. The president formally appoints all 11 members, but the National Assembly chooses four members, and the chief justice of the Supreme Court designates three.[65] The chairperson must undergo a confirmation hearing at the National Assembly, and the law specifically provides that not more than six-tenths of the commissioners shall be of the same gender.[66]

The commission's *sui generis* status as independent from all three government branches has caused some confusion. Although not part of the executive branch, its dispositions are considered 'administrative measures'. Consequently, one must first exhaust all administrative appeals process before challenging a commission's decision by filing a constitutional complaint.[67] Further, since the commission was established by

---

[64] S-Y Hwang, 'Advancing Human Rights, Advancing a Nation: Becoming a *Seonjinguk* via the National Human Rights Commission of Korea' in CL Arrington and P Goedde (eds), *Rights Claiming in South Korea* (Cambridge University Press 2021).

[65] National Human Rights Commission of Korea Act, art 5(2) (Law No 17126, 24 March 2020).

[66] National Human Rights Commission of Korea Act, art 5(5) and (7).

[67] Const Ct 2013 Hun-Ma 214 (26 March 2015).

statute and not constitutional authorisation, it cannot file a competence dispute against other state agencies or local governments. For example, when the commission sought to contest the government's reduction of public officials assigned to it, the Constitutional Court held that, as a statutory agency with no constitutional basis, the commission had no standing to file a competence dispute.[68]

The commission has the power to investigate human rights violations and recommend remedies via correction or improvement of existing practices. It may present opinions to the courts, including the Constitutional Court, when the case's outcome will seriously affect human rights. It may express opinions on legislative bills and the government's policy proposals. Over the years, it has issued opinions criticising the proposed bill for the Counter-Terrorism Act and the government's decision to send troops to Iraq. It has urged repealing the National Security Law, abolishing the death penalty, instituting alternative forms of military service for conscientious objectors,[69] and adopting a comprehensive anti-discrimination law. On the other hand, during its early years, the commission was criticised for reluctance to express concern or condemnation regarding North Korea's human rights violations.

While its findings and opinions lack legally binding force, the commission's main contribution may have been in introducing international human rights norms to Korea. By frequently citing international standards, it has enhanced state agencies' and ordinary citizens' awareness of the importance of human rights in an 'advanced' country.

VII. CONCLUSION

Proper protection of basic rights requires much more than the judiciary's conscientious interpretation of constitutional provisions or scrupulous application of the proportionality principle. Institutional frameworks, government policies, and cultural attitudes also matter. Since democratic transition, South Korea's first principle is no longer anti-communism or economic development. The establishment of the National Human Rights Commission helped to bring Korea in line with international human rights standards. The government's embrace

---

[68] Const Ct 2009 Hun-Ra 6 (28 October 2010).

[69] D-K Yoon, *Law and Democracy in South Korea: Democratic Development Since 1987* (Kyungnam University Press 2010) 193–202.

of multiculturalism and social diversity has encouraged various non-conformists to claim their rights. Expansion of rights claims, however, has galvanised opponents wishing to preserve traditional notions of moral propriety and social order. Korean society is becoming increasingly polarised.

With polarisation comes the risk that sound bites and dogmatic assertions will displace genuine deliberation and the spirit of moderation. An example is the recent clash over 'feminism'. There is a mutually reinforcing opposition between militant 'man-hating' women's rights activists, who some argue have hijacked feminism, and equally militant 'misogynistic' men who claim to be victims of reverse discrimination. Many politicians unfortunately capitalise on this antagonism rather than promote reason and moderation.

Similarly, discussions about reforming the prosecutors' office have increasingly become dogmatic. The side for reining in the prosecutors' powers has created the myth that Korea is the only country where prosecutors have authority over both investigation and indictment and that true democracy requires transferring their investigative powers exclusively to the police. Reform advocates' self-interest became apparent when prosecutors started investigating corruption charges against politicians and government officials promoting this myth. Advocates also have ignored the risk of police corruption or ineptitude and refused to heed warnings that crimes committed by the politically and economically powerful will not be effectively tackled if prosecutors cannot supervise police investigations. By contrast, those arguing for equipping prosecutors with the effective power to investigate and charge even the highest and most powerful officials have tended to ignore the call for democratic oversight of prosecutorial authority. For them, concerns about possible abuse tend to give way to arguments for efficacy and independence.

In such a polarised environment where dogmatic assertions pass for political debate, the rights of ordinary citizens will likely suffer. While courts will hopefully provide a voice of reason and moderation, citizens are also realising that judges are political beings too. That judges can have political beliefs will matter less as long as judicial decisions are rigorous and principled. The Constitutional Court has meaningfully expanded rights protection through its jurisprudence on human dignity, but its decisions could be better reasoned. More importantly, it must assuage the fear that it is just another partisan institution.

FURTHER READING

Arrington CL and Goedde P (eds), *Rights Claiming in South Korea* (Cambridge University Press 2021).

Chandra V, 'Korean Human-Rights Consciousness in an Era of Transition: A Survey of Late-Nineteenth-Century Developments' in W Shaw (ed), *Human Rights in Korea* (Harvard Council on East Asian Studies 1991).

Choi D, 'The State of Fundamental Rights Protection in Korea' in L Mayali and J Yoo (eds), *Current Issues in Korean Law* (The Robbins Collection 2014).

Chung Y-H, 'Confucianism and Human Rights: The Reception of the Concept of People's Rights During the Enlightenment Period in Korea' (2000) 27 *Korean Social Science Journal* 1.

Hahm C, 'Human Rights in Korea' in R Peerenboom, CJ Petersen, and A HY Chen (eds), *Human Rights in Asia: A Comparative Legal Study of Twelve Asian Jurisdictions, France and the USA* (Routledge 2006).

Hahm C, 'Constitutional Discourse on Human Dignity in South Korea: A Critical Appraisal' in J C-S Hsu (ed), *Human Dignity in Asia: Dialogue between Law and Culture* (Cambridge University Press 2022).

Shaw W, 'Korea before Rights' in W Shaw (ed), *Human Rights in Korea* (Harvard Council on East Asian Studies 1991).

Shin YJ, 'Proportionality in South Korea: Contextualizing the Cosmopolitan Rights Grammar' in PJ Yap (ed), *Proportionality in Asia* (Cambridge University Press 2020).

9

A Constitution between Past and Future

Weight of the Past – Transitional Justice – Constitutional Continuity amidst Rupture – 'Social Vices' and Promotion of Traditional Culture – Confucianism and Constitutional Order – Korean Diaspora's Claims on the Korean State – Overseas Citizens' Voting Rights

A CONSTITUTION IS a product of its times. It embodies the drafters' hopes for the future, which are unavoidably shaped by the lessons they took from the past. It thus provides a glimpse into the way a nation narrates its own history. Necessarily caught between past and future, the Korean constitution is at times invoked to stand in judgment of the nation's past, while at others it is asked to provide a means to imagine a better, more democratic future. By way of illustrating the constitution's relation to the past and the future, this chapter will look at three issues. The first issue is transitional justice or, in Korean parlance, the demands for 'settling' or 'liquidating' the past. Second is the relevance and compatibility of traditional Confucian values for modern Korea. And the third is the issue of who counts as a 'Korean' in a globalised world where overseas Korean communities are growing. Although there are no constitutional provisions that directly speak to these issues, citizens are turning to the constitution to seek answers to questions regarding the weight of the past and the path toward to the future.

I. TRANSITIONAL JUSTICE AND CONSTITUTIONAL CONTINUITY

The 1987 Constitution is a symbol of South Korea's democratic transition. However, due to Roh Tae-woo's election as the first president under the new constitution, calls for repudiating the previous authoritarian government were rather muted during the early years of the transition. To be sure, the National Assembly held a year-long special hearing in 1988 to investigate corruption under Chun Doo-hwan's Fifth Republic and the killing of civilians during the 1980 Kwangju Uprising. Yet, no legal action was taken against Chun or other members of the military group that seized power in 1980.

A. Prosecuting and Convicting Former Presidents

When Kim Young-sam succeeded Roh as president in 1993, he initially continued the stance of not taking any legal action against the ex-generals. Even though he sought to distance himself from his predecessors by calling his administration the 'Civilian Government' and although he had been persecuted under military governments, he insisted that national reconciliation demanded avoiding any action that could be seen as political retribution. He said that it was up to future generations to cast any judgment on the military leaders.

When it was revealed, however, that both Roh and Chun had accumulated, during their terms in office, astronomical amounts of secret 'slush fund' through bribery and other illegal means, Kim Young-sam had no choice but to switch course. In 1995, he called on the National Assembly to enact special laws authorising the prosecution of members of the military junta that came to power through the mutiny of 12 December 1979 and massacre of 18 May 1980.

i. Prosecutors' Decision and the Constitutional Court's Response

Demands for transitional justice had been made even before the special law's enactment. In July 1993, victims of the 12.12 Mutiny filed criminal charges against Chun, Roh, and their associates. In May 1994, victims of the 5.18 Kwangju massacre did the same. When the prosecutors decided against indicting the leaders of the military regime, the victims sought, separately, to cancel the prosecutors' decision by filing constitutional complaints on the grounds that the prosecutors had abused their discretion. In the case involving the victims of the 12.12 Mutiny, the Constitutional Court held that there was no abuse of prosecutorial discretion in deciding not to indict. It stated that the prosecutors had reached that decision after properly weighing the potential benefit of rectifying past wrongs via the criminal process, against the foreseeable cost of social turmoil and political polarisation likely to arise from prosecuting former presidents.[1] The Court evidently chose to respect President Kim's preference at the time for not taking any legal action.

In the case involving the victims of the 5.18 Kwangju uprising, however, the Court seemed to agree with the complainants.[2] It rejected the prosecutors' reasoning that in the case of a 'successful coup d'état' the state has no power to prosecute. The prosecutors argued that Chun and Roh's coup had established a new constitutional order, and that the prosecutors could not question the legitimacy of the foundational act which created the new order from which the prosecutors derived their powers. The Court, however, insisted that a coup remains unlawful even when it is successful and that the prosecutors have a duty to prosecute any act that subverts the constitution. The military coup did not create any new constitutional order, and the fact that its leaders were in office as presidents and other government officials was just a practical impediment to prosecution. As soon as such impediments were gone, the disruptors of the constitutional order had to be punished. The constitutional order could not be replaced by an unlawful seizure of power. The Court stressed the military coup's unlawfulness, thereby supporting the process of transitional justice.

Technically, however, the Court's rejection of the prosecutors' argument that successful coup d'états cannot be prosecuted had no binding force, as this was included in a 'minority opinion' attached to an announcement that the case had been closed. This was because the complainants withdrew the case before the Court could render a final decision. Faced with the extraordinary situation of having no case to decide, the Court had to announce the 'termination of proceedings'. Yet, it evidently wished to make known its views on successful coups and decided to release them as a 'minority opinion' although there was no majority opinion.

The more important aspect of this case, however, is how the Court invoked the idea of constitutional order, which does not necessarily refer to the constitution then in force. When Chun and Roh staged their coup d'état, the *Yushin* Constitution was in force, and it is improbable that the Court wished to safeguard the continuity of that constitution. The constitutional order apparently exists above and beyond both the *Yushin* Constitution and the 1980 Constitution. It is an ideational norm that is unaffected by actual constitutions or their revisions.

---

[1] Const Ct 95 Hun-Ma 246 (20 January 1995).
[2] Const Ct 95 Hun-Ma 221 (15 December 1995).

ii. Statute of Limitations and the Enactment of Special Law

In the previous case involving the victims of the 12.12 Mutiny, the Constitutional Court held that, for crimes committed by presidents, the statute of limitations must be deemed to have been tolled (ie, paused) during the period that they are in office. For crimes of insurrection and treason, however, the statute of limitations continues to run during their term. This was, according to the Court, the meaning of article 84 which states: 'The President shall not be charged with a criminal offence during his or her term of office, except for the crime of insurrection or treason.'

In practical terms, this meant that Chun and Roh could no longer be prosecuted for crimes of insurrection or treason due to expiration of the statute of limitations, but they could theoretically be prosecuted for other crimes (such as murder or mutiny under the Military Criminal Code). Yet, that depended on when to start counting the 15-year statute of limitations. Some argued that it should start running on 12 December 1979, when Chun, Roh, and associates staged their coup by arresting the martial law commander and took control of the military. Others claimed that the 15 years should be counted from 17 May 1980, when they imposed martial law on the entire territory of South Korea, or 18 May 1980, when they committed the massacre in Kwangju and suppressed all dissenting voices. Still others contended that, since the usurpation of power was consummated on 1 September 1980, when Chun was inaugurated as president, that date should be the starting point for calculating the time limit. Some even claimed that, since the usurpation lasted throughout Roh Tae-woo's presidency, the day he left office (24 February 1993) should be the starting point. Put differently, there was disagreement over when Korea's constitutional order had been disrupted, and for how long.

The special law enacted at the request of Kim Young-sam put an end to this disagreement. It stipulated that, during the period when 'impediments existed for the exercise of state's prosecutorial power', the statute of limitations shall be deemed to have been tolled for 'crimes destructive of constitutional order'.[3] Further, this period was defined as having lasted until 24 February 1993.[4] According to a companion special law, the 'crimes destructive of constitutional order' included the crimes of insurrection and treason under the Criminal Code as well as the crimes

---

[3] Special Act on the May 18th Democratisation Movement, art 2(1) (Law No 5029, 21 December 1995).
[4] Special Act on the May 18th Democratisation Movement, art 2(2).

of mutiny and benefitting the enemy as provided for in the Military Criminal Code.[5] The upshot was that prosecution was now possible even for the crimes of insurrection and treason, which had been thought to be time-barred according to the Constitutional Court's previous decision.

Not surprisingly, Chun, Roh, and associates challenged the special laws as unconstitutional *ex post facto* laws that permitted retroactive punishment. The Constitutional Court rendered a decision that allowed the prosecution to proceed.[6] While acknowledging the element of retro-activity, the justices were split as to the 'degree' of retroactivity. Five justices said that if the special laws extended the statute of limitations after the original 15-year time limit had already expired, that would be unconstitutional. The other four reasoned that, even if retroactivity existed, a law could be constitutional in exceptional cases where there is overwhelming public interest outweighing the harm to the individual defendants. As six votes are needed to strike down a statute, this meant that the opinion of the four justices was controlling. The Court also said that whether the time limit was extended after the original 15 years had elapsed was not a constitutional issue, but a factual issue to be deter-mined by the trial court. In effect, this decision enabled the prosecutors and ordinary courts to sidestep the issue of statute of limitations and to proceed with the substantive issue of whether the defendants' actions constituted crimes destructive of the constitutional order. In February 1996, the prosecutors finally indicted the two former presidents, Chun and Roh, and 14 other individuals. The trial and appeals process lasted until 17 April 1997, when the Supreme Court affirmed the high court's ruling of a life sentence for Chun and 17-year imprisonment for Roh.

B. Rejecting the Past by Constructing Constitutional Continuity

The Constitutional Court may have facilitated the process of transitional justice by clearing the way for the prosecution of former presidents.[7] Yet, much of the nation's effort to rectify past wrongs proceeded outside the Court. In the National Assembly, many legislations were passed for the

---

[5] Special Act on the Statute of Limitations for the Crime of Destruction of Constitutional Order, art 2 (Law No 5028, 21 December 1995).

[6] Const Ct 96 Hun-Ka 2 (consolidated) (16 February 1996).

[7] Chun and Roh were eventually pardoned by Kim Young-sam in December 1997 at the request of Kim Dae-jung who was elected the next president. Kim Dae-jung reportedly wished to start his presidency on a note of national reconciliation. Many citizens thought the pardon was premature and did not serve justice.

purpose of revisiting repressions under past governments. Numerous commissions were established to uncover miscarriage of justice by various state agencies. These commissions were mandated to make compensation for and to restore the honour of the victims.[8] Many government agencies, such as the police, the prosecutors' office, and the national intelligence agency, set up internal probes to investigate their own transgressions under authoritarian regimes. The judiciary accepted requests to retry prior cases in which defendants were allegedly convicted unjustly. Efforts to 'liquidate' the nation's dark past and to embark on a new path were made over many years by various groups and institutions.[9]

Another characteristic of the Korean experience with transitional justice is the variety of past wrongs calling for redress. The entire span of Korea's modern history apparently required reckoning and rectification. For example, there have been demands for compensating those who suffered for participating in various 'democracy movements' going back to the Park Chung-hee era; for investigating alleged civilian killings (by South Korean and American soldiers) during the Korean War and during the 4.3 Incident in Cheju Island; for punishing pro-Japanese collaborators who enriched themselves at the expense of their compatriots; for compensating those who suffered during the colonial period, such as the 'comfort women' forced into sex slavery by the Japanese military and labourers conscripted to work in mines and military plants; and even for redressing injustice caused by the military during the Tonghak Rebellion at the end of the nineteenth century, when Korea was still under dynastic rule. To be sure, not all of these raised constitutional issues. Some cases, however, reached the Constitutional Court, resulting in interesting judicial pronouncements regarding the historical continuity of Korea's constitutional order.

i. Continuing Utility of the Yushin Constitution

One issue adjudicated by both the Constitutional Court and the Supreme Court was the lawfulness of emergency measures issued by the president under the *Yushin* Constitution, which, in practice, criminalised all forms of criticism of the government.[10] During the mid-1970s, numerous

---

[8] Eg, Framework Act on Settling the Past for Truth and Reconciliation, art 34 (Law No 7542, 31 May 2005); Act on the Honour Restoration of and Compensation to Persons Related to Democratisation Movements, art 1 (Law No 6123, 12 January 2000).

[9] For a good overview, see D-K Yoon, *Law and Democracy in South Korea: Democratic Development Since 1987* (Kyungnam University Press 2010) 172–92.

[10] For more on *Yushin* era emergency powers, see ch 4.

individuals were convicted under these measures for protesting the Park regime. When they challenged the convictions, as well as the constitutionality of the emergency measures, the courts consistently dismissed the cases because the *Yushin* Constitution's article 53(4) specifically excluded emergency measures from judicial review. After more than three decades, a few individuals filed for retrial, seeking nullification of their convictions and/or reparations for injuries.

In 2010, the Supreme Court declared that a person who had been convicted of violating Emergency Measure No 1 (issued 8 January 1974) was not guilty because the measure itself was unconstitutional.[11] It began by noting that article 53(4), which precluded the courts' review of emergency measures, was a mere procedural rule blocking judicial review rather than an affirmation of the measures' constitutionality. Since the law to be applied on retrial was the law in force at the time of retrial, this provision did not need not be followed, as the *Yushin* Constitution was no longer in force. Further, the Supreme Court stated that even under *Yushin* Constitution, the said emergency measure was invalid because the requirements for issuing emergency measures had not been met. Specifically, no national emergency existed at the time which could justify the restrictions imposed on the freedom of speech, the right to physical freedom, and the right to make petitions – all of which were guaranteed by the *Yushin* Constitution. In other words, the emergency measure was unconstitutional *ab initio*.

This decision is noteworthy because it departed from the Supreme Court's well-established line of precedents. Previously, it had studiously avoided pronouncing on the constitutionality of *Yushin* era emergency measures.[12] It would rule that the measures no longer had any force because the *Yushin* Constitution had been replaced by a new constitution in 1980.[13] In the 2010 decision, the Court chose to directly review the constitutionality of the emergency measure.

More importantly, this decision implied that, although the *Yushin* Constitution was no longer binding, it might still be employed as a yardstick in certain cases. Its rights provisions were apparently still worth invoking in determining the substantive validity of emergency measures, even though the provision precluding judicial review of emergency decrees

---

[11] Sup Ct 2010 To 5986 (16 December 2010).
[12] M S-H Kim, *Constitutional Transition and the Travail of Judges: The Courts of South Korea* (Cambridge University Press 2019).
[13] Eg Sup Ct 74 To 3501 (29 January 1985).

was no longer worthy of respect. In a later case involving a different emergency measure, the Supreme Court maintained the same approach and suggested the continuing relevance of the *Yushin* Constitution.[14] To be sure, the Court also mentioned that the emergency measures would be unconstitutional under the current 1987 Constitution's rights provisions. Yet, it devoted much more space to analysing the measures' constitutionality under the *Yushin* Constitution.

The Constitutional Court, however, took a different approach when deciding on the same issue. In a 2013 decision, it declared that the constitution now in force is the only applicable yardstick for determining the constitutionality of *Yushin* era emergency measures.[15] On this view, there was no need to invoke the rights provisions of the defunct *Yushin* Constitution. Adoption of the current constitution in 1987 was a clear expression of the people's decision to reject that constitution. As such, using the *Yushin* Constitution cannot permitted, as it goes against the sovereign will of the people who chose to repudiate it in 1980, and again in 1987. The Constitutional Court repeatedly stressed that criticising the constitution or demanding a constitutional revision, which the emergency measures had prohibited, was the sovereign people's fundamental right and prerogative. As such, they could revise the constitution whenever they chose. The Court stated that shielding the *Yushin* Constitution from all criticism served no legitimate end. Even assuming there was a legitimate end, restricting and criminalising the exercise of the sovereign people's prerogative was not a means proportionate to that end. While the Constitutional Court referred to infringement of many other constitutional rights and freedoms, its primary reason for finding the emergency measures unconstitutional was that they violated the principle of popular sovereignty.

For the Supreme Court, the emergency measures were invalid from the beginning. It thus reasoned that the measures were unconstitutional even under the *Yushin* Constitution. To that end, certain parts of that constitution could be invoked as standard. By contrast, for the Constitutional Court, a break had been made in the nation's constitutional order by the people's decision to abolish the *Yushin* Constitution. The only criterion for judging the constitutionality of any law must be the current constitution. While it sidestepped the question of whether the *Yushin* Constitution itself was unconstitutional (particularly article 53(4), which

---

[14] Sup Ct 2011 Ch'ogi 689 (18 April 2013).
[15] Const Ct 2010 Hun-Ba 70, 132, 170 (consolidated) (21 March 2013).

precluded judicial review),[16] the Court's unmistakable premise seems to be that it was an aberration in the history of Korean constitutionalism. The *Yushin* Constitution contained provisions, it pointed out, which contravened the cardinal value of the nation's constitution – free democratic basic order – which has remained constant ever since the Founding Constitution.

This decision is noteworthy because, by underscoring the people's rejection of the *Yushin* Constitution, the Constitutional Court sought to highlight the continuity of Korea's constitutional order. By way of showing the abnormality, if not unconstitutionality, of the *Yushin* Constitution,[17] it stressed that the Korean constitution has always maintained 'sameness and continuity'. To support this proposition, it invoked the passage in the preamble which states that the Republic's constitution adopted at founding had been revised nine times.

ii. Pre-constitutional Free Democratic Basic Order

The Constitutional Court claims that 'free democratic basic order' has been the constitution's constant and most fundamental principle ever since 1948. On this view, the fact that the phrase only became part of the constitution's text in 1972 is immaterial since the constitution had always been geared toward realising and maintaining free democratic basic order since the Republic's founding.

Indeed, the Court has suggested that even before the official founding in August 1948, Korea's constitutional identity has been marked by its commitment to free democratic basic order. In a 2001 decision, it stated that those who were harmed while engaging in armed resistance to block the founding of the Republic cannot be regarded as victims of state violence.[18] Anyone opposing the creation of a state dedicated to free democratic basic order did not merit compensation or recognition. The case dealt with the '4.3 Incident', an insurgency on the island of Cheju undertaken by communists intent on preventing the establishment of the South Korean government. With a view to blocking the 10 May 1948 general election, armed communist insurgents carried out a series

---

[16] The complainants had requested the Court's official pronouncement of unconstitutionality regarding the *Yushin* Constitution's provision on emergency decrees, but the Court stated that such a ruling is not necessary to find the emergency decrees unconstitutional.

[17] Marie Kim describes this case as a Korean instantiation of the oft-discussed concept of unconstitutional constitution. Kim (n 12) 309.

[18] Const Ct 2000 Hun-Ma 238 and 302 (consolidated) (27 September 2001).

of violent raids, beginning on 3 April, in which they ransacked police stations throughout the island, burned school buildings and government officials' residences, and killed dozens of police officers and election officials, while kidnapping many more. The insurgents succeeded to the extent that elections could not be held in two of the three electoral districts in Cheju.[19] Violent attacks by armed guerrillas persisted after the Republic's founding in August 1948, and throughout the Korean War, until the last insurgent was apprehended in 1957. To deal with this prolonged crisis, the newly formed Republic declared martial law and deployed thousands of troops. In the process of subduing the armed rebellion, innocent civilians also suffered. Claims of brutal killings by soldiers who failed to distinguish between civilians and insurgents continued to be made through the years. After the democratic transition in 1987, calls emerged for investigating the extent of civilian casualties and collateral damage during the military operation. A special law was enacted in 2000 to uncover the truth and provide restitution for victims of state violence.[20]

The case decided by the Constitutional Court arose when former policemen and military service men (and their family) protested that those who died during the military operation should not be deemed 'victims' if they opposed the creation of the Republic of Korea or resisted the legitimate authority of the newly created state by taking up arms or actively aiding the insurgents. To the claimants, the special law mischaracterised the 4.3 Incident as an instance of illegitimate use of state force against innocent civilians, when in fact the incident at its core was an unlawful attack on Korea's first democratically established government. Civilian casualties deserve verification and compensation, but they remain regrettable collateral damage sustained in the process of a lawful exercise of state power. By casting the rebellion as a morally justified resistance to state violence, the law was dishonouring those who fought and died in defence of the Republic. The Court agreed that those who took up arms to block the establishment of the Republic of Korea or to contest its legitimacy should not be honoured.[21] It stated that such

---

[19] This is why two seats were vacant at the opening of the first National Assembly on 30 May 1948.

[20] Special Act on Discovering the Truth of the Cheju 4.3 Incident and the Restoration of Victims' Honour (Law No 6117, 12 January 2000).

[21] The special law, however, was held not unconstitutional because by itself, ie, without any process of implementation, the law did not dishonour the former members of the police or armed forces. Any potential for dishonouring them will become a reality only when the fact-finding committee, established under the special law, decides to honour an unworthy individual as a 'victim' of the 4.3 Incident.

persons cannot be protected under the constitution and laws of Korea. They were not 'victims' under the meaning of the special law.

According to the reasoning of this case, free democratic basic order is a governing principle that permeates the Korean constitutional order, not only today but also throughout the past and future. That the constitution had not even been drafted when the insurgency broke out is immaterial. Free democratic basic order is a timeless ideal to which the Korean people have always been committed, even before the Republic's founding.

iii. Victims of Colonialism and Continuity of the Korean State

When applied to the colonial period, this view that posits an unbroken constitutional order irrespective of the actual political regime in place leads to the denial of Japan's occupation. Just as Chun's 1980 Constitution could not affect the continuity of the constitutional order, the colonial regime could not supplant Korea's rightful constitutional order. If this seems fanciful, it is in fact the Korean government's official position. Korea has always maintained that the 1910 annexation treaty was invalid from the beginning. This means that there was never a lapse in Korea's national sovereignty. Upon resuming diplomatic relations with Japan in 1965, Korea signed an agreement with Japan which stated that the annexation was 'already null and void'.[22] On this view, the Korean state never ceased to exist even during colonial occupation. The Republic of Korea thus confirmed the continuing validity of several multilateral treaties acceded to by the Great Han Empire at the turn of the twentieth century.

Similarly, the continued existence of the Korean state during colonial occupation seems to be the premise of a couple of decisions rendered by the Constitutional Court. One case involved claims brought by the former 'comfort women' who had been forced to work in wartime brothels operated by the Japanese imperial army.[23] The other involved claims by former conscripts who had been stationed in Hiroshima and Nagasaki when the atomic bomb was dropped in those cities at the end of the war.[24] In both cases, the Court affirmed the Korean government's

---

[22] Treaty on Basic Relations Between the Republic of Korea and Japan (22 June 1965), art 2. By contrast, Japan has read 'already null and void' as meaning that as of 1965 the treaty of annexation had already lost validity. It thus maintains that Japan's occupation of Korea until 1945 had been lawful.

[23] Const Ct 2006 Hun-Ma 788 (30 August 2011).

[24] Const Ct 2008 Hun-Ma 648 (30 August 2011).

duty to redeem the human dignity and worth of those who had suffered under the colonial regime, and it described that period as a time when the 'state was unable to carry out even the most basic duty' of protecting its citizens. Previously, it was common for the Court to describe the Republic of Korea and its constitutional order as having been built on the toils and sacrifice of patriots who fought for independence against Japanese imperialism.[25] By stating, however, that the 'state' had a duty to protect the citizens' rights during colonial times, the Court is apparently affirming that Korea's sovereignty, rather than being restored after Japan's surrender, continued unabated throughout the occupation.

On this basis, the Court concluded that the rights of the former comfort women and conscripts had been violated because of the Korean government's inaction. It reasoned that the Korean government had done nothing to resolve a dispute between Korea and Japan regarding whether these victims of colonialism still had a right to compensation for their sufferings. Specifically, the dispute was over the interpretation of another treaty signed in 1965 to resume diplomatic relationship.[26] Whereas Japan claimed that Korea had agreed to forego all claims of its individual citizens against Japan in return for a lump sum economic 'contribution' and several long-term low-interest loans, Korea maintained that the treaty was never intended to extinguish individuals' claims arising from wartime sexual slavery or from injuries caused by nuclear explosions. The Court then pointed to a provision in the treaty on actions to be taken in case of interpretive disagreement (ie, negotiation and arbitration), and concluded that the Korean government's failure to initiate any action was a cause of the victims' continuing pains and indignity.

Transitional justice is often understood to require a negation of the past, a radical break in the nation's history. Yet, these cases suggest that in order to achieve transitional justice, it is also necessary to posit or construct continuity in the constitutional order even as one is repudiating and condemning the past. Evidently, the wrongfulness and injustice of certain acts and historical periods are better highlighted when held up against a righteous order (and statehood) that endures and persists even at the nation's darkest hour.

---

[25] Const Ct 2008 Hun-Ba 141 (31 March 2011). For support, the Court cited the passage in the Constitution's preamble which describes the Korean people as the 'rightful successor' to the Provisional Government of the Republic of Korea created in the wake of the March 1st Movement.

[26] Agreement on the Settlement of Problems Concerning Property and Claims and on Economic Cooperation between the Republic of Korea and Japan (22 June 1965).

II. CONSTITUTIONAL SIGNIFICANCE OF THE
CONFUCIAN TRADITION

The adoption of South Korea's constitution in 1948 signified an attempt to modernise not only law and politics but also its culture and social practices. The preamble has always contained a statement that the Korean people are determined 'to destroy all social vices'. The term 'vices' in the original Korean is *p'yesŭp*, literally 'harmful customs', which typically refers to received social customs and practices considered undemocratic and unscientific. For most of the twentieth century, Koreans sought to cast off their traditions and to adopt a modern lifestyle. It is thus interesting that, during the revision of 1980, an article was inserted which declares that the state must 'strive to sustain and develop traditional culture and to propagate national culture' (art 9).[27] Perhaps this reflects a change in the people's attitude toward things traditional. It may be an expression of a resolve to correct any distortion of the nation's cultural heritage during colonial occupation or the period of single-minded pursuit of 'modernity'.

One cultural issue that has received constitutional notice is whether Confucianism is a 'traditional culture' worthy of preservation and promotion or a 'social vice' that should be destroyed. During the Chosŏn Dynasty, Confucianism was essentially equated with civilisation. Confucian teachings thus permeated all aspects of society, including the government, intellectual life, and family relations.[28] Today, Confucianism is no longer so prominent in the Republic's public discourse or scholarly pursuits. Yet, conceptions of a decent personal relationship and a well-ordered family tend to be still informed with Confucian values or vocabulary. This raises the question whether Confucian family and interpersonal norms are compatible with the basic principles of a constitutional democracy, especially when legal means are used to enforce them. The Constitutional Court's view has not always been consistent.

A. Confucian Tradition at Odds with Constitutional Values

At times, the Court has held that legal provisions designed to promote Confucian family norms are inconsistent with the constitution's

---

[27] Similarly, since the 1980 revision, the text of the presidential oath of office has included a pledge to 'advance national culture' (art 69).
[28] See ch 1.

principles. In a 1997 decision, it concluded that the legally enforced system of 'exogamy' was not in conformity with the constitution. Inspired by the Confucian teaching that one's spouse should be sought outside one's own clan, article 809(1) of the Civil Code banned marriage between persons of the same surname and same 'ancestral origin' (*pon'gwan*). Ancestral origin meant the city or village where one's clan purportedly originated from, and the assumption was that if two persons' surname and ancestral origin were the same, they were members of the same clan. As a person's *pon'gwan* was prominently recorded in the government-maintained family registry, couples sharing the same surname and same ancestral origin could not register their marriage at the local district office.[29] When such couples challenged the provision, the Constitutional Court concluded that the marriage ban resulted in an unconstitutional restraint on the individual's right to choose one's marriage partner, a right that can be inferred from article 10's guarantee of the right to personhood and the right to pursue happiness.[30] Deciding who to marry was a part of the 'right to sexual self-determination'.

The Court stated that traditional culture that deserves protection under the constitution refers to 'traditional ethical or moral principles which are compatible with today's overall social and economic setting, and which still have universal applicability in the present'.[31] As the marriage prohibition originated in a bygone era to maintain a pre-modern social order characterised by patriarchy, monarchy, hierarchy, and an agrarian economy, it could no longer be justified or applied in the modern age. The decision even characterised the Confucian teaching on exogamy as something imported from China, the implication being that it was not a 'national culture' protected under article 9. Two justices, however, dissented and argued that the custom of marrying outside one's own clan is a time-honoured tradition of Korea going back to pre-Confucian times, and that there was nothing to suggest that marriage customs and social conditions have become incompatible. Further, since family law is inevitably heavily influenced by traditions and customs, the legislature must be accorded considerable leeway in shaping the legal rules that govern family relations. The dissent thus argued that legalising

---

[29] C Hahm, 'Law, Culture, and the Politics of Confucianism' (2003) 16 *Columbia Journal of Asian Law* 253.

[30] To use an extreme example, persons with the surname Kim and *pon'gwan* of Kimhae numbered over four million, and the marriage ban meant that all of them were off limits to each other as potential marriage partners.

[31] Const Ct 95 Hun-Ka 6 (consolidated) (16 July 1997).

traditional marriage custom to preserve social order is a legitimate legislative purpose, and that this did not cause any arbitrary restraint on the right to choose one's spouse.

In 2005, the Constitutional Court decided another case that raised questions of the continuing relevance of Confucian-inspired family norms. It held that the traditional patriarchal household registry system mandated by the Civil Code was not in conformity with the constitution. At issue was a system that required each family to be registered under a 'head of the household' (*hoju*), a position usually held by the father and passed on to the eldest son. Daughters were not allowed to hold the position unless there was no male heir. Younger sons stayed within their father's or eldest brother's household until they were married, when they became heads of their own households. Upon marriage, a woman was automatically transferred to her husband's household registry. A divorced woman could either revert to her father's household or establish a new household and become its head. In sum, women could become a *hoju* only when their father had no son or when they obtained a divorce. Further, the law required children to assume the surname of their father and become members of the father's household. This remained so even when their parents divorced, and their mother took custody. If the mother remarried and wished to have her children from previous marriage registered as members of the stepfather's household, the consent of both the stepfather and the biological father was required.

In striking down this household registry system, the Constitutional Court reaffirmed its pronouncement on traditional culture made in 1997. Even a family system that has the sanction of tradition must conform to the constitutional ideals of individual dignity and sexual equality. If a historical tradition contravenes the principles of today's constitution, it might be an instance of 'social vice' meriting destruction as per the preamble, but certainly not a traditional culture to be 'sustained and developed' under article 9.[32] The Court stressed that the Republic was founded on a determination to repudiate the traditional patriarchal 'feudal' family system, as can be seen in the provision that marriage be based on 'equality of the two sexes' (art 36(1)). It concluded that the idea of household head and the registry system violated not only the principle of equality but also the ideal of human dignity. Besides discriminating against women, the *hoju* system disrespected all family members by treating them as a mere means to maintain a state-sanctioned family

---

[32] Const Ct 2001 Hun-Ka 9 (consolidated) (3 February 2005).

system rather than as independent individuals endowed with human dignity. The Court also stated that the pre-modern social and economic setting from which the Confucian-inspired patriarchal family system originated is no longer extant. In this case, too, there were dissenting justices who wished to retain the household registry while eliminating its sexist and patriarchic elements. For them, the registration system was part of Korea's venerable tradition, which could be operated democratically and less hierarchically. The majority responded by stressing that abolishing the registry system was in no way intended to undermine such laudable traditional practices as veneration of one's ancestors, respect for the elders, and filiality toward one's parents.

In 2015, the Constitutional Court held that criminalising adultery was unconstitutional.[33] This case is interesting because there was not a single mention of the Confucian background for punishing adulterous behaviour, even though many understood it as a legacy of the Confucian tradition. Even the Court's previous decisions had acknowledged that in Korea the punishment of an adulterous woman was a dictate of Confucian ethics which taught that 'chastity is more important than life itself'.[34] Rather than characterising it as a Confucian influence, the Court only referred to 'traditional ethos' which emphasised the virtue of chastity and faithfulness between marriage partners. It then stated that such ethos had considerably weakened in the modern world where sexual behaviour is more regarded as a matter of individual freedom. By pointing out that other countries used to have similar laws criminalising adultery, the Court apparently wished to frame the issue as a universal phenomenon rather than something specific to the Confucian tradition. It thus invoked the individual's right to sexual self-determination and the democratic state's limited role in enforcing marital devotion through law. Despite the lack of any reference to Confucianism, however, the decision made it clear that that a rule that used to be justified by Confucian teachings has no place in a modern democracy.

These cases may give the impression that the Constitutional Court is 'modernist' in the sense of emphasising the priority of individual rights and human dignity over traditional practices rooted in Confucianism. Especially, the invocation of the right to sexual self-determination appears intended to reform, if not eliminate, the conservative social

---

[33] Const Ct 2009 Hun-Ba 17 (26 February 2015).
[34] Prior to this decision, on four different occasions, the Court had upheld criminalisation of adultery.

mores of the Confucian tradition. Other cases, however, paint a different picture.

B. Confucian Tradition Worth Preserving

The Constitutional Court has held that the Confucian virtue of filiality (respecting one's parents) and remembering one's ancestors may be encouraged by the legal system. In 2008, for example, it affirmed the continuing importance of the Confucian ancestor rituals (*chesa*).[35] These are memorial services in honour of one's deceased ancestors, held on the anniversary of their passing and certain traditional holidays such as the Lunar New Year and the Mid-Autumn Festival. Previously, the head of the household presided over these rituals and only male descendants were allowed to participate. Since *chesa* was usually held at the *hoju*'s residence and involved preparation of food and drinks offered to the ancestors' spirits as well as the extended family, the law had a special rule to compensate for the financial burden borne by the *hoju* and his family.[36] Specifically, the *hoju* was entitled to real property marked out for providing material resources to support the periodic performance of the ancestor ritual. This property was succeeded by the next *hoju*. Even after the household head system was abolished, this rule was maintained, although it now provided that the property would pass to the next 'presider of *chesa*' who was to be decided by agreement among the heirs. The law thus provided an exception to the general rule that property be divided equally among the heirs of the deceased.

When this rule was challenged, the Constitutional Court held that it was not an arbitrary encroachment on the inheritance rights of other heirs, nor was it a violation of the principle of equality. It was a reasonable means of pursuing the legitimate goal of preserving the worthwhile tradition of venerating one's ancestors through the performance ancestor rituals. The Court stressed that if the property were to be split up among the heirs, the continued performance of *chesa* would become impossible. Ancestral ritual was a traditional culture that deserved protection under article 9. At the same time, the Court explained, this was not a

---

[35] Const Ct 2005 Hun-Ba 7 (28 February 2008).

[36] In traditional times, the *hoju* was expected to honour four generations of patrilineal ancestors and their wives, through regular performance of *chesa*. That amounted to eight ancestor rituals a year, plus the seasonal *chesa* when all ancestors were remembered collectively.

promotion of Confucianism because the law does not impose a duty to perform ancestor rituals, nor does it mandate that the presider of *chesa* be a male heir. Also rejecting the argument that followers of other religions are being disadvantaged, it stated that they were free to remember their ancestors according to the dictates of their own faith. Whatever the outward expression, showing respect toward one's deceased forebears was a tradition worth preserving.[37]

Along similar lines, the Court has held that filiality toward one's living parents and grandparents is a cultural tradition that deserves legal promotion. In a case decided in 2002, it stated that an offspring's duty to respect, love, and take care of their progenitor is a universal norm that has existed ever since humankind formed societies and that particularly in Korea, with its Confucian heritage, this norm comprises an essential part of the society's current ethical system.[38] Regarding the crime of death resulting from bodily injury, the Criminal Code has a special provision prescribing harsher punishments in cases where the victim was the offender's 'linear ascendant'. The Court unanimously held that, given the heightened depravity and blameworthiness of such a crime, it was not a violation of equality for the legislator to prescribe a heavier minimum sentence.[39] It thus rejected the argument that children were being singled out for worse treatment because the exact same act resulted in lighter sentences when perpetrated by others. The Court also stated that the law was not treating linear ascendants as a special 'class' deserving preferential treatment, and that the law's promotion of respect and love for one's parents should not be viewed as a remnant of an outdated 'feudal' family ethics.

The same line of reasoning was repeated in 2013, in response to a challenge to the Criminal Code's provision specifying higher minimum sentence for the murder of one's lineal ascendants.[40] In a brief historical survey of legal treatment of the crime of parricide, the Court acknowledged that the Confucian emphasis on the virtue of filial piety had a role in prescribing heavier punishments. It then went on to describe respect and love for one's ascendants as a virtue that is still relevant in today's world such that there is sufficient reason for heavier punishment given the heightened depravity of the crime of parricide.[41] Unlike the

[37] M S-H Kim, 'In the Name of Custom, Culture, and the Constitution: Korean Customary Law in Flux' (2013) 48 *Texas International Law Journal* 357.
[38] Const Ct 2000 Hun-Ba 53 (28 March 2002).
[39] Criminal Code, art 259(2).
[40] Criminal Code, art 250(2).
[41] Const Ct 2011 Hun-Ba 267 (25 July 2013).

2002 decision, however, there were two dissenting justices in this case. They pointed out that heavier punishment for parricide had its root in the feudal period as a means for maintaining an authoritarian and patriarchal family structure based on domination and obedience. As such, the provision was inconsistent with the constitution's mandate that family life be 'established and maintained on the basis of dignity of the individual' (art 36(1)). The dissent even offered sociological data to argue that in most cases the killers were either mentally troubled or had endured chronic abuse by the victim, which made it difficult to characterise the crime as particularly depraved or more blameworthy than ordinary murder. Singling out murderers of linear ascendants for heavier punishment was thus unconstitutional, according to the dissent.

Legal enforcement of the Confucian virtue of filiality was also upheld in a 2011 decision regarding a provision in the Criminal Procedure Act that made it illegal to file a criminal complaint against one's lineal ascendants.[42] The Court pointed out that family is a sphere in which traditional ethics play a more important role than law, and that traditional ethics is inevitably influenced more by local cultural traditions and ethical sensitivity unique to each society than by universal ethics common to all humanity. It then stated that in Korea the Confucian tradition has been accepted and internalised over a long period and still forms an undeniable part of society's ethical sensitivity. It thus concluded that suppressing the children's 'unethical act' of asking the state to punish their own parents, and thereby preserving the traditional value of filial piety, was an acceptable discrimination with a rational basis.[43]

For the Court, having a rational basis was sufficient because the right to file a criminal complaint was a statutory right rather than a constitutional right. The dissenting justices, however, pointed out that the discrimination had a direct effect on a basic right protected by the constitution, namely, the 'victim's right to make a statement at trial' (art 27(5)). If the victim cannot even file a criminal complaint because the offender is the victim's lineal ascendant, there will be diminished chances of a trial where the victim can make a statement against the offender. As such, stricter scrutiny under the proportionality test should have been applied.[44] That is, even if maintaining a family system founded on the Confucian virtue of filiality were a legitimate legislative goal, depriving

---

[42] Criminal Procedure Act, art 224 (Law No 341, 23 September 1954).
[43] Const Ct 2008 Hun-Ba 56 (24 February 2011).
[44] On the Court's use of proportionality and rational basis tests, see ch 8.

the children's right to file a criminal complaint was not the least restrictive means to pursue that goal. For the dissent, this resulted in the abdication of the state's penal power even for unworthy linear ascendants who did not deserve respect and filiality from their offspring.

As can be seen from the dissents, the Constitutional Court's decisions have rarely been unanimous. This reflects the variety of viewpoints within Korean society regarding the meaning and relevance of Confucianism. For some, the law may be used to preserve and promote Confucian values, but for others that goes against the values and ideals of a constitutional democracy. When the Constitutional Court is called on to adjudicate such issues, it must decide if a Confucian-inspired legal provision is 'traditional culture' worth preserving or a 'social vice' that must be overcome. Sometimes, the Court examines whether the legally supported Confucian norm violates equality, human dignity, or the right to determine one's own life. At others, it seems to focus more on whether the norm still coheres with the society-wide ethical sensibilities. It is not clear which approach is taken when. One commentator has noted that the Court tends to be wary of invalidating norms designed to promote filial piety.[45] Whatever conclusion it reaches, the Court must construct a narrative about the place of Confucianism in Korea's past and future using the constitution as its framework. It must decide how much weight to accord historical traditions while imagining where Korea should be headed in the future. Whether that warrants designating Confucianism as Korea's 'constitutional identity' may be debatable.[46] What seems clear is that Korea's constitution is playing an important role in assessing and pronouncing on the worth of Confucianism as the nation's cultural tradition.

III. CONSTITUTIONAL STATUS OF THE KOREAN DIASPORA

Another area where the weight of history and uncertainty of future are acutely felt is the relationship between ethnic Koreans living abroad and their motherland. The phenomenon of Koreans emigrating to foreign lands has a very long, and sometimes painful, history. Even before the Japanese occupation, many left the country in search of better conditions and opportunities. Between 1903 and 1905, several thousand Koreans relocated to Hawaii as labourers at sugar plantations. That was the first

---

[45] Kim (n 37) 373.
[46] GJ Jacobsohn, *Constitutional Identity* (Harvard University Press 2010) 338–46.

time that official passports were issued, but many more had already left Korea toward the end of the nineteenth century. By 1910, according to some estimates, more than a hundred thousand Koreans were residing in Manchuria and the Russian Far East. This number grew rapidly after Japan's colonial rule began. In 1937, Stalin deported all Koreans living in the territory of Soviet Union, estimated to be over 170 thousand, to Central Asia. During the colonial period, more Koreans were drawn to Japan, such that by 1945, more than two million were residing in Japan. Some had relocated voluntarily, but many had been forcibly conscripted to work in factories, mines, and battlefields. These overseas Koreans faced different hardships after independence. Those residing in China and the former Soviet Union were not able to return because South Korea did not have diplomatic relations with these countries until decades later. Many thus acquired the nationality of the country where they resided. For Koreans in Japan, many were repatriated, but as many as 650,000 remained, even though they were stripped of their Japanese nationality following the war. Japan unilaterally changed their nationality to 'Chosŏn' in their documentation and treated them as foreigners. After liberation, the number of Koreans emigrating to North America increased dramatically to reach over two million. Overseas Koreans thus comprise a variety of groups with different histories. Their relationship to the Republic of Korea is bound to be different as well.

Against this background, the Constitutional Court's decision in 2001 regarding overseas Koreans was rather sweeping in its scope and reasoning. It essentially declared that ethnic background is more important than legal documentation to be eligible for benefits provided by the South Korean government.[47] It held that the law must not discriminate among overseas ethnic Koreans when it provides easier entry into the Republic (compared to other foreigners) or grant them preferred status in real estate and financial transactions. At issue was a statute intended to enable overseas Koreans to take advantage of their relationship with Korea in their business relations. But the law defined its beneficiaries as Korean nationals who were permanent residents of foreign countries, plus individuals who had once held Korean nationality and their descendants.[48] This effectively excluded from the scope of its beneficiaries ethnic Koreans who had left Korea before the establishment of

---

[47] Const Ct 99 Hun-Ma 494 (29 November 2001).
[48] Act on the Immigration and Legal Status of Overseas Koreans, art 2(2) (Law No 6015, 2 September 1999).

the Republic of Korea.[49] Those residing in China and the former Soviet Union thus claimed that the motherland was discriminating against them. The Court agreed. It pointed out that most of them (or their ancestors) had emigrated either to flee the Japanese colonial regime's conscription and exploitation or to join the independence movement abroad. Compared to those who emigrated after 1948, mostly to North America and other more affluent countries, these overseas Koreans were, if anything, more in need of assistance from the motherland. The law's discrimination against them was thus intolerable. Distinguishing overseas Koreans according to the time of their departure – before or after the establishment of the Korean government – lacked rational basis. For the Court, all of them were essentially the same in being 'our compatriots', or in Korean, *tongp'o*, literally 'of the same womb'. The implication is that common ethnic heritage should be the basis of membership in the extended Korean nation.[50] On this view, the Republic of Korea has a duty to protect and treat equally all ethnic Koreans no matter what passport they happen to carry.[51]

In 2007, the Court took a similarly expansive view regarding the voting rights of overseas Koreans. It declared that all Korean citizens, wherever they may be on election day, should be able to exercise their right to vote. This right belongs only to those who carry Korean passports, and so common ethnic heritage is not a sufficient basis for exercising this right. Nevertheless, the Court's approach was quite sweeping in that it proclaimed that the right to vote is an essential component of citizenship such that, so long as one is a member of the sovereign people of Korea, one must not be denied the chance to participate in the nation's decision-making process. It thus held unconstitutional an election law that failed to provide any means for Korean nationals living abroad to cast their ballots.[52] Whether the person is

[49] Technically, this was because the law's enforcement decree provided that persons of foreign nationality must have had their Korean nationality 'expressly ascertained by a Korean diplomatic mission' before acquiring the foreign nationality. Given that Korea did not have diplomatic relations with China or Soviet Union until the 1990s, that would have been impossible for most ethnic Koreans who had emigrated to those countries in the early twentieth century or before.

[50] C Lee, 'South Korea: The Transformation of Citizenship and the State-Nation Nexus' (2010) 40 *Journal of Contemporary Asia* 230.

[51] Indeed, the statute's definition of 'overseas Korean' encompassed both Korean nationals living abroad and ethnic Koreans of foreign nationality.

[52] Public Official Elections Act, arts 15(2), 16(4), and 38(1) (Law No 7681, 4 August 2005).

travelling or residing permanently in a foreign country, a person of Korean nationality should be able to vote.[53]

With this ruling, the Court reversed its previous decision on the same issue. In 1999, it had ruled that the legislature has broad legislative discretion in establishing the electoral system, such that not setting up voting booths for overseas Korean citizens was permissible, given the cost and risk involved in administering elections at embassies and consulates abroad.[54] Now, in 2007, it declared that the right to vote cannot be limited based on considerations of administrative expedience. This was because, said the Court, voting rights are a dictate of the principle of popular sovereignty. It thereby rejected the argument that voters must maintain a registered address in Korea so that they may have some familiarity with the local conditions. Similarly, the Court rejected the argument that anyone who does not pay local taxes or serve in the military should not be allowed to participate in elections.[55] The performance of such duties, said the Court, was never a condition for exercising one's right as a member of the sovereign people. It thus ruled that one need not have a registered residence in Korea to participate in presidential elections and the party representation portion of National Assembly elections. This was welcomed by many overseas Koreans, especially those residing in Japan, who could vote in neither Japanese elections as they had been made foreigners, nor Korean elections as they had no registered residence in Korea.[56]

In 2014, the Constitutional Court applied the same reasoning to participation in national referendums. It was unconstitutional to disallow overseas citizens from voting in a national referendum on grounds that they do not have a registered address in Korea.[57] Since a referendum is held on issues of national significance, the Court stated, one need not have a connection to, or be familiar with, a particular location in Korea. A corollary of this logic was that, in choosing a National Assembly member to represent one's electoral district, familiarity with the conditions of that district is needed. The Court thus held that it was

---

[53] Const Ct 2004 Hun-Ma 644 (consolidated) (28 June 2007).

[54] Const Ct 97 Hun-Ma 253 and 270 (consolidated) (28 January 1999).

[55] Korean nationals who were permanent residents of other countries were exempt from local tax and military duty.

[56] After living as nationals of 'Chosŏn' after the war, Koreans in Japan could adopt the nationality of the Republic of Korea. Yet, even after adopting Korean nationality, they had been prevented from participating in Korean elections due to the residence requirement.

[57] Const Ct 2009 Hun-Ma 256 (consolidated) (24 July 2014).

constitutional to require a registered address for voting in district elections for choosing the district's representative.

Dispensing with the requirement that voters be connected to the land may reflect the growing trend toward a world of ever-increasing mobility, remote work, and inter-connectivity. With newer means of staying connected virtually, people may be able to make informed decisions wherever they live. To that extent, the Court's rulings on voting rights may be regarded as bringing Korea's election system into the future. For critics, however, this may lead to the nation's future being influenced by a growing number of overseas citizens who are less familiar with the issues and more attached, emotionally and economically, to the country of their residence. The quality of the political process may suffer with the participation of distant and ill-informed voters who have less at stake in the decisions made in Korea. More importantly, for critics, the Court's invocation of popular sovereignty to justify its decision may be too simplistic. According to the constitution, both the eligibility for Korean nationality and the extent of protection afforded overseas Korean nationals are to be defined statutorily by the legislature (art 2). Also, voting rights are guaranteed under conditions set by the legislature (art 24). The conditions for exercising voting rights as a Korean national are thus a matter of legislative policy, which should not be confused with the principle of popular sovereignty which is about the source of legitimate state power.

The issues raised by these cases require the Constitutional Court to consider the weight of the past – ethnic Koreans' painful experience when the state was unable to protect them. What should be done to compensate for their sufferings? The cases also compel the Court to ask how the state should relate to the transborder community of ethnic Koreans in the future. What stance should the Republic take toward the growing Korean diaspora throughout the world?

IV. CONCLUSION

The past is still very much alive in Korea and the constitution is sometimes made to bear its weight. Yet, the constitution was not primarily designed to deal with the past. It has very few clauses that can be invoked to resolve issues of transitional justice, Confucian tradition, or reparations for overseas Koreans. These are what some scholars have called 'mega-political' issues about the identity and legitimacy of the entire polity.[58] Not surprisingly, when the Constitutional Court decides these cases, they reflect deep divisions within the larger society. Koreans are divided about how to understand and assess their history. They are also divided about how to chart their course for the future. As such, when the constitution is called into such contested territory, it sometimes acts as a conduit for preserving the inheritance of the past into the future; at other times it provides justification for repudiating the past in favour of a more enlightened future. It functions as a framework for narrating and evaluating the nation's past, as well as for imagining what sort of society Korea should become in the future. The Korean constitution is inescapably caught between past and future.

FURTHER READING

Guex S, 'Legality or Legitimacy: Revisiting Debates on the Korea-Japan Annexation Treaties' in M S-H Kim (ed), *The Spirit of Korean Law: Korean Legal History in Context* (Brill 2016).

Kim HJ, 'Transitional Justice in South Korea' in R Jeffery and HJ Kim (eds), *Transitional Justice in the Asia-Pacific* (Cambridge University Press 2014).

Kim J, *Contested Embrace: Transborder Membership Politics in Twentieth Century Korea* (Stanford University Press 2016).

Kim M S-H, 'History Is Not Destiny: Colonial Compensation Litigation and South Korea–Japan Relations' (2022) 81 *The Journal of Asian Studies* 475.

Lee C, 'How Can You Say You're Korean? Law, Governmentality and National Membership in South Korea' (2012) 16 *Citizenship Studies* 85.

West J, 'Martial Lawlessness: The Legal Aftermath of Kwangju' (1997) 6 *Washington International Law Journal* 85.

---

[58] R Hirschl, 'The Judicialization of Mega-Politics and the Rise of Political Courts' (2008) 11 *Annual Review of Political Science* 93.

Conclusion

SOUTH KOREA HAS achieved the rare feat of attaining economic development and political democratisation in a period of slightly over half a century. During that period, its constitutional system has also matured. The constitution has gone from a formalistic declaration of the nation's basic principles and aspirations to a living and enforceable norm that regulates the citizens' lives and the government. Commentators point out that Korea's transition to constitutional democracy was made possible by the emergence of a middle class through the years of 'developmental dictatorship'. The single-minded pursuit of economic development and national security, while postponing democracy and human rights, produced a thriving and politically demanding citizenry that increasingly became impatient for democracy and human rights.

According to Machiavelli, in the case of a new state, the prince should not hesitate to do whatever is necessary to preserve the state. He also suggests that the prince will likely be ruined if 'he does not change his mode of proceeding' to adapt to changing 'times and affairs'.[1] In its early years, the new Republic of Korea needed leaders with Machiavellian *virtù* to ensure the state's survival in the face of military threats and abject poverty. With the spectacular success of their policies, however, times and affairs changed such that the state could no longer be governed through the same approach. No longer an underdeveloped country, Korea is now home to a contentious, internet-savvy citizenry with a growing diversity of interests, who will go to great lengths to hold their political leaders to account. The mere rejection of authoritarian rulers, however, does not lead to perfect self-government or unadulterated freedom. Nor does it mean that the constitutional system will function without a hitch. Indeed, tensions and incongruities latent in the system may become more salient as more citizens utilise it. We will conclude our examination of the Korean constitutional system by noting three tensions which have characterised its development, and which may be becoming more salient.

---

[1] N Machiavelli, *The Prince* (HC Mansfield tr, 2nd edn, University of Chicago Press 1998) 100.

I. THE PERSISTENCE OF HYBRIDITY

First is the issue of 'hybridity'. South Korea was established in 1948 with a constitution that embodied a compromise between presidential and parliamentary forms of government. This hybridity, however, permitted different interpretations of the constitution, which led to political instability and even constitutional crisis. Members of the National Assembly assumed that the basic organising principle of the government was parliamentarism, with some elements of presidentialism sprinkled in to mollify Syngman Rhee. By contrast, Rhee took it for granted that the constitution's basic structure was a strong presidential system based on strict separation of powers. As such, any attempt by the legislature to influence the president's decision-making process (eg, personnel decisions) was an unacceptable encroachment on the president's prerogatives. Rhee's interpretation prevailed as he resorted to strong-arm tactics and direct appeals to the people. This seemed to be formalised with the 1954 revision, which eliminated the office of the prime minister and strengthened the president's power. In 1960, however, the constitution was changed to launch the Second Republic which adopted the parliamentary form of government. Then, in 1961, this experimentation with parliamentarism was cut short by Park Chung-hee's coup and the return of the presidential form of government under the Third Republic. With the further strengthening of the president's powers under the 1972 *Yushin* Constitution, the National Assembly seemed to become all but irrelevant.

Yet, during these years, the legislature succeeded in propagating the idea that presidentialism contained an inherent danger of dictatorship, and that true democracy was only possible under parliamentarism. Alternatively, the powers of the National Assembly had to be boosted to restrain the overbearing president. Some incremental changes were made in that direction during the 1980 revision, as Chun Doo-hwan wished to distance himself from the *Yushin* system. When the current constitution was adopted in 1987, a parliamentary form of government was out of the question, due to the citizens' overwhelming demand for direct popular election of the president. Nevertheless, the president had to be weakened by enhancing the role of the National Assembly.

Ironically, the result was to return, after all those years, to a hybrid form of government akin to the Founding Constitution. The National Assembly is now empowered to conduct annual inspections of state affairs to monitor the activities of the executive branch. Assembly members are allowed to sit as cabinet ministers. To enhance the legislature's role in the government, the number of government offices has been increased, which require confirmation hearings at the National Assembly. On several occasions, legislative bills have been proposed which would empower the legislature to review administrative regulations and enforcement decrees issued by the executive branch. The legislature, in other words, has become more assertive over the years. In response, the president often claims the National Assembly is transgressing its constitutionally defined role.

It is thus doubtful if the return of hybridity has restored the proper balance between the legislature and the executive or succeeded in restraining the president. If anything, it is now difficult to know the exact scope of legislative and executive powers, leading to more clashes between the two branches. Moreover, as seen in Chapter 4, the hybrid elements may be enhancing, rather than reducing, the president's status over the legislature. It appears we have come full circle. With the legislature criticising the president for acting like a dictator and the president attacking the legislature for violating the separation of powers, political clashes stemming from the hybrid form of government may have become a regular feature of Korea's constitutional system.

II. DEMOCRACY AND THE RULE OF LAW

The second tension is that between democracy and the rule of law. It is well known that the two ideals may pull in different directions. An important role of a constitutional system is to maintain a proper balance between them. Korea's Founding Constitution was also adopted on the premise that the new Republic must practice both democracy and the rule of law. While proclaiming popular sovereignty, it also specified legal processes and institutions. Yet, from the beginning, the Korean system showed that the demands of democracy and the rule of law may not always coincide. During the drafting of the Founding Constitution, the people's demands for punishing pro-Japanese collaborators was so great that an exception had to be made to an important rule of law principle. The constitution itself provided that legislation could be adopted to enable retroactive punishment of traitors to the nation. Similarly, after Syngman Rhee's resignation in 1960, impatient student leaders forced the government of the Second Republic to adopt a constitutional revision that enabled retroactive punishment of those responsible for corruption under Rhee's administration. Democracy demanded an exception to the rule of law.

Under the current constitution, calls for democracy seemed to coincide with the dictates of the rule of law – for a while. Efforts to correct abuses of state power and to rectify miscarriages of justice under author-itarian regimes were seen as advancing both democracy and the rule of law. More recently, however, tensions may be arising between the two ideals. Whenever the judiciary, especially the Constitutional Court, strikes down laws enacted by the legislature, charges are often made about the justices' so-called 'democratic deficiency' and the dangers of 'judicialisation of politics'. When a former Supreme Court chief justice was accused of abusing his administrative powers, many called for making the judiciary more democratic and responsive to the people. In this context, arguments were made that individual judges should not only have more autonomy from the senior judges, but also be freer to express their political viewpoints both inside and outside the courtroom. Now, a body consisting of judges representing all the judges throughout the national court system is supposed to participate in the governance of the judiciary. Limited elections are held to select the chief judges of district courts. These trends raise difficult questions about the meaning of judicial independence and the ultimate source of the courts' legiti-macy. What is the relationship between the individual judges' right to political viewpoints and the requirement that judges adjudicate cases free of external pressure or interference? Does the rule of law imply certain limits to democratising the courts? What if the constitution dictates a decision that conflicts with the will of the people?

From the perspective of the constitutional system, these are troubling questions. It may, of course, be pointed out that even the people's will can only be articulated and represented though the procedures and insti-tutional arrangements provided by the constitution. The constitutional system, in other words, must be seen not as an external hinderance to the implementation of the people's will, but as a framework that enables the people to form a coherent will. This perspective may be what is needed to manage the tension between democracy and the rule of law. The trend in South Korea, however, may be toward underscoring the primacy of the people's sovereign will. If the constitution is regarded as a mere crea-tion of the sovereign people, and if judges must ultimately heed their desires, this may not bode well for long-term integrity of the constitu-tional system. It remains to be seen which perspective will win out.

III. MANY FACES OF NATIONALISM

The third issue is the influence of nationalism. Adoption of the Founding Constitution in 1948 was doubtless a culmination of the nationalist desire to reject foreign domination and to regain sovereignty. Yet, the Republic's founding took place in the context of national division. Over the years, nationalism has been utilised by different actors for different purposes. For example, during the Korean War, Syngman Rhee resisted signing the ceasefire agreement on grounds that the communist aggressors must be fully vanquished, and the entire nation unified under the Republic of Korea. Although the war began with North Korea's unlawful and unprovoked invasion, this was an opportunity to realise his nationalist conviction that the nation should be united as a free democracy. During the Second Republic, students who spearheaded the ouster of Rhee called for softening the government's hardline anti-communist stance and argued for a meeting between university students from both sides of the DMZ, where they could discuss the nation's reunification. The students' nationalism called for a conciliatory stance toward the North Korean regime. This was derided by others, like Park Chung-hee, who contended that such a stance would only encourage communists to foment social unrest and chaos. Anti-communism was thus given renewed emphasis under the Third and Fourth Republic, and anyone suspected of being sympathetic to the North was repressed as a threat to national security. Park's nationalism required industrialisation and rapid economic growth under absolute stability, which justified silencing all challenges to state authority. Such policy enabled the Korean nation to enjoy unprecedented prosperity, but stifling all critics of the government as communist sympathisers had an unfortunate effect. Even genuine followers of North Korea could claim that their only demand was better respect for freedom and democracy. Since pursuing democracy meant opposing the anti-communist authoritarian government, it could be argued that being sympathetic toward the North went hand in hand with democracy. This co-mingling of 'pro-North' and 'pro-democracy' was reinforced during the Fifth Republic, when numerous student organisations imbibed the *Juche Sasang*, the official ideology of North Korea. For them, protesting the Chun Doo-hwan regime was justified in the name of not only democracy but also national self-determination.

Even after democratic transition, the pro-North nationalist camp claims to be the 'pro-democracy' camp. It prides itself as having played a major role in Korea's transition to democracy and often casts its critics as holdovers from the authoritarian era. Sceptical of the South Korea–US alliance, this camp tends to be sympathetic toward the North's argument that US armed forces stationed in South Korea should be withdrawn so that the two Koreas can work toward unification, without foreign interference. Believing that a hawkish stance is not conducive to peace on the Korean Peninsula or reconciliation with the Northern regime, it is generally less critical of the North's frequent military provocations.

Critics, by contrast, charge that the rhetoric of peace and reconciliation disregards the North's ongoing provocations that threaten the lives of South Korean citizens. Aside from its persistent testing of nuclear weapons, the North's planting of wooden-box landmines along the DMZ in 2015, its sinking of South Korean Navy ship *Cheonan*, and its bombardment of Yŏnp'yŏng Island in 2010 are but a few recent, incontrovertible proof that North Korea is the real threat to peace. Critics also claim that a totalitarian regime that commits unspeakable human rights violations, including mass starvation, against its inhabitants is the ultimate enemy of the Korean nation. Nevertheless, the staying power of the nationalist rhetoric is remarkably strong, such that the South Korean political scene has become extremely polarised. Claiming the mantel of Korea's democracy movement, the pro-North nationalist camp regularly casts its opponents as 'deep-rooted evil' (*chŏkp'ye*) in need of eradication, whereas the opponents point out that the pro-North nationalists are wantonly endangering South Korea's national integrity, political freedom, and economic prosperity just to pursue reconciliation with the North.

South Korea's current constitution declares national unification as a state goal, which entails reconciliation with the North. Yet, the constitution also mandates that unification be pursued on the basis of 'free democratic basic order', which requires repudiating the North's inhumane totalitarian system and its ideology. Nationalism cannot but be a complicated issue for Korea's constitutional order. It is further complicated by the fact that the strange pairing of 'pro-North' and 'pro-democracy' continues to have currency even after South Korea's transition to democracy.

IV. CONCLUSION

Writing in 1969, a leading Korean jurist of the day observed that frequent constitutional revisions had a detrimental effect on the authority of the constitution.

> [B]eing a piece of written document, there was no reason why the Constitution could not be amended. But the elites have also found to their dismay that the more the document was amended to comply with the exigencies of the time,

the less authority the document came to possess. Although a constitutional amendment permitted legality in the instant case, legality, and therefore legitimacy, itself became less meaningful.[2]

Political leaders' abuse of the constitution for their own interest only succeeded in undermining its relevance. The constitution was merely a formalisation of existing power dynamics or an expression of abstract political ideals and values. Few believed that it could be used to rein in the political leaders or defend the rights of ordinary citizens. The current Korean constitutional system has come a long way since then. It is being utilised by citizens for all sorts of purposes – to contest state laws and policies, to obtain redress for past wrongs, to impeach public officials, to challenge received notions of family relationships, etc. As it responds to new demands, the system must constantly evolve. In that sense, the Korean constitution has become much more dynamic.

Yet, it bears noting that this dynamism is the result of the constitution having remained unchanged since 1987. Of course, Korea's constitution is not perfect. The three tensions discussed above show that it has important issues that must be managed, if not fully resolved. But the constancy of the constitution for more than three decades has been a vital factor in the development of its ability to evolve and to manage its own tensions. Not tampering with the constitution enhanced its relevance. The Constitutional Court has no doubt played an important role in this, but not because its decisions were always correct or uncontroversial. Rather, by offering its interpretations of the constitution which were contested and critiqued by the legal community, politicians, and civil society, it enabled a 'constitutional dialogue' in which every citizen felt entitled to participate. The long-term health of Korea's constitutional order will depend on the quality of this dialogue. So long as this constitutional dialogue endures, there will be less of a need to change the constitution. Indeed, so long as South Koreans can maintain that dialogue, the tensions caused by hybridity, democracy, and nationalism will continue to energise and stimulate the evolution of their constitution.

---

[2] PC Hahm, 'Political Legitimacy Yesterday and Today' in *Korean Jurisprudence, Politics, and Culture* (Yonsei University Press 1986) 195.

Index

244   *Index*